"SWORDS
IN MYRTLE
DRESS'D"

"SWORDS IN MYRTLE DRESS'D"

Toward a Rhetoric of Sodom

Gay Readings
of Homosexual Politics and Poetics
in the Eighteenth Century

Jon Thomas Rowland

Madison • Teaneck
Fairleigh Dickinson University Press
London: Associated University Presses

Associated University Presses
440 Forsgate Drive
Cranbury, NJ 08512

Associated University Presses
16 Barter Street
London WC1A 2AH, England

Associated University Presses
P.O. Box 338, Port Credit
Mississauga, Ontario
Canada L5G 4L8

The paper used in this publication meets the requirements
of the American National Standard for Permanence of Paper
for Printed Library Materials Z39.48-1984.]

Library of Congress Cataloging-in-Publication Data

Rowland, Jon Thomas, 1956–
    Swords in myrtle dress'd : toward a rhetoric of Sodom : gay
readings of homosexual politics and poetics in the eighteenth
century / Jon Thomas Rowland.
        p.   cm.
    Includes bibliographical references and index.
    ISBN 0-8386-3760-4 (alk. paper)
1. English literature—18th century—History and criticism.
2. Homosexuality and literature—Great Britain—History—18th
century. 3. Politics and literature—Great Britain—History—18th
century. 4. English language—18th century—Rhetoric. 5. Gay men
in literature. 6. Sex in literature. 7. Poetics. I. Title.
PR448.H65R69   1998
820.9'353—dc21   97-21641
                                                                         CIP

PRINTED IN THE UNITED STATES OF AMERICA

Contents

Part III: Wilkes, Churchill, and George III:
The Politics of Homophobia (2)
(A Late-Century Coda)

Preface

In the following pages my main endeavor has been to bring to the attention of a larger audience a whole series of unfamiliar texts that in some way constitute homosexual expression. Many of these texts are homophobic, but some are homoerotic at the same time; some of these latter were even written by people who today would almost certainly be regarded as "homosexual." This immediately leads to a problem: the probability of a discrepancy between what eighteenth-century texts mean and what their readers interpret. What the writers and the people they wrote about "really" were might ultimately be unknowable, and the homosexuality of an expression unascertainable. However, such statements suggest a kind of solution, since any such historical meaning, apart from interpretation, apart from *reading*, must also be unknowable (or simply an impossibility). Thus, I have called this book "readings," because that is what I believe it must be. Similarly, what constitutes a "homosexual expression" ultimately depends on what this reader, himself homosexual, *reads* as one. Such an emphasis on the readings and the reader is to me consistent with the work, or rather the spirit, of Michel Foucault; indeed, to me it is the *corollary* of it.

Michel Foucault has already argued, I think very persuasively, that what we mean by "sexuality" is largely a function of discourses. Thus, judging the sexuality of an important midcentury poet like Mark Akenside on the basis of information besides his poetry, or on the basis of archival matter (as literary historians like George Rousseau have done), seems almost anachronistic. One might prove by biographical research that Akenside had never buggered anyone, or (which is much more likely) that it could not be proved that he had (or disproved either), but such information could have little bearing on the sexuality of the *poet*, and indeed probably only very little on the sexuality of the *man*. If sexuality in general is a construct of writing, then I think it is reasonable to assume that the sexuality of writers is, too; more significantly, it must be a construct of *reading*. Thus, I have tried to confine myself to matters of presentation and perception, and not concerned myself with matters of some sort of "sexuality" apart from such things, which I believe I am at one with Foucault in disregarding.

While I regard this text as ultimately, and indeed necessarily, comprised of my readings, the readings of a modern subject or indeed a postmodern one, part of whose inescapable postmodernism is a high degree of skepticism about the possibility of historical objectivity, there may be other than "ultimate" considerations. A principal one for this "reader" is the bearing of other eighteenth-century readings on these texts. Thus, I have paid a great deal of attention to context, perhaps not what we conventionally mean by it, but what we probably should mean at least a little more often: other texts, other readings, organized into sections that subsequently become contexts themselves. These, filtered as they are through my own late-twentieth-century subjectivity, suggest to me a degree of continuity between them and myself, and a degree of agreement, which together indicate that at least some of what I read really exists.

Various critics like Trumbach and Rousseau have argued that the idea of homosexuality, which ranges from covert homophilia to homophobia, emerged early in the century. My argument (my "reading" of these texts) is that it is actually bound up with many of the era's key concepts and institutions: patronage, politics, academic life, aesthetics, and religion are all dealt with in the following texts, and variously either express homosexuality or in some way are seen to be expressions of it. The difference is subtle at times but not merely a function of modern or indeed postmodern abstraction and obfuscation. Eighteenth-century writers themselves charged their contemporaries with not just "expressing" homosexuality when they were attacking it but with promoting homosexuality and even with being homosexual for doing so; whatever else they were expressing, they were always expressing homosexuality. At least a part of what Foucault means by the principle of the polyvalency of discourse would have been no surprise to Churchill's answerer in *The Anti-Times*. In ways that corroborate at least some of Foucault's analysis of what happens to discourse as it "immerses" itself in the field of power relations, the most virulent attack on homosexuality could be perceived by a contemporary as an expression and even, depending on the form, as advocacy.

That the forms of such expression often appeared so subversive is no doubt one reason why. The idea of homosexuality seems to overload the systems in which it occurs, in which it is expressed. Using it to express an abuse can result in its becoming itself the abuse to which all others are subordinate, ancillary, illustrative. Complaining about it often seems to get the complainers into trouble; they go too far, jeopardizing homosocial arrangements that either facilitated homosexuality in the first place or that they sought to preserve, and so for their own sakes have to be suppressed.

In his influential *History of Sexuality,* Michel Foucault can occasionally seem to obfuscate, as when he remarks "there can be no misunderstanding that is not based on a fundamental relation to truth" (55). But the obfuscation involved in the use of such a phrase as "fundamental relation" should be overlooked for the sake of the novelty of his approach to "truth." Perhaps the wholesale equality of all discourses implicit in such a remark is consistent with the attitude that finds enlightenment in "repressive" and indeed *repressed* discourse. The good thing about such an approach is that it has prepared us to open our eyes and read elsewhere, or indeed *everywhere.* The bad thing is that it has probably diminished our perception of the need to do so, at least in any quantity, since the same "truth" can be found in so many different places. Perhaps this explains his rather small inductive base. Foucault's spirit is good as far as it goes, but that is not far enough—which is only to say that he remains an inspiration, but not an example or even an "adequate sample."

Foucault suggests that he himself suffers from complicity with repression, as the advocates of the "repressive hypothesis" identify freedom about sex with other freedoms to be achieved "the day after tomorrow" and "sex too is placed on the agenda for the future" (6):

> A suspicious mind might wonder if taking so many precautions in order to give the history of sex such an impressive filiation does not bear traces of the same old prudishness: as if those valorizing correlations were necessary before such a discourse could be formulated or accepted. (6)

I suspect some critics, the followers of Foucault especially, of a similar collusion, with the difference that not "valorizing correlations" but Foucault's *History* itself becomes their excuse postponing or obviating "other" texts, "other" readings. Perhaps all hypotheses become "repressive."

I have taken as a kind of motto what Foucault writes that we should do:

> The central issue, then (at least in the first instance), is not to determine whether one says yes or no to sex, whether one formulates prohibitions or permissions, whether one asserts its importance or denies its effects, or whether one refines the words one uses to designate it; but to account for the fact that it is spoken about, to discover who does the speaking, the positions and viewpoints from which they speak, the institutions which prompt people to speak about it and which store and distribute the things that are said. (11)

I have been especially interested in this question of "who does the speaking" about homosexuality in the eighteenth century. The way I would like to formulate an answer is reflected in the organization of my readings into three parts, ostensibly discontinuous except for their chronology. They are at least symmetrical however, with Akenside's somewhat suspect poetics sandwiched between somewhat suspecting work of lower-class writers and politicians. And I trust they are also at least a little less discontinuous than meets the eye, if only because what I suspect Akenside of is just what the hacks (not that Smollett is only a hack) and politicians suspected all along.

Foucault is equally good at debunking old myths and creating new ones, as when he mocks the prelapsarian terms of "the repressive hypothesis" in language no less fictive:

> At the beginning of the seventeenth century a certain frankness was still common, it would seem. . . . But twilight soon fell upon this bright day, followed by the monotonous nights of the Victorian bourgeoisie. (3)

The danger of such debunking technique, however entertaining the results, is the suspicion it leaves with the reader of the debunker's own rhetoric. Foucault's own discourse undergoes a certain polyvalency. Perhaps part of his fiction is that prior theories of sexuality really were such fiction, or that if they were—and what is not?—they were *this* fiction.

One of Foucault's main hypotheses, which he poses as a rhetorical question, is that contemporary attitudes to sexuality are continuous with a long past (which has been everything but merely repressive of sexuality):

> But have we not liberated ourselves from those two long centuries in which the history of sexuality must be seen first of all as the chronicle of an increasing repression? (5)

Part of my own endeavor has been to delineate, through the reading of a number of obscure texts, a part of this continuity of sexual discourse, which hitherto has been rather more assumed than investigated and explored, and partly because Foucault's own great influence seems almost to have precluded such activity. He himself, as he challenges the quasi-mythical assumption that more recent discourse is really a liberation, implicates his own discourse in processes that could rightly be termed repressive. Sex remains the unexpressed (or inexpressible) sin we pretend to have got rid of, if only through the guilt we feel over having made it a sin in the first place:

> How does one account for the displacement which, while claiming to
> free us from the sinful nature of sex, taxes us with a great historical wrong
> which consists precisely in imagining that nature to be blameworthy and
> in drawing disastrous consequences from that belief? (9)

Moreover, repression itself might be a myth, the "workings of power" might *not* belong to the category of repression, and by calling some of the discourse on sex "repression," one might just repress it too and so become "part of the same historical network" as the thing one denounces (10). But the fact remains that for many years we believed otherwise, and read accordingly. The mere assertion of error does not free us from its consequences, any more than the assumption of liberation makes us free. Now, the widespread acceptance of the discursiveness of sexuality seems to have resulted in something like the effects of the old repression, as we ignore sex not because we believe it is absent but because we believe it is ubiquitous and take it for granted. Or perhaps we simply forget that the discursiveness of sexuality cannot occur, certainly cannot be experienced or understood, unless we read. Such texts as the ones read here suggest that the eighteenth-century printed discourse on sex was a lot less repressive than most of us probably assume, and they tend to confirm some of Foucault's other suspicions too. But we "know" that already, just from our reading of Foucault. We need to know more however, and for that we have to read *them*.

"SWORDS
IN MYRTLE
DRESS'D"

Part I:
Gays in Polemical Literature of
the Early Eighteenth Century:
The Politics of Homophobia (1)

1

Introductory: Three Homophobic Tracts:
Plain Reasons, Strict Observations,
and *Hell upon Earth*

I use the following tracts as the starting point for what I hope will become the groundwork for the first handbook of the rhetoric of homosexual expression in the eighteenth century. Because they are relatively unknown and difficult to obtain, I have chosen to read them fairly closely, in the hope that from such careful attention what will eventually emerge will be the commonplaces of one kind of homosexual expression. At the end of this chapter (really something of a second preface), I will attempt to summarize precisely and succinctly what I feel these tracts reveal in common.

I appreciate that my judgment of what constitutes a commonplace is prejudiced by other, later readings. I trust that my reader will appreciate that one of the handicaps of reconstructing almost any history is knowing in advance how at least some of it turns out. A part of what one tells, perhaps the best part, is the story of the telling itself, the "history" of what one knew as one knew it. My task is complicated by the desire somehow to do justice to these often rather unusual sources as texts in themselves, without detracting too much from the unity of my own argument.

PLAIN REASONS FOR THE GROWTH OF SODOMY (1730)

The "Essentially" Masculine Heterosexual

The pamphlet begins by describing the masculine man as capable of playing a number of different roles while violating none, of maintaining balanced antitheses that never threaten to "deconstruct" and subvert the system of which they are a part. More significantly, he is capable of playing these numerous roles without blurring them or, above all, losing his own autonomy. He is "train'd up to Arts and Arms . . . equally fit for the Council as the Camp" and moreover, initially at least, is a mere "Boy" as well as "a Baronet's son" (*Plain Reasons* 1730, 2). He is amphibious without being amorphous; moreover that amphibiousness is only an attribute of some essential "he" which is not itself amphibious but fixed, rock solid.

The writer describes the masculine man's boyhood in terms of an almost democratic austerity, at least compared to the "aristocratic" upbringing attributed to Hervey in other (only slightly later) tracts that we will read in this section.

> [T]he Boy, (tho' perhaps a Baronet's Son) was taken early from the Nursery and Sent to the Grammar-School, with his Breakfast in his Hand, and his Satchel at his Back: subject to Order and Correction, he went regularly through his Studies; and, if Tardy, spurr'd up: The School-Hours over, and his Exercise made, he had his Moments of Play allotted him, for Relaxtion [*sic*]; then sought he the resort of other Boys, either in the Fields, or publick Squares of the City; where he hard'ned himself against the inclemency of Weather, and innur'd himself to athletic Exercises; wholsome, as well, as pleasant: this has sent him home with his Blood in a fine Circulation, and his Stomach, as sharp as a Plowman's: Supper over, and jogg'd down with t'other Frolick, he went to Bed and slept sweetly; after which he rose early the next Morning, fresh, and fit for Study, hurry'd on his Cloaths, and away to School again: No matter if his Hands and Face were now and then a little Dirty, so his Understanding was clean: If his Cloaths were sometimes torn with some Skirmish, his Heart was whole, and the frequent Battles between School and School; (which were then in Vogue) innur'd him to Courage, gave him a Thirst after Honour, and a Proneness to warlike Exercises. (4)

Here, then, is a compendium of the attributes of young manliness: an emphasis on regularity of routine, lots of healthy play, plenty of physical exercise, public companionship of other boys, outdoor activities, hardiness in bad weather, good circulation, keen appetite, sound sleeping, rough-and-ready-ness, scorn for clothing and matters of physical hygiene and appearance in general, and pugilism (one can appreciate why the writer thought it necessary to add that he "would not from this have my little Hero esteem'd a Bully" [4]).

While all this masculinity is said to occur in a past for which the writer is obviously nostalgic, it is more likely or even more logical that it is occurring only at the time the writer imagines and writes it, not recreating but actually creating the past. For clearly this rise of sodomy is accompanied from the outset by the rise of masculinity, and it is only in opposition to this that the sodomite himself emerges. It is a good question whether this kind of manliness has ever been previously expressed this way, with such an emphasis on details like hand- and face-washing, and routine. I think not. This kind of gender—if that is not tautological—seems to exist mainly as a counterbalance to its opposite; this masculinity makes sense mainly as a (frightened?) response to (a threatening?) femininity, though it is impossible to know which threatened first and which answered. Perhaps both involve the same sort of trivializing insistence and overstatement that characterize dogmatic opposition.

Consistent with the underlying idea here and throughout much of this tract, and indeed throughout many of the tracts that follow—namely, that the "straight" or masculine man can be defined by having an essence that remains fixed whatever his social role or category—this brief sketch emphasizes the inviolateness of the boy's character.

That this character is actually the more affirmed the worse its role is illustrated by the strangely mixed contrast between "dirty" hands and "clean" understanding, which in its underlying physical and spiritual opposition suggests not just resistance to adversity, to "dirt," but to any perceivable role at all. The boy is "defined" by spirit—and the quotes are necessary, because to be defined *this* way is to elude definition almost entirely.

The narrative of this masculine "little Hero" (4) continues, to describe how,

> as he grew to riper Years, where the virtuous Object of his first Wishes crown'd his virtuous Love, there, in the Flower of his Health, and Vigour of his Youth, stampt he his Makers's Image: Behold our School-Boy now become a Father, blest with an endearing Wife, and a dutiful, beautiful Off-spring; his Love and care for them, now makes him ready to pursue whatever State of Life Heaven has alotted him. (5)

Observing that the preceding "shews the Advantages of a proper Education; I am sorry to say an old fashioned One" (5), the writer proceeds to complete the contrast with the predictable opposite: the "modern Modish way of bringing up Young Gentlemen" (6).

The "Nonessential" and Effeminate Sodomite

"Little Master" stays too long in the nursery: "is kept in the Nursery 'till he is Five or Six Years Old" (6), where he is presumably feminized by predominately female company. Then he is sent to the wrong kind of school:

"to a Girl's School" (6) where he gets even more female company. And he learns the wrong subjects, "Dancing and Reading, and, generally speaking, gets his Minuet before his Letters" (6).

He begins to lead an irregular, nearly nocturnal existence, in marked, symmetrical opposition to the previous routine that makes (or at least *used* to make) one healthy and wise: "[W]hereas Boys of Old went to School at Six in the Morning and came home at Eleven; Master goes at Eleven and stays till Twelve" (6). These bad habits lead to others—principally, an undue emphasis on matters of hygiene and appearance, and a taste for female company—quite opposite to those of the "Boy of Old" above: "[T]he poor Child must not get up till all it's Things are aired, and 'tis Barbarous to let him Breakfast without his Mamma; so that if he is Drest by Tea time, 'tis well enough" (6). His diet is not simple either: "to let him have Milk-porridge, Water-gruel, or such like, spoon Meats is vulgar and Unpolite" (6). When they do get up early, it is only to "Dance in a Morning" (6).

At school, he "stands by his Mistress, who is generally working and looking another way all the while"—and does his lessons carelessly. He stays at this "Girls' School" till "the Age at which Boys formerly went to the Universities" (7), when he is "sent to a Master, probably to a writing School, for fear he should break his Head with *Latin*, besides *Grammar-Masters* are harsh" (7). By now quite the opposite of the "Boy of Old," he is characterized by a "tender Constitution," poisoned with "apothecary's *Slip Slops*" (7), and an appetite that "has been spoiled with Tea" (7).

Already he suffers from "early Intemperance, sitting up late on Nights, eating Meat *Suppers*, and drinking Wine, and other strong Liquors of most pernicious Consequence to Infant Constitutions" (7). This is aggravated by the effect of too little exercise, since, for one thing, "at the Mistress's *School* he was brought up in all respects like a *Girl*, (Needleworks excepted) for his Mamma had charg'd him not to play with rude Boys, for fear of spoiling his *Cloaths*; so that hitherto our young Gentleman has amused himself with Dolls . . . insomuch, that his whole Life hitherto has been one Series of Ignorance, Indolence, and Intemperance" (8). Such solicitude for his appearance seems necessitated by his being only an appearance, by his having no masculine essence, or an essence that is (almost paradoxically) nonessential.

Ultimately, of course, all this leads to sexual difficulties: "When our young Gentleman arrives to Marriage; I wish I could say fit for it, What can be expected from such an enervated effeminate Animal? What Satisfaction can a Woman have in the Embraces of this Figure of a Man" (9). Consistent with the idea expressed above that there really is some sort of masculine essence, a spirit that remains fixed and inviolable yet apart through many kinds of roles, the one role a truly masculine man cannot "play" is *man*. Man is essence, not body or container or, as in this incriminating phrase, "figure." To be the "Figure of a Man" is not *really* to be a man at all.

Thus, here the "reason" for homosexuality is entirely negative. Effeminate men prefer sex with one another not because they find each other attractive but because they are less exacting, more forgiving of each other's weaknesses (which, presumably, would include weaker appetites) than a woman would be: "Thus, unfit to serve his King, his Country, or his Family, this Man of *Clouts* dwindles into nothing, and leaves a Race as effeminate as himself; who, unable to please the Women, chuse rather to run into unnatural Vices with one another, than to attempt what they are but too sensible they cannot perform" (10).

Sartorial Satire

In the second chapter, "The Effeminacy of our Men's Dress, and Manners, particularly their Kissing each other," the writer narrows his focus to the issue of appearances and surfaces. Consistent with this emphasis, which amounts to the perception of a (perverse) privileging of signification over "significance," he remarks that men can be women by virtue of "a Suit of Pinners"; the addition of something as trivial as the latter can make the "difference" between being a man and being a woman:

> I am confident no Age can produce any thing so preposterous as the present Dress of those Gentlemen who call themselves pretty Fellows: Their Head-Dress Especially, which wants nothing but a Suit of Pinners to make 'em down-right Women. (10)

Such a distinction hardly seems significant, yet it is.

It is important, in terms of the "polyvalency" of many of the other texts in this study, that some of these "reasons" are supposedly offered from the standpoint of the sodomites themselves, so it is probably stretching the term to call them reasons at all. At the same time it is evident that the sodomites begin to "speak" in them, however ironically. Thus their motive for dressing effeminately (and for the writer of this tract any preoccupation at all with dress or appearance is almost by definition, and in ways that must eventually prove self-incriminating, effeminate) is mutual identification: "[T]hey would appear, as soft as possible to each other any thing of *Manliness* being diametrically opposite to such unnatural Practices, so they cannot too much invade the Dress of the Sex they would represent" (10). But the reason such softness, such concern with surfaces, identifies them is that they have no "hardness," no core or essence; their essence is "nonessentialness"; they would "represent"—*period.*

Homosexuals communicating their involvement in "unnatural Practices" through clothing, and the way this "language" among themselves becomes a language to others like the writer, indicates something approaching a distinct orientation, one incriminating for any writer but especially for one so virulently opposed to the phenomenon. This is a discourse the nature of which it is hard to separate from the allegedly more unnatural intercourse it ostensibly impugns. Typically, "their" language means one thing to its "native speakers," and another to its non-native interpreter, the author of the *Reasons*, who analyzes, even *allegorizes,* it:

> 'Tis a Difficulty to know a Gentleman from a Footman, by their present Habits: The low-heel'd Pump is an Emblem of their low Spirits; the great Harness Buckle is the Height of Affectation; the Silk Wastcoat all belac'd, with a scurvey blue Coat like a Livery Frock, has something so poorly preposterous it quite enrages me; I blush to se'em Aping the Running Footmen, and poising a great Oaken Plant, fitter for a Bailiff's Follower than a Gentleman. (11)

For the author the sodomite's dress is "read" literally or allegorically, depending on the author's whim; either way, the meaning of a piece of clothing is partly a function of its location on the body. Usually some perceived discrepancy between the two helps to underline the sodomite's deliberate violation of "essence." The "low-heel'd Pump" simply stands for what appears to be the generalized "effeteness," the lack of spirit, attributed to sodomites from early on; it is interpreted literally, but perhaps is unlike a "natural" heel in its lack of elevation. The "Harness Buckle," while it appears to indicate higher spirits, is more ironically interpreted as the "Height of Affectation"; perhaps that is why it is interpreted arbitrarily. Rather arbitrarily, the author privileges some signifiers while discounting others. Clothing can either be an escape from or an approach toward, a desired meaning. Finally, the sodomite's dress seems to betray him doubly, by identifying him not only to but also with the very individuals who are both his inferiors and his worst enemies. His attire ultimately seems to tell others important things that the sodomite himself (unfortunately) is always the last to know.

The sodomite's concern with appearance does him a disservice even as our author fashions a self-serving system out of it, a "language" that works largely by arbitrarily forcing some signifiers to stand for themselves while converting others into their opposites. Those we reject we designate "affectation," in much the same way that critics "ironize" a meaning that refuses to "fit." Our author takes greater pains to fit the meaning of the sodomite's clothing to his scheme of sexuality than any real tailor ever did to fit the actual clothing itself to his body. Of course, these pains are obvious, and it is partly through them that the sodomite begins to speak.

Curiously, considering his own arbitrariness, what troubles our author about the sodomite's attire, his "language," is its very instability, its facilitating a kind of sexual amorphousness; it stands for too much, or nothing at all. He takes special offense at the sodomite's hair, or more precisely the way dressing it on "quilted *Hair Caps*" facilitates the hated instant sex change: "Master *Molly* has nothing to do but slip on his *Head-Cloaths* and he is an errant Woman, his rueful Face excepted" (11). This too can be rectified, "with Paint." This difference too, however crucial, can easily—literally—be made up, and this time without even crossing gender-lines, as in the case of "Pinners," since "Paint . . . is as much in Vogue among our Gentlemen, as with the Ladies in *France*" (11). At times the author himself comes close to betraying the "essentialness" of masculinity.

Later, the author exploits the difference between the article of clothing and its location in terms of the whole body as an illustration of the sodomite's lack of essence and another indication of his "unnaturalness." He himself jokes about the sodomites' "*Joke Hats*" (11), which, he tells us, "plainly demonstrating," indicate "That notwithstanding the *Bustle* they make about *Jokes*, they have 'em only about their *Heads*" (11). The author's pun makes connections among female posteriors, male anteriors, and the sodomitical "head" for—preoccupation with?—such things. To this reader he invokes the spectacle of buttocks wriggling with merriment over headgear.

Of course, the pun is also on "Jokes," the identification of the site of homosexual intercourse with absurdity, with strange notions; no doubt for him the site of homosexual intercourse is a joke. Perhaps his idea is that sodomites should adorn their buttocks too. The paradox of high and low is reiterated by his own response, a high aversion—a high point for "them," a low point for him: "But to see 'em dress'd for a *Ball*, or Assembly in a *Party-colour'd Silk Coat*, is the Height of my Aversion: They had better have a *Mantua* and *Petticoat* at once, than to mince the Matter thus, or do Things by Halves" (11).

A reader might wonder why, unless the sodomite represented something more disturbing than "even women" were—depending on whether the "whole" means imitating or *being* women, which is far from clear. At times the author's aversion to homosexuals resembles their own (imputed) aversion to women.

Xenophobia and Anti-Catholic Bigotry

Much greater is his xenophobic aversion to kissing: "But of all the Customs *Effeminacy* has produc'd, none more hateful, predominant, and pernicious, than that of Men's *Kissing* each other. This *Fashion* was brought over from *Italy*, (The Mother and *Nurse* of *Sodomy*); where the *Master* is oftner *Intriguing* with his *Page*, than a *fair Lady*" (12). Again, his concern with their appearance at times resembles theirs, even though he persistently implies that such a preoccupation with appearance only indicates the absence of masculine character.

From this the author leaps to an indictment of Catholicism, for Lesbianism—the "*Contagion* . . . diversify'd" (12). The author simultaneously claims to be so "partial" to his own "*Country-Women*" (12) as to exempt them form any charge of Lesbianism, and so sensitive to Lesbianism as to be "shock'd to the last Degree" when "I see two Ladies *Kissing* and *Slopping* each other, in a *lascivious Manner*, and *frequently* repeating it" (12). I wonder at whom he is looking, and wonder too about the looker, himself a kind of "reader." His "last Degree" of indignation is still less than what he feels when he sees "two *fulsome* Fellows *Slavering* every Time they meet, *Squeezing* each other's Hand, and other like *indecent Symptoms*" (12). To the author, kissing is "the first *Inlet* to the detestable Sin of *Sodomy*" (12), the sexual equivalent of our "soft" drugs; it "naturally" leads to harder things.

The alleged Italian origin of the practice of kissing among men, serves as the bridge to the equally xenophobic discussion of opera and the arts in "Chapter III: The Italian *Opera's*, and Corruption of the *English* Stage, and other Publick Diversions." After his opening statement that "how infamous Italy has been in all Ages, and still continues in the Odious Practice of *Sodomy* needs no Explanation" (17), he proceeds to attack a tolerance that probably looks a lot more attractive to us today than it did to him in the eighteenth century:

> [I]t is there esteemed so modish a Sin, that not a Cardinal or Churchman of note but has his *Ganymede*; no sooner does a stranger of Condition set his Foot in *Rome*, but he is surrounded by a crowd of *Panders*, who ask him if he chuses a *Woman* or a *Boy*. (17)

As above, at least some of the writer's anger seems to originate from a sense that sodomy has complicated other kinds of intercourse besides the sexual: language and business as well as sex. He specifically objects to its "*Casto* and *Culo* which they intermix with almost every Sentence" (17), the way "on never so serious a Subject, these two Syllables must come in" (18), as if with its anal as well as phallic orientation sodomy has doubled the capacity for scurrilous allusion and "penetrated" discourse in ways that heterosexual scurrility never could.

"Nay," he continues, "There are those who will intermingle it word for word" (18). He argues that with the introduction of Italian opera, things will soon be as bad in England; it will have an effect on virtuous Englishmen analogous to the softening influence of "Chromatic Music" on the Greeks. Again, the sign of this "homosexualization" is an obsession with the sign itself, "their sweet Faces" (19), the conspicuousness of their effort to look *like* something only confirming their *not* being it, their becoming a look till all it takes is a look to destroy them:

> [T]hey grew so *Womanish* in Mind, Gesture, and Attire; and withal so fearful of hurting their sweet Faces, which were nurs'd up with all the *Cosmetics* Art or Nature could invent or produce, that their Enemies kill'd 'em with their very Looks, and for Fear of having their *Faces* gash'd, or their *fine Cloaths* spoil'd, they turn'd their Backs upon those *ugly dirty Fellows*, and gave up their Liberty to preserve their *Effeminacy*. (19)

In essence what they surrender is that "spirit," that "essentialness," which defines the masculine man above. The writer prays "Heav'n grant the Application may never extend to *England*," but English theater has already followed Italian opera, accompanied by "*Masquerades, Ridotto's*, and *Assemblies*" (20). Their effect on "private Conversation" is already discernible in its reduction to "two important Heads, *Tittle Tattle* and *QUADRILLE*" (21).

Misogyny

Given the instability that the writer himself exhibits throughout the text—inveighing against femininity in a way that itself suggests the very misogyny he blames sodomites for, dwelling on their appearances in a way that resembles their own alleged obsession with looks, etc.—it is not surprising to find him exposing himself more directly to the charge of misogyny in "Chapter IV: The Persecutions of *Prudes*, and Barbarity of *Women* one to another."

Specifically, he blames the prudery of some women for creating a climate in which men "dread more the *Scandal* of a *Child*, than the *Charge* [of "*unmanly Practices*"]" (23). His solution is to "Let the *Ladies* be more *merciful*, the *Gentlemen* more *manly*" (24). In other words, if only women would let men sow their seed out of wedlock, fewer men would resort to sodomy. As we shall read in other works on the subject, the idea of sodomy is sufficient to upset conventional morality, to facilitate a realignment of virtue and vice. Moreover, what in his concluding paragraph he attributes to charity actually seems to be the work of sodomy itself, its heinousness "teaching us to walk in the *Paths* of *Virtue* ourselves, without being so uncharitably *vain-glorious* of our own Merits, to lose all Compassion for the *Venial Offences* of our Fellow Creatures." Sadly, but typically, sodomy causes charity to be extended to everything *but* itself.

A Treatise, wherein are Strict Observations Upon That detestable and most shocking Sin of Sodomy, Blasphemy, and Atheism (1728)

Sterility and "Backwards" Creation

This tract begins as a diatribe against atheism, which the writer considers the root of the age's wickedness. In the middle of it he identifies atheists, not very logically or clearly, with sodomites: "We have Reason to believe, you are the Sodomitical Dogs, and a Dung-hole is the fittest for you" (*A Treatise* 1728, 28). In the next sentence, in what proves to be an only too typical non sequitur, he seems to both lament that they are fertile and gloat that they are not (or cannot be): "['T]is a pity your Seed shou'd ever be sown where it can take Root; we want no such corrupt Branches" (28). One good thing about sodomites, to this writer at least, is that they cannot populate the world with their own kind. He fails to determine why heterosexuals cannot always either.

As he rails for some pages against atheists, it becomes unclear whether this identification of them with sodomites is glancing or permanent. On page 31, however, he drops atheism to attack sodomy especially, in language that suggests that the one is merely an aspect of the other, that he is never *not* talking about sodomy: "Oh! I cou'd live upon this Subject, but must not, for fear of tiring the Readers. Thou unnatural Monster, I can't leave thee yet. Is this the Return of Gratitude to the Fair-Sex for giving thee Birth?" (31–32). Thus, here a large part of sodomy's wickedness is its perceived ingratitude to women, as if maternal love were a debt that should (and could) be repaid (hetero)sexually:

> Hast thou never heard of the racking Torments, and lingering Miseries, and very often that throbbing Pangs of Death seize them, to give thee a

Being in order for eternal Happiness? Is this the Reward thou givest to thy tender Nurse for giving thee her warm Breast to nourish thee? Is this thy Reward to the Female at thy Baptism, that prest thee with a thousand Kisses, and ten thousand kind Wishes, hoping some Female might be the better for thee? (32)

Perhaps the pleasure of sexual intercourse is some compensation to women for the pain of childbirth, but if so then one could easily object that the sodomite's mother has already been "repaid" by his father. One could even argue that the sodomite has done women a favor by *sparing* them the pangs of childbirth, especially when such pangs cannot be compensated in one generation. It is typical of the role of homosexuality in these tracts that it not only raises questions but suggests answers to them, too. The idea of homosexuality causes the order to question itself in the very process of self-defense. This happens through nothing so much as its own would-be proponents' transparent speciousness.

An additional but related objection is to sodomy's unnaturalness in terms of what all other living things do:

Vipers ingender in their Kind; but thou, rational noble Creature Man, to forsake that charming, sweet, delightful, heavenly Creature, that breeds thy own Likeness, to go to that unnatural Dunghill, sowing thy Seed for a Breed of Cockatrices, Snakes or Devils, if it shou'd take Root. . . . (32)

Of course it *cannot* take root, but it is nevertheless all the worse for what it would produce if it could. Thus, with the inconsistency that is all too typical of homophobic texts, the writer fears not so much the sodomite's sterility as his power to create a whole "new Creation":

If all were to go on at this rate, God must begin a new Creation, and the King wou'd not have Subjects to defend his Throne. Women wou'd not stay with you, but violently destroy themselves, and your vile corrupt Seed would raise such a Sett of Devils in their room, if it should take Root, as wou'd torment you worse than the Damn'd. (32)

Women's troubles are aggravated by the fact that, while many sodomites are "dead to Women" (33), heterosexual men are busily killing themselves with war and hard drinking so that "by a moderate Computation there cannot be less than fifteen Women to one Man" (33); numerically superior as they are, why they do not simply "cut us all off, for fear one of those Wretches should escape" (33) is incomprehensible.

After a brief lecture on hell on page 36, in which sodomites seem to

stand first among equals as an illustration why there must be degrees of
hell—"All offend God, and without true Repentance must be lost for ever.
I hope you do not think lost in such dreadful Torments as the Sodomites,
that endeavour to destroy the World backward, whom God has so beauti-
fully created, by stopping Procreation" (37)—the writer returns to the (to
me, at least) rather surprising notion that the sodomite is not so much sterile as fertile in unnatural ways. The key to the passage is the punning on
"backward" and "procreation." The sodomite does not so much stop creation as stop *frontal* creation, or rather replace it with "backward" anal
intercourse, which destroys the world as we know it but which is not necessarily sterile. Finally, sodomites, blasphemers, and atheists will not even
be judged, but summarily damned, as the devil himself was after his rebel-
lion.

Atheism

After a brief panegyric on women's innocence (violated by heartless
men) and an injunction to men to show a "tender regard how they use
them" (34), the writer attacks the next group on his agenda, blasphemers,
whose existence he finds it hard to believe in apart from "those who are
raving in *Bedlam* for Liberty" (34), since they "every day hear and see his
wonderful Goodness to themselves and their Fellow-Creatures" (34). He
concludes that all blasphemers secretly believe in God but deny his existence to escape punishment because "their own lives have been spent so
notoriously contrary to the Orders of our divine Preachers" (34). He then
reiterates his identification of one sinner with another: "If there be such a
Sett of Miserables in the World as *Blasphemers*, *Atheists*, and *Sodomites*,
'tis my real Opinion there is a separate Hell for the Punishment of such
Wretches" (36). Note that in this separate hell they are not separated from
one another (unless perhaps by cells) so that "they may . . . be Witnesses to
each other's Torments" (37).

Anticlericalism

There follows a long digression on the clergy (42–51), the implication
of which seems to be that they are somehow responsible for the age's wickedness: "[T]he World was never so much fill'd with Clergymen, nor never
half so wicked as wicked as it is now; nay, a great many don't stick to say
they do more Hurt than Good, by setting ill Examples as some few of them
perhaps do; but that I look upon to be Malice and entirely false" (51). The

connection of the clergy with sodomy, here faint and inchoate at most, will become more pronounced in the next decade (especially in the *Codex* material discussed in the next chapter).

Misogyny and Praise of Women

With typical quirkiness the writer digresses to talk about the management of the king's household, on the grounds that there is some analogy between the effect that God would have on atheists if he were visible and the effect that the king would have on his subjects if only he were more public. This occasions some criticism of the meanness of the royal managers, which "gives a great Concern to many People, for fear it should lessen the glory of so beautiful a Family" (40). Among its beauties is Princess Amelia. The panegyric addressed to her is at least consistent with the tract's vindication of female beauty, though it is doubtless even more consistent with the writer's desire to flatter; it is, after all, 1728 and George II has only recently been crowned: "[T]his I do believe, if she would have represented an *Amazon* Queen, and declar'd for War, she could have raised Fifty thousand Men" (39).

After a further series of digressions or "fill"—a defense of the poor ostensibly delivered in a tavern (52–54), an allegorical dream "to fright a Girl" (54–57) about a romantic hell for those who murder their beloved, a series of turgidly amorous letters to women and girls (58–62)—the writer begins a long paean to moderation. It concludes with a panegyric on women, or rather heterosexuality, as among the principal joys of a simple but wholesome life:

> The only Man I can think of for Happiness on this side the Grave, is he who enjoys about a hundred Pounds a Year, and the dear, constant Woman for his Wife, that ought to be of more Value than his Estate, if he thinks her so, as all ought; then he has doubled his Happiness at once. (68)

The tract includes this portrait of domestic bliss, in implicit contrast to the misery of sodomites and other sinners.

Such oppositions tend to confirm the hunch of critics like Trumbach that homosexuality emerged as a third gender or "orientation" partly in reaction to increased parity between men and women. The parity of the man and woman here, in this intensely homophobic tract, is striking. The one thing that distinguishes *this* man from his spouse is his love for "womankind":

[A]fter the moderate Fatigues of the Day, when he returns at Night, he is welcomed home with innocent open Arms, eager to grasp him to her swelling warm Breast. Then he returns it with a thousand close kind Kisses, and as many sincere kind Wishes, hoping and requiring to know of each other whether any Disappointments have happened since the Morning Departure. Finding all has been well of each side, supper is set to Table, where they enjoy all the Pleasure eating and drinking can afford. (68)

The climax of these domestic pleasures is heterosexual love, described in a passage that is hard to distinguish from absurd parody, or from what today we might call soft pornography:

In Innocence the Evening is spent like Turtle Doves, 'till the place of Rest is proposed. Immediately both are agreed, and up Stairs they nimbly trip; and then all the small Vessels of the Body are waken'd, and while they are both undressing, 'tis when all the little Fibres and Tendons of each Party are swelling and pouting, in order to cast up the superfluous Nourishment to the larger ones; till charg'd so high, that the great Vessels are ready to burst, by a Stoppage in those tender Parts, which often causes a Stagnation in the Blood, without it retracts or discharges itself: Then, for want of Circulation, the strutting Veins with Desire are ready to burst through the Skin, for want of Copulation; which often occasions a high Fever, by the Extacy of what's to come. Now both being prepar'd, and equally inraged with scorching Desire at once, in the storm of Love, they plunge themselves into each other's Arms, there roll in a Tempest of the highest Tide of Pleasures, 'till by the Surges of each other's fierce Blows above, the Superficies of the Skin throws out the Foam. 'Tis then you might behold the gloomy Eye-balls roll, and all the true Passions of the dying Man. There is sighing, and twisting, and winding, grasping as close as grasp can 'till the Fury of the Battle is ended, and then 'tis all calm again. (68–69)

Despite the ferocity of the language, there is little indication of the genre of the lovers (or combatants) before the comparison of their passion to "the death throes of the dying Man." Even this is equally applicable to either partner, either gender. It is as if the difference that must be crucial to such a scene, and that would account for at least some of its violence if not for all of its violent language, now lies entirely elsewhere. Among other possibilities, it "lies" here, in this very text, in the homophobic passages especially.

When the spouse of the heterosexual couple rises the next morning, he has a vision of all nature in his wife, whose body is (not very subtly) allegorized into Eden:

> The first Place you discover, is a fine large Hill; and just under that Hill, there is a Vale, covered with Broom, Furze, Brambles, and Flowers of every Kind, at the proper Season of the Year. A little below that Vale, under the Shade, there is a Fountain of a surprising depth. . . . And just behind this Fountain, there you may discover two large fine rising Mountains as white as when cover'd with Snow in the midst of Winter. . . . (70)

Part of the point of the allegory is to further vilify the sodomite, since in rejecting women he thus rejects the whole creation that she metaphorically is (and that the sodomite would, of course, reverse):

> What Monster can there be, that will not adore this glorious Creature, that so much resembles the irregular Form of the whole World, whom God has so beautifully ordered, and from whom we have received all our Beings? (75)

Nevertheless, despite their ecstasy, these pleasures are well integrated into a business-like routine; afterwards, the male kisses his partner and heads off in time for work. With a combination of fulsome sentimentality and attention to business, the writer describes the heterosexual male as he, metaphorically,

> grasps the whole Globe a second time, takes his leave; leaves the dear Creature in a dose, goes to his Industry with that Contentment for her Service, with the pleasing Expectation of the same Happiness the ensuing Night. (75)

One might wonder whether his real world is the one he is leaving or the one he is going to. Similarly, the "ecstasies" described in the penultimate quotation seem to be part of a routine, indeed to derive their intensity *from* routine, so that one might also wonder whether, just as his contentment with work comes from her, at least some of his contentment with her comes from work. There are other oppositions at work here besides gender and sexual orientation; moreover, it seems likely that they are *all* working together, as the parts of a self-sustaining system.

HELL UPON EARTH, OR THE TOWN IN AN UPROAR (1729)

On the title page, a paragraph identifies sodomy among a series of "horrible scenes" that include forgery, perjury, street robbery, and murder. Other "blurbs" depict the vices of London graphically, as if the writer took the expression "horrible Scenes" quite theatrically. Many of these blurbs amount to little tableaux, and their spiritedness makes this "hell" not an uninteresting place, the site of a not entirely one-sided contest between good and evil. People who would rob citizens on their way to church are confronted by churchgoers carrying guns instead of prayer books; men die by drinking while other men, publicans, live by it; and, as the writer sums it up, there is a "vast plenty of Diseases *and* Doctors" (my italics). Generally, vice exists in some sort of complementary relationship to virtue; it will be interesting to see to what extent sodomy shares such "complementariness," or is disqualified from it by its peculiar heinousness.

It is incidentally amusing to note that among the "blurbs" on the title page is a "Subscribing Coffee-Mens pretty Project for printing their Customers Prittle Prattle," which is little more than what *this* tract is. Similarly, the description of "News-Mongers *inventing* Stories of Rapes, Riots, Robberies, etc., for their next Papers" (*Hell* 1729, 2), might also apply to this writer's own interest in vice, or in exaggerating it, as a means of selling copies of his tract. This writer is already in complicity with vice, and only advertises it by attacking fellow scandal mongers.

The main body of the text is presented almost as a series of entries in a daily journal: a day, indeed a Sabbath, in the life of a harried urbanite. The traffic between classes amounts to a kind of class corollary of vice and virtue. Coachmen prepare for "citizens and their Wives, Doxies and Daughters," demonstrating the same interrelationship of high and low that is indicated by "tradesmen stealing from their Maid Servants Garrets to their own Bed-Chambers" (2). What we are presented with is a kind of *economy* of vice that is pervasive enough to include virtue as well.

Some of this commerce is "wicked," but much of it neutral (though colorful), like the "Half-Pay Officers laundresses scolding and refusing to deliver their Linnen without *ready Money*" (2–3), and occasionally it facilitates a calm moment, about as virtuous as can be, like that of the "Innocent People of more Merit than Fortune, sitting down to homely wholesome Food with *Calm Consciences*" (6). Consistently, these moments of virtue, calm as they are, occur in the flux of (often rather "wicked") business, without introduction or modulation, as simply another part of it. Similarly, in the midst of all this life, there is death, "Drunken Christenings *and* Funerals" (italics added).

This "diurnal" portion of the text concludes—appropriately, considering its emphasis on kinds of traffic and commerce between apparent opposites (high class and low class, masters and servants, rich people and poor people, doctors and diseased people)—with an eighteenth-century version of gridlock. Traffic is arrested not because there is no space but because it has become impossible to determine, in all the flux, who should take *first* place; finally, traffic among the low becomes snarled and congested by what it has trafficked from the high, a traffic occluded by what it traffics in (class), a kind of class embolism in the narrow streets of London: "Drunken Quarrels at all Corners of the Streets amongst the Mob about Precedency" (10).

The writer inveighs for several pages against alcoholism, then turns to other sources of "moral defection." First of these are "the unreasonable Gallantries now going forward amongst us" (13), by which he seems to refer to opportunistic and hence quickly broken marriages. Next he attacks swearing, slander, political gossip, female gossip, and male vanity. His criticism of the latter leads to a portrait of a foppish soldier, which is more pertinent to our discussion:

> I was surpriz'd on a nearer View to see him stagger in his Gate, his Knees contending with every little Breeze, and his Wire-drawn Legs hardly able to support him; by a black Patch on his Nose, and a flannel Bandage round his Neck, I soon guess'd the unhappy Creature's Condition. (25)

Any compassion for the "unhappy Creature" seems secondary to indignation at the fraud he represents to the state, since he is a soldier who cannot fight.

Evidently the writer is proceeding on some principle of association. Perhaps it is the effeminacy of his last subject that suggests opera to him; perhaps a man who cannot fight suggests men who cannot procreate. At any rate, opera is his next topic. He notes its decline without regret but with a trace of tenderness or even sympathy quite absent from *Plain Reasons*. There is something oddly touching about the inventory he gives of the goods for sale outside an opera house in the Hay Market: "A Rising-Sun, second-hand, eclips'd five Digits by the dirty Hands of an Opera-Porter" (26). Among the other items, I note the following articles of men's clothing, feminized and even travestied for the castrati who wore them, and not insignificantly "transformed" and reduced to the lowest articles of women's clothing, their shoes: "Four Brocade Breeches, worn by *Nicolini* and *Senesino*, cut into upper leathers for ladies Slippers" (27). It is as if the castrati were being metaphorically kicked, via their own betraying splendor, in the very seat of their offense.

Perhaps the "extravagance" of opera suggests his next topic, the "present luxurious and fantastical manner of Eating" (28). But finally, after presenting the elaborately decadent bill of fare from a "Person of Quality's" banquet, he seems to "zero-in" on a topic he can warm to, "The Character of a Fop." This "fop" is marked by the same traits that stigmatize the sodomite, the homosexual in the previous tracts, especially by what I describe above as "nonessentialness," an identification with surfaces: "He is the Superficies of a man, and the Magazine of Superfluities, and consults his Taylor with as much Care as the ancient *Greeks* did the Oracle at *Delphi*" (33). While this fop keeps a mistress, he would "rather be gelt than discommode a *Flanders* Lace Chitterling" (34). Naturally, he is obsessed with clothing, to the extent that "he is the only Person that rejoiceth at *Adam's* Fall, otherwise he must have gone naked" (35). Because he fears "a Coat that is wore Thread-bare" more than death itself, in adversity he is apt to be suicidal: "Thus a supercilious Life brings an ignominous [*sic*] Death, and for want of Reason to guide his Passions, Sir Foppington falls into Despair, and dies in suicide" (36). Consistently, a few pages later, the "Beau" is marked, for all his obsession with dress, by an "*inward Nakedness,*" which he is apt to expose in his speech.

Perhaps inevitably, the fop leads to an encounter, on a Bristol stagecoach, with two men in drag. The two impersonators embarrass another traveling companion, who brags about having "been happy in their Embraces" (36). After a brief digression on indolence, connected to the foregoing concern for surfaces and matters of presentation by a concern for language and its abuse, the author inveighs against sodomites proper. He recounts the story of "one Tolson" (42) who caught his wife in bed with a soldier, whom he agreed to forgive if he would let him bugger him. The author seems to call out for harsh punishment of sodomites, at the same time he deplores it:

> The greatest Criminal has some People that may drop some pitying Expressions for his unhappy and untimely Fate and condole his dismal Circumstances; while those Persons who fall by the Laws for *Sodomy*, can expect neither Pity or Compassion. (42)

With similar inconsistency, he remarks that condemned sodomites are "Men in full Strength and Vigour," while characterizing them elsewhere as effeminate Mollies:

> It would be a pretty Scene to behold them in their Clubs and Cabals, how they assume the Air and affect the Name of *Madam* or *Miss, Betty* or *Molly*, with a chuck under the Chin, and *O you bold Pullet Ill break your Eggs*, and then frisk and walk away to make room for another, who thus accosts the accosted Lady, with *Where have you been you saucy Queen?* (43)

It would be interesting to know how the writer knows these things.

In increasingly scattered fashion, the writer next discusses the general amorality of the parish and the powerlessness of the clergy to do anything about it, ghosts in the parish, a famous housebreaker named Sheppard, various examples of men who enslaved themselves to their passions, the scheme of some tradesmen to start a newspaper, samples from that newspaper, etc. I believe that the tract, loose as it is, maintains some degree of unity as the writer approaches, albeit circuitously, the most heinous example of "Hell on Earth," and that after the discussion of this—the discussion of the sodomite on pages 41 to 43—the author has effectively spent his shot. Sodomy is the high point of his text, after which there is a marked falling off. Moreover, the traits associated with sodomy provide a kind of progression, from fop through impersonator to downright sodomite; we always seem to know where we are headed. Considering that this fairly obvious progression is traced through another progression not so obvious— from vain women to vain men—and from such vanity to the vanity of highly suspect art forms like opera, sodomy can indeed be seen to occupy a central role in this text.

This centrality of sodomy, out of proportion to the space devoted to its overt discussion, is consistent with the vital role that "vice" plays in the economy of the city, at least as it is described at the beginning of the tract. This sense of the complementariness of vice, this exuberance, is dissipated at the same time as sodomy is exposed, almost as if "vice" were now quintessentially sodomitical. Vice disappears as sodomy emerges, as if they were one all along. Or vice complements, even energizes, until it seems to progress into something the complementariness of which is unacceptable. At this point, the tract (perhaps understandably) unravels. If this is vice, and the logic of the tract suggests it is, then it is not something about which we can *afford* exuberance.

SOME OBSERVATIONS

These texts are complementary, though in different ways. The maudlin or exaggerated domesticity of *A Treatise* would alone be enough to occasion the rather strident emphasis on masculinity in *Plain Reasons*. *Hell upon Earth* seems to overlook the personal and the domestic for a view of the whole city that is bound to be more tolerant, even if the author cannot consciously accept such a vision or even recognize it as the "structural principle" of his own piece.

These are but some of the poles in a complicated system of oppositions in which homosexuality emerges as a negative or as a contradiction. All of these texts are contradictory, inconsistent, ill-logical. The nature of their subject must be determined indirectly, as we would that of a black hole, through the physical irregularities of other bodies.

With its panegyrics on specific women and on women in general, and in the abstract, *A Treatise* seems to respond to the imputation of misogyny to which the writer of the first text exposed himself. It is as if early writers on the subject of sodomy found themselves caught in a kind of bond or contradiction, partly a function of the oppositional system with which they dealt and within which they wrote, and which they themselves helped to create or at least intensified. Thus some of them complain about women while blaming other men for their aversion, while others eulogize women fulsomely and argue for the existence of a wrong or a debt that could be used to *defend* homosexuality.

To me the most striking thing about these texts is the way they seem to implicate their writers in the very linguistic confusions that they themselves blame on homosexuality. Homosexual expression takes many forms of language, but seems marked by an overemphasis on the signifier at the expense of a signified; this overemphasis, in turn, corresponds to the homosexual's being himself a kind of signifier *without* a signified, a nonessential essence. The basic confusion that results from this, the tendency for the nonessential to masquerade as the essential, afflicts the authors themselves as they cite as "reasons" or causes what are plainly effects; as they themselves dwell on appearances, or otherwise exhibit their own marked preference for signifiers over signifieds, by their obvious fondness for allegory, puns, fulsome hyperbole, and other verbal excesses.

2

Formal Strain: Problems of Homosexual Expression in William Arnall's *Letter to Dr. Codex,* Philalethes' *The Parson and His Clerk,* and Thomas Gilbert's *A View of the Town*

On 27 February 1733 Edmund Gibson, bishop of London, had published in the *London Daily Journal* his "Instruction to the Crown" (as William Arnall presumes to call it), in which he expressed his opposition to the Whig government's intention to elevate Thomas Rundle to the vacant see of Gloucester.[1] While, according to Norman Sykes, "the true reasons for his opposition were theological . . . they referred to the general character of Rundle's opinions" (1926, 266–67), Gibson's expression of opposition was seen as yet another instance of the clergy's interference in affairs of state, of their perennial unwillingness to subordinate ecclesiastical to secular power.

In subsequent replies by William Arnall,[2] "Philalethes," and (probably) Thomas Gilbert, the dangers of the church's alleged insubordination are depicted in the most lurid sexual and homophobic terms. Ultimately, it becomes unclear whether in these arguments homosexuality illustrates a constitutional danger or vice versa. At times these arguments seem to be more about homosexuality than the church; certainly, they are striking for the information they provide us about midcentury attitudes, and in particular about a nexus between politics and "perversion" that is striking enough to warrant further research. At the very least, appreciating this nexus helps us to understand a curious if minor piece of literature by Thomas Gilbert: his *A View of the Town,* part of which has recently been anthologized by Lonsdale (1984, 283).

Like *Plain Reasons* and *Strict Observations,* these pieces are marked by an instability that could aptly be called "playful," if only it were always deliberate; usually such instability proves less playful than subversive, or morally confusing. Thanks to it, homosexuality itself, as an illustration intended to convey the luridness of particular widespread abuses, seems to proliferate by association; what it illustrates, illustrates itself. Usually the author is himself implicated in the very process of writing. He himself makes or at least implies an identification between a preoccupation with appearances or "signification," which any writer might share but which *these* writers exhibit almost glaringly, and homosexuality. Then, in ways that illustrate Foucault's principle of "polyvalency," he makes special "allowances" against homosexuality that sufficiently subvert notions of virtue and vice to draw attitudes to both homosexuality and heterosexuality into question.

Perhaps it is no coincidence that the most successful of these *Codex* pieces, *The Parson and his Clerk,* is also the least "serious." Perhaps the playfulness of the author gave him, if not greater sympathy, greater understanding of the "play" of the phenomenon, an insight unoccluded by indignation. In fact, such "unseriousness" characterizes the shrewdest pieces in the other controversies we will explore, in particular *College-Wit Sharpen'd* (about homosexuality in academe), as if playfulness were the one prerequisite for successfully handling the subject.

In the following pages I will principally indicate how Arnall uses homosexuality to oppose Gibson, how "Philalethes"—rightly, I think— extracts the most lurid, homophobic part of Arnall's *Letter to Dr. Codex* for his *Parson and his Clerk,* and finally how these works help us to understand the way homosexuality is used in Gilbert's poem.

Arnall's general tactic is to turn the tables on his opponent, first by reapplying Gibson's parallel to Gibson himself and supplying some parallels of his own, then by suggesting that Gibson's "preferment project" (as Arnall describes it) would pose worse dangers than the present system.

The parallel—published in the *Daily Journal*—uses the vehicle of Anne's decision not to make a man a bishop after other bishops had objected to his character to show how Gibson thinks George II should resolve the current controversy—i.e., by not promoting Rundle:

> If such a *Paragraph* can be REMARKABLE *more than any other,* if such an *Example* can be *fit for Imitation* more *than any other mention'd by the* Reverend *Historian,* it can be so in no other View than this, that particular Princes have now a *parallel Case* before them. (Arnall 1734, 6)

While taking pains to attack the application of the past vehicle to the present tenor, he is careful not to attack the conduct of Anne. What he attacks is the use of the past as a vehicle for the present, the past abstracted from its extenuating circumstances. By implication one cannot apply the past without applying these too, but these are nowhere to be found in the present (7).

Of course, it could be objected to Arnall's procedure that it contributes to Gibson's purpose by broadcasting the meaning of the analogy to everyone who might not have understood it:

> [I]f you mean any thing at all, you must intend to suggest, that there is a *present* Recommendation to a *vacant See* which appears to you in the same Light with *Lord Sidney's* Recommendation to a *Bishoprick in Ireland.* You thus suggest that a GREAT COUNSELLOR *of the Crown* hath recommended a Person to the *Favour of the Crown*, with an *undue Representation of* his *Character.* (6)

It is clear that what Arnall principally objects to in the parallel is the implication, or what he chooses to see as the implication, that the power to choose bishops should reside in the bishops themselves ("*if they . . . agree* he labours under an *ill Fame*, he is not to be promoted" [6]).

One should note how skillfully Arnall turns the tables on Gibson, reapplying his vehicle to a negative tenor:

> [T]he Person set aside *did labour under an ill Fame* . . . the QUEEN *heard it* from no *malicious Whisperers*, or *interested Tale-bearers* . . . the *Six Bishops* who were refer'd to, and who certified their ill Opinion of him, were equal *unbias'd indifferent Judges*, incapable of an Intention *to shake off their* due Dependency *on the ROYAL SUPREMACY*; incapable of any Scheme or Project *to turn their* Hierarchy *into an* ARISTOCRACY. (7)

Arnall turns the tables even further by supplying parallels to the most famous interfering cleric of them all, Archbishop Laud, and to a previous bishop of London, Edmund, who made himself so unpopular with his interference that it became possible for him to destroy a man's career merely by recommending him.

However, Arnall's most effective ploy involves a different kind of reversal, whereby he suggests that just as anyone Gibson would recommend must be a sinner, anyone he would be oppose must be a saint. Even more destructively, throughout the *Letter* Arnall drops phrases the purport of which becomes clear only in the final pages concerning Gibson's alleged protection of a sodomite: *"Cabal of Churchmen"* (14), *"vile Cabal"* (19), "THE PLEASURE OF PRIESTS" (20), "SIN *exceeding* SINFUL" (23), etc. This anticipatory innuendo becomes more pointed in his use of one Dr. Green's *Letter*,[3] where he quotes him on the danger of exempting the clergy from the law:

> [I]t is his Interest that his *Sacred Office* be not regarded in the *Question*, lest it serve only to *aggravate* the Crimes proved against him; or to speak in the Language of the *Great St. Paul, to make his* SIN *exceeding* SIN-FUL. (23)

The parson's sodomy is the "SIN"—already quite sinful—made even more heinous by Gibson's protection, which stands metaphorically for his entire church policy. Sodomy becomes the best gauge of the worst—political—depravity.

Moreover, Dr. Green's letter is excerpted in ways that make Gibson's "crime" all the more telling, as when Green is cited on wanting to belong to a society where

> every Man *who enters into such Measures* as endanger my *Liberty*, my *Property*, or my *Religion*, be he *Civil* or SACRED, wear he a *Garter* or a MITRE, is upon *Discovery of his Designs*, brought to a fair *Trial*, and does upon *Conviction*, pay that DEBT OF PUNISHMENT which the known *Laws of his Country demand.* (24)

The parson's sodomy is similarly anticipated in a quotation urging clergymen as *"Teachers of Religion"* to "endeavour to *support the Society* in which we are to happily planted" (26). Thus sodomy is exploited to illustrate the sort of crime—politically unacceptable in its failure to subordinate church to state, socially unacceptable in its flagrant violation of sexual mores—that thanks to Gibson remains unpunished.

Thus, homosexuality unpunished comes to stand for ecclesiastical tyranny. All of the abuses that Arnall cites as consequences of a church not subordinated to its state, lead in a rather theatrical way to Gibson's alleged protection of a homosexual priest. Specifically, Gibson is accused of deliberately transferring the priest's case to "Spiritual Court," where the prosecution would be so delayed that "it would have had no Countenance in the *Civil Courts*, had an *Indictment* been preferred so long after the *Fact* was Committed" (33). The allegation comes last, because in curious ways it is the climax of Gibson's argument. It, and the fact that the priest eventually gets off with a £100 fine and a warning "not to commit such filthy Sins in Time to come" (33), is what finally clinches Arnall's argument:

> Thus was *Justice* disarmed of her Power to punish the *worst Offences*! Thus did an *intriguing Ecclesiastical*, SCREEN Enormities in his *own Order*, which he had followed with all the *Vengeance of Law* in the *Case of other Men*! And do you not think, that were such a Man to be entrusted with *Supreme Power in the Church*, he would employ it as wickedly and as *partially*, in STIGMATIZING some, as he hath employed it in SCREENING of others? (34)

I am not sure that it is merely a trick of time that the constitutional point the allegation was intended to illustrate—however luridly—is now obscured for us by its sociological interest. From the beginning the illustration had a tendency to usurp the argument.

THE PARSON AND HIS CLERK

This, I believe, is what happens with the "Philalethes" poem, *The Parson and His Clerk,* a versification of the homophobic part of Arnall's *Letter*—its unintended core.

The poem begins by asserting a connection between the rise of sodomy and the priesthood:

> No Wonder then if *Flocks* do STRAY,
> When *Evil Pastors* lead the *Way*.
>
> (1)

This particular homosexual priest owes some of his lustiness to the high living, especially drinking, associated with the clergy:

> A *Priest*, who Rector was, or Vicar,
> And lov'd a Cup of humming Liquor;
>
> . . . .
>
> Now rosey grew, robust, and jolly,
> Whose chief Delight was in a M—[oll]—y;
> To his *Superiour* a mere *Bigot*,
> And play'd at *Fosset* and at *Spiggot*.
>
> (1–2)

He not only uses religion as a cloak, but his cassock to conceal an erection:

> A Cloak he made it to conceal
> The *firey Itching* of his T——.

(2)

At times Philalethes precisely echoes the political poetry of *Poems on Affairs of State*, but with a risqué punning humor that suggests that religion means almost as little for the writer as, it is alleged, for the sodomite:

> No Man more zealous for the *Church*,
> Yet always left her in the Lurch.

(2)

One imagines the embarrassed priest not deserting his church over some ideological issue, but physically lurching out of it—after his clerk. Priests previously deserted the church for political issues; now they desert it for boys—curiously, the change seems not entirely for the worse. The parodic element pervades the poem, for example in lines that describe the priest's sexual appetite in terms of religious dissent and inward light:

> In outward Shew this *Holy Teacher*,
> But inwardly a zealous Leacher.

(7)

The point might be that homosexuality in an established priest is doubly wrong, or rather that a homosexual priest is virtually a contradiction in terms, since he would almost certainly have to be a dissenter—in more ways than one. At points this priest resembles less the Anglican than the dourly hypocritical Puritan of Anglican polemic. But the parody becomes satire when the flesh and blood of Christ are doubly "transubstantiated," first in the Anglican mass and second in the twice-perjured member of the hypocritical sodomite who celebrates it:

> This perjur'd Piece of Flesh and Blood
> Who nought had in him that was good:

(8)

It is apparent that Philalethes himself connects the problem of the hypocritical, sodomizing priest to the problem of patronage, since the latter protects the former:

> This *Priest* . . .
> To all the World was too well known,
> By each *immortal Practice* shewn;
> And by his steddy Disaffection,
> Yet after all he found Protection.

(6)

It is equally apparent that the priest was suspected of sodomy long before he was apprehended:

> By his *Amours* so shocking he
> Long branded was with *Infamy*;
> Yet valued not the *odious Shame*,
> And said, 'twas nought but *common Fame*.
> Then *common Fame* he call'd a Lyar,
> So gratify'd his curs'd Desire.

(6)

He is not apprehended until he is exposed, accidentally it seems, by another sodomite in orders:

> At length by one of flagrant Kind,
>
> .   .   .   .
> This pious Priest, this holy Widgeon,
> Who made a May-game of Religion,
> Detected was, and then expos'd,
> Spurn'd, and by all the Parish nos'd.

(7)

The truth might never have emerged, if his lover, the "passive . . . simple Noddy" had not "been rode too fast," so violently that he had to visit the surgeon.

While the priest is exposed, he remains unpunished, for reasons not specified but clearly incriminating to the clergy:

> But as the Clergy made no Pother
> In prosecuting this false Brother,
> For Reasons to themselves best known,
> Which they in Prudence will not own;

(14)

The idea that the clergy are merely protecting one of their own sexual orientation is taken up again later, when the priest appears to get off scot-free, thanks to his superior's chicanery, by being tried first in the ecclesiastical court:

> With a kind Brotherly Affection,
> And by good Offices, Direction
> Did humbly give to moderate
> The vile Delinquent's rigid State;
> And, as his Heart was now grown tender,
> From Justice *Screen* the Black Offender.
>
> (14)

On must note how Christian commonplaces like "Brotherly Affection" are given a new meaning. One must appreciate too how they are treated as commonplaces in the most negative sense, as clichés in fact, and how consequently being revived with even a sodomitical meaning seems like an improvement. But finally, the wickedness of the clergy's toleration of sodomy among their own sodomizing kind is compounded by their hypocritical intolerance of it among the laity:

> Thus an Intriguing Man we've seen
> In his *Own Order* Vices *Screen*,
> Which he, with Reverential Awe,
> And all the Vengeance of the law,
> In Lay-mens Cases did pursue,
> With utmost Rage, a Thing not new!
>
> (15)

The poem is curious for its striking reapplication of the language of religious satire to sex, for its peculiar exploitation of anti-Puritan (and probably, too, Jacobite) stereotypes in a secular, homophobic context. Finally, the way it develops a few pages of homophobic allegations against Gibson and his priest into a broadside against the whole clergy raises many questions about contemporary attitudes to the Anglican priesthood. Perhaps Arnall's shot hit a larger mark than he intended.

A VIEW OF THE TOWN

Thomas Gilbert's *A View of the Town* is a homophobic, anticlerical satire, exactly contemporary with the preceding works. One needs to have read them to understand Gilbert's work.

I first became acquainted with Gilbert's poem in a truncated version, number 192 in Lonsdale's *The New Oxford Book of Eighteenth-Century Verse*. The excerpt contains a sketch about a woman ("Saphira") recently deserted by her homosexual husband, and the conventional comparison of London to Sodom and Gomorrah. I wondered, because it was an excerpt, just what kind of poem would contain such a passage, what its relationship to the whole might be, or in other words what homosexuality could be doing in such a poem.

The very spareness of the reality that Gilbert accords homosexuals in this poem—even their blame oddly wedged between praise of abstinence and blame of (hetero)sexuality, between praise of men and blame of women—creates problems both in the preface and in the poem proper. While the poem is overtly a homophobic diatribe, when it would have been appropriate to say something about homosexuality in the preface Gilbert is oddly silent; instead, he treats his poem as a potentially anticlerical expression, specifically arguing that it is not *really* anticlerical.

The effect of this evasive defensiveness is, I think, to award the otherwise unsignified "homosexuality" a clerical signifier. Since (1) he apologizes here for something he might appear to have said against the *entire* priesthood, and (2) the poem's sharpest satire is directed against homosexuals, it unintentionally suggests that what he means by "priesthood" is something significantly homosexual. Whether many people thought so, or even whether *he* thought so, is a question for further historical research; my point is that he would *appear* to think so, by virtue of the problematic expression of this "vice."

Gilbert is concerned from the beginning that readers will put a "bad Construction" on his poem, but evasive about precisely what that construction is:

> As there are some of my Well-wishers who may in all Probability put a bad Construction on some Passages in the following Poem, I must beg the Reader's pardon for troubling him with a short Preface. (1735, 2)

I will return to what I think this "bad Construction" is later; for now, I will only indicate that what he says it is—anticlericalism—is not really what I think most readers would take to be the issue of the poem. That it must be *homophobia*, or a peculiar breed of *homophobic* anticlericalism, becomes more likely considering the lengths he goes to to prevent that relation. Moreover, he seems to want to prevent counterattack, by exploiting the heinousness that would adhere to even the *accusation* of sodomy, insisting that only those who deserve censure will be offended by the poem: "[I]f none of them are guilty of the Crimes mentioned in the following Pages, no

one can be offended; but if they are, they deserve Censure." That his criticism of the priesthood could be a severer attack than he indicates becomes
more apparent in lines that seem to mean something opposite to his intention, or at least to his *avowed* intention:

> [I]f there are Men, who only make use of Religion as a Veil, and while
> they are lifting up their Eyes with the most apparent Ardour to God, are
> serving the Devil in their Hearts, why should their deviating by the vile
> Practice of their Lives from the Precepts of that Religion they profess,
> serve them a Shield for their Iniquity? (preface, n.p.)

On the surface this is just a defense for satire of the priesthood, precedents
for which had long since been established by satirists, including Milton,
Marvell, and Swift—himself a priest. However, the defense is worded—
"why should their deviating . . . serve them as a Shield"—as if the *deviation,* the crime itself, were the shield, when logically it must be their priesthood. I suggest that this particular expression is not simply a result of bad
grammar or poor choice of words, but homosexual expression that is "bad,"
almost as if the expression of a deviation itself had to be devious—deviant.
Deviation would normally be the thing shielded, rather than the thing shielding, but here the "deviating"—by which he might mean just the usual heterosexual crimes—is indeed a shield, as these particular "deviants" themselves are probably, for a worse deviation, closer to what *we* mean by sexual
deviancy. Moreover, another "deviant," almost as conspicuous as the others, at least in Gilbert's "Preface," is Gilbert himself, as he deviates from
the crux of his own poem to shield *himself.*

The addressee's being in the country enables the writer to contrast rural naturalness with urban unnaturalness and perversion:

> Fortune has thee to happier scenes convey'd,
> By nature fit for contemplation made,
> There may'st thou live, exploring of her laws,
> And neither meet with censure or applause.
>
> (lines 5–8)

It is curious that the writer's point is that his addressee must abandon such
naturalness for the unnatural perversions of the city in order to "shew the
virtues of the man I love" (line 10)—a telling phrase, given the prevalence
of the love of allegedly nonvirtuous men in the rest of the poem, which
suggests that even the nature of the relationship between the writer and the
addressee depends contrastively on more negative relationships in the city.

The reason for this, as for the addressee's abandonment of rural nature, is that such "naturalness" provides no opportunity for "censure or applause." What is *most* curious is that (as I hope to show) the same thing could be said, only perhaps more strongly, for unnaturalness, too, or that it subverts the whole bipolar system of praise and blame of which this poem is an expression.

Some of the ambivalence about naturalness/unnaturalness that underlies the poem can be detected in the following sequence of a shipwreck that in stormy seas (unnaturalness) disgorges its treasure onto the peaceful shore (of naturalness),

> But when the surges rage and billows roar
> The seas discharge their spoils upon the shore.
>
> (lines 15–16)

This is followed by a topical allusion to a criminal (one Thompson) taken and tried:

> So here such various follies rush to sight,
> Dark deeds that seek the covert of the night,
>
> (lines 21–22)

The idea might be that "storms" of uncertainty divulge both vice and virtue, but I note that the more "natural" disturbance produces "treasure" while the "unnatural" urban example produces dross in the form of some sort of highwayman. Is the point one of comparison or contrast? The language of light and dark suggests at least the possibility that the highwayman's dross serves as a kind of foil for the good.

Developing the series of contrasts on which the poem appears to be based, virtuous love seems to characterize the relationship of this writer and his addressee in the country, but patronage is associated with the city, and in general with homosexuality; both patronage and homosexuality are associated with the church:

> Pimps, b—[isho]—ps, pathicks, parasites attend,
> Each vice still finds some patron for a friend:
>
> (lines 33–34)

Eventually preferment is so closely associated with the church as to become almost a metaphor for it. Note that the equation is never simply "homosexuality = clergy," but rather "homosexuality = preferment and patronage

= clergy." Gilbert's formula always has a convenient third term—conveniently elided.

Lines 47-64 describe the preferment-seeking divines of Catholic and more recent Anglican history, in ways that remind one of Marvell or that anticipate Churchill. Priests sin with impunity,

> Hypocrisy, that bastard of their zeal,
> Serves as a veil, base actions to conceal;
>
> (lines 71–72)

but their sins, at this point, appear to be things like masquerading, gluttony, alcoholism, atheism—the usual (lines 79–100). In their wicked pursuit of patronage, the clergy have potentially enslaved a whole society. By sanctioning wicked patrons (ultimately the king himself), they compel everyone else to become a wicked client. The words associated with clergymen are effeminate or suggestive of the kind of female character both satirized and perpetuated by Pope: "pampered prelates" (75); "negligent to please" (54).

Lines 111–40 comprise a kind of "Directions" to the would-be flatterers, like Swift's "Directions for a Birthday Song," or Marvell's "Instructions" to the painter. This is literally "fucking panegyric"—panegyric in praise of fornication:

> On fornication panegyrics make,
> And swear his Lordship's the most finish'd rake
> That ever revel'd in the arms of *Cox*,
> Or went to *Missauban* to get a pox.
>
> (lines 129–32)

What follow are more truly characters of "unnaturalness"—a weak man who would like to be a reveler, a man of sense who prevaricates, and, more significantly, a sufficiently robust man who still refuses to be a lover, because he is a "fop":

> Such coxcombs love a theory intrigue
> But think the practice is too much fatigue.
>
> (lines 173–74)

Later lines indicate that for Gilbert the fop's unnaturalness consists of a kind of narcissism, a love of love which is really a love of the lover himself, but certainly not of women. The characters have the effect of equating

flattery, false praise, and intellectual unnaturalness with sexual unnaturalness—a kind of impotence that occurs as a result of a failure to fulfill one's
nature.

While women would obviously appear to share some of the guilt here,
Gilbert is unusually—at least for this kind of satire—reluctant to blame
women:

> Perhaps a despicable race of men
> Expect the female sex should feel my pen;
> The charms of beauty all their faults excuse,
> And claim protection from a youthful muse.

(lines 288–91)

Ostensibly his satire of women is constrained by the fact that he is in love
with a woman who, while she appears to be in love with someone else,
may *not* fall. It is more probable that his constraint is due to the obvious
rhetorical need (illustrated by the author of *Plain Reasons,* among others)
not to appear misogynistic just before his attack on presumably misogynistic homosexuals. It is as if homosexuality introduces a third alternative into
the essentially dualistic system of eighteenth-century formal verse satire.
The system shows signs of stress here, especially when Gilbert begins a
long section of blame, deflected from women onto male homosexual targets, by invoking Pope, an exponent of the tradition notorious for misogyny
and his own kind of eccentric sexuality:

> O *Pope*, thou scourge to a licentious age,
> Inspire these lines with thy severest rage;
> Arm me with satire keen as *Oldham* wrote
> Against the curst *Divan*, with poignant thought;
> To lash a crime which filthy lechers use,
> Sworn foes to mother *Haywood's* and the stews;
> Inverting nature to a foul design,
> They stop the propagation of their kind.

(lines 304–11)

He also invokes Oldham, who had satirized a kind of priesthood in his
Satires of the Jesuits. This would suggest a connection between the subject
of the beginning of the poem, the principal subject of the preface, and its
strong conclusion. Typically, however, Gilbert immediately shifts his
ground, from opposing the Jesuits/priests, to invoking them—though in
opposition to a clerical enemy that looks strikingly jesuitical:

> Bold race of men! whom nothing can affright,
> Not e'en their consciences in dead of night.
> Let *Jesuits* some subtler pains invent,
> For hanging is too mild a punishment:
> Let them ly groaning on the racking-wheel,
> Or feel the tortures of the burning steel;
> Whips, poisons, daggers, inquisitions, flames,
> This crime the most exalted vengeance claims;
> Or else be banish'd to some desart place.
> And perish in each other's foul embrace.

(lines 324–33)

Some Hypotheses

I hope some useful questions have arisen here. Why does Gilbert appear to describe a very different poem in his preface from the one he wrote? Why, in a satire ostensibly aimed at an abusive priesthood, does he conclude by invoking as a corrective what stood for precisely such abuses? More generally, why does his satire seem so scattered, unable to establish clear opposition, for example between fornication and chastity, in a form that depended on such symmetry? It becomes almost impossible to blame heterosexual promiscuity in the context of any sort of homosexual activity, since the latter, given the cultural values of the day, seems to make the former positive by comparison.

I suggest that there is no clear answer to such questions that is not simultaneously inter- and extratextual, or perhaps simply *contextual*. It is at least highly probable that Gilbert exploits an identification of the priesthood with sodomy that had already been established for him by Arnall and "Philalethes," and that was at least glanced at by the author of *Strict Observations*. It is also highly probable that he could only express such a charge against the priesthood indirectly, almost metonymically, or through a complicated formula the meaning of which could only be arrived at through elision of certain central terms. The existence of these other poems would have provided such a formula, whose very beauty was precisely its intertextuality. Gilbert's poem is fascinating for the way it articulates such relationships.

However, and this might be the most interesting aspect of these poems, there must have been considerable public awareness of homosexuality and some rather strong feeling about it for different writers to pick up on Arnall's illustration—as they obviously did. The texts would have provided the wiring, but this feeling must have supplied the current. And that must have been an *alternating* current, constantly reversing its polarity, making homosexuality now the vehicle of priestcraft, and now its tenor.

3

The Wadhamites: Homosocial versus Homosexual in *College-Wit Sharpen'd* and *A Faithful Narrative*

In a chapter entitled "The University and Social Life" in *The History of the University of Oxford: The Eighteenth Century*, V. H. H. Green observes that "In a society statutorily celibate there were inevitably some occasions of scandal. . . . In a predominantly youthful male society some degree of homosexual affection and activity was inevitable." Green then relates the following events described more circumstantially below: "The most widely publicized scandal concerned the warden of Wadham, Robert Thistlethwayte, accused of sodomy with a college servant and one of his undergraduates, Mr French, the latter unwillingly, in 1739. Another fellow, a Mr Swinton, seems to have escaped prosecution for the same offence" (Green 1986, 350). The following is a discussion of how this "society statutorily celibate," an intensely "homosocial" one, is addressed in two texts, *College-Wit Sharpen'd* and *A Faithful Narrative of the Proceedings*.

Ultimately I would like to consider how these works characterize not just the society they directly address, but the larger society too—which they address in a different way. This larger eighteenth-century society is, of course, the one for which these (not to mention other, similarly homophobic works) were printed. As we shall see, the larger one is what the university administrators themselves seem to have appealed to by allowing Baker's recantation to be published in the newspapers.

I know little about Robert Thistlethwayte, warden of Wadham College, beyond his dates: 1691–1744. A note in I. G. Doolittle's chapter, "College Administration," indicates what might have been a factor in there being homosexual wardens at Wadham. While heads of some colleges were allowed to marry, "Wardens of Wadham were unable to marry until 1806" (Doolittle 1986, 230). At the same time, as warden of a college, Thistlethwayte would have enjoyed sufficient wealth and privilege to discourage exposure. The *Dictionary of National Biography* indicates that the man who narrated his exposure, George Costard (1710–82), entered Wadham College about 1726 and became an "astronomical writer. . . . the drift of [whose] arguments was to show that exact astronomy was a product of Greek genius, beginning with Thales, and owed little to either to Egypt or Babylon." That his opponent in the Thistlethwaite affair, John Swinton, who entered Wadham in 1729, was an orientalist suggests that his animosity, while overtly homophobic, might have been aggravated by professional jealousies—such as the direction of Arab studies at the university, the intrinsic merit of Islamic learning, etc. The vacancy of the Laudian professorship of Arabic in 1738, and the installation of John Wallis, might have disturbed things. At least there are indications that from the outset the homosexual might have been secondary to the homosocial, but of course this is difficult for the nonspecialist to prove.[1]

One locus classicus for discussions of the homosocial is, of course, Eve Kosofsky Sedgwick's *Between Men: English Literature and Male Homosocial Desire*. In her opening pages she offers a kind of definition of the term, indicating its paradoxical nature:

> "Homosocial" is a word occasionally used in history and the social sciences, where it describes social bonds between persons of the same sex; it is a neologism, obviously formed by analogy with "homosexual," and just as obviously meant to be distinguished from "homosexual." (1985, 1)

Much of the tenor of Sedgwick's book is that the homosocial is increasingly removed from the homosexual, though perhaps never entirely. This might seem unexceptionable enough, given that with today's greater tolerance the homosocial and the homosexual could even be complementary. But in the eighteenth century, at least in the case of those "Wadhamites" John Swinton and George Baker, the relationship seems to have been more complicated than a simple opposition between two forms of mutually exclusive desire. The complexity of this relationship between the homosocial and the homosexual, in itself as complicated and as interesting as anything between the people involved, is indicated by the surprising outcome of the event: John Swinton, probably a homosexual, continued to enjoy homosocial life at Wadham College, while George Baker, his accuser and would-be exposer, was ostracized and himself exposed as a violator of homosocial bonds and boundaries. This raises many questions, the most important of which concern not only the nature of the relationship of the homosocial and the homosexual, but also the nature of the latter's role in contemporary life and thought. Without anticipating myself too much, I suggest at the beginning that the outcome of the events referred to by Green indicates that the homosexual might well have been opposite, but at the same time *subordinate,* to the homosocial, and moreover that, like most subordinate beings, he could also have continued to be serviceable to the order to which, after all, he still (somehow) belonged.[2]

These pieces extend our exploration of "homosexual expression" into the area of academic life. Slightly later as they are, they also seem at least a little more sophisticated. For one thing, they show how one important and fairly recent source of "expression" was the press, represented by the newspaper, which Baker's fellow academics knew better how to manipulate than he did. The "News Papers" become the ultimate arbiters of the contest between "the homosocial" and "the homosexual."

COLLEGE-WIT SHARPEN'D

The poem begins as if at the conclusion of a long-standing competition between Oxford and Cambridge over which university is the gayest. Oxford has won:

> At length, the *Quaere* is decided;
> And Disputants, long since divided,
> Must now in one Opinion join,
> Oxford does Cambridge far out-shine.
> There reigns, and thrives, an antient ART,
> T'improve the Health, and chear the Heart.
>
> (1)

In a reference to George Whitefield the poet suggests that if the English Methodist had only stayed at Wadham a little longer he would not only have learned how to be gay but how to get away with it:

> O! *Whitefield*, had you tarry'd longer,
> Your Party might have been much stronger.
> Could you, dear Sir, abet this Cause,
> You'd skreen your self from penal Laws;
> W[a]rd[e]ns, and C[hance]ll[o]r, would be-friend you;
> B[i]sh[o]ps at *Kennington* attend you:
> Nay, in their holy Arms embrace,
> Squeeze your white Hand, and kiss your Face:
>
> (2)

The poet makes connections between the clergy, preferment, and sodomy, similar to what we encountered in the *Codex* pieces; moreover, as in other midcentury works with homosexual subject matter, there is a tension here between the crime itself and the crime as illustration or vehicle, between what it is and what it stands for.[3] Here the poet seems more disturbed by Whitefield's learning the knack of "getting away with it" than by whatever it is he gets away with. In the poet's mind the thing itself is metonymically replaced by the thing—legal immunity—associated with it:

> Could you, dear Sir, abet this Cause,
> You'd skreen your self from penal Laws;
>
> (2)

The poet immediately focuses this trend of using homosexuality to illustrate the evil of more widespread abuses by associating it with patronage and its material benefits. The protecting embrace of power, of investiture, is equated with the penetrating sexual embrace of the homosexual, the client's full pockets with the patron's fondling hand in his breeches:

> Nay, more, they'd grope your virgin Breeches
> And lign your Pockets well with Riches.
>
> (3)

The problem with such equations is that with such extremely "charged" moral qualities, they become unstable and incriminating. If homosexuality here becomes principally illustrative, it probably does so the only way it can, by suggesting that there is something perverted about fundamental social arrangements like patronage—and that, conversely, homosexuality must consequently be nearly as pervasive. The identity between the two, between perversion and patronage, is reinforced by the obvious puns like the one on "rise":

> I only Hint, I don't advise:
> (Since ev'ry Man's not born to rise:)
>
> (3)

The naturalness implied in "ev'ry Man's not *born* to rise" (italics added) must immediately be qualified by whether "rise" means preferment or erection, and by whether—if the latter—it is for a woman or for a man. Some men might be "not born to rise" because they are heterosexual, and others because they are homosexual—depending. The really curious thing is the way the illustration of the social by the sexual consistently seems to naturalize the latter, if only by allowing for the reading that suggests that people could indeed be "born to rise" for loved ones of their own sex. With a similar effect, of spreading and normalizing homosexuality, the following lines associate it with the widespread elitism of "Taste":

> For should your Genius prove too low,
> Your Skull too thick, your Wit too slow;
> Should *Sw—nt—n* after taking Pains,
> T'infuse his Skill into your Brains,
> For want of Tast, mispend his Time,
> Your heavy Soul would be your Crime.

(3)

Thus, homosexuality seems to stand for "other" things, like the arbitrariness of preferment, or the elitism of "Tast," at the cost of enabling such things to stand, in lesser degree, for the homosexual. It is as if while homosexuality lends its "artificiality" to political and cultural arrangements, it acquires some of their diffuseness and pervasiveness. Something uncontrollable happens on the level of signification, akin to the process that Foucault and others call "sexualization," and which I will consider more elaborately in the following sections. For now I would only observe that, if it is always unclear just what is illustration and what is "text," some sort of crude equation is made between homosexuality and central concepts of Augustan society.

This subversion, especially through such concepts as "art" and "taste," continues in the next section, where Dr. Thistlethwayte's homosexuality is described in terms of a "virtuous" chastity:

> Deeply in this rare ART acquainted;
> Virtuous; no Vice his Soul e'er tainted:
> Nay, more, abhors a pretty Wench.
> Pleas'd with the sprightly Air of *Fr——ch*,
> Kindly determines to impart
> To him, the Secrets of his ART.

(4)

When one "French" proves a stupid, recalcitrant pupil, the poet moralizes:

> What one esteems a useful ART,
> Another values not a Fart.
>
> .   .   .   .

> Hard Fate, O! *Th—stle—th—te*, is thine,
> To cast thy Pearls, before such Swine.
>
> (6)

Thistlethwayte takes on two new pupils, who protest when he buggers them that "[they] cannot learn" and beg him to let him get him a whore—better to be pimps than catamites, bawds than buggerers. Thistlethwayte's speech seems to reinforce earlier identifications between preferment and perversion, through indication of a "role model" in another "Wadhamite," John Swinton, and through a pun on "interest" as self-interest and homosexual interest, reinforced by the same pun on "embrace" encountered earlier:

> View but how *Sw—nt—n spends* his Time;
> Pleasure and Profit, both combine,
> To make his Days one single Scene,
> Of perfect Bliss; then what d'ye mean?
> Embrace the present happy Time;
> Int'rest can never be a Crime.
>
> (10)

Again, the language blends moral platitude with innuendo as exhausted neoclassical Horatianisms ("to instruct and delight") are reapplied to a homosexual relationship—and, one should note, somewhat revived in the process.

Less than delighted with their teacher's "lesson," the students beat him. Curiously, but perhaps consistently with the poem's surprising neutrality, a function of the way homosexuality seems to be normalized by what it is associated with, by what illustrates it, and by what it illustrates in return, the students are next shown "screening" themselves, or doing the very thing that initially seemed more distasteful to the poet than homosexuality itself. If homosexuality equals screening and these pupils screen, then what are they? The question is especially insistent, given the earlier identification of homosexuality with screening from the law. These "stupid" pupils hear of that other "stupid" pupil French, "stupidity" now a code-word for homophobia, or at least a too-doctrinaire heterosexuality, which results in heterosexuals behaving like homosexuals. Such codedness contributes, along with the reflexiveness of the poem's comparisons (taste and art, for example, which point to the poem itself as a work of art), to an atmosphere less indignant than morally compromised and even complicitous:

> They heard by Chance, Oh happy Day!
> That *Fr——ch* as stupid was, as they;
> That after all the *W—rd—n's* Pains,
> He curs'd the ART, and cal'd him Names.
>
> (12)

The poet's own "ethos" is not spared the contagion that obviously infects his language. The trio's subsequent exposure of Thistlethwayte is offered as an instance of how "sometime's the Case, / Virtue and Learning meet Disgrace." But, the poet adds, in the same corrupted terms, "[It] very often gets the best / Of Vice and Falshood: Hear the rest."

The "rest" consists of the story of another Wadham sodomite, John Swinton, and his outwitting of a homophobe. Swinton is described, at least more sympathetically than Thistlethwayte, as a kind of homosexual "talent scout":

> *Sw—nt—n* desiring for to spread
> The skill, in which he's deeply read,
> To all around both Rich and Poor;
> No Indication can be truer,
> Of a diffusive publick Spirit,
> Which few are born for to inherit,
> After his ART with great Success
> He'd taught to twenty, more or less,
> Some Rich, some Poor, as he could find
> Their Genius was thereto inclin'd;
> Beheld with Sympathy a Youth
> Poor, yet unprejudic'd to Truth;
>
> (16–17)

Curiously, here the indifference of homosexual interest to "privilege" almost makes that interest look positive. Sodomy can illustrate something corrupt about patronage, and vice versa; however, it can also suggest new relationships replacing worn-out arrangements, an alternative system, and even perhaps a frame of mind in which almost any change is a change for the better. At least the "Youth" in question, Bob, appears to live happily with Swinton, until one Baker—described as "of Genius mean, / Crafty and base"—exposes Swinton to the chancellor and prevails on "Bob" to support him. The "Man's" reasons are curious because, while they repeat a standard argument against homosexuality, one that we have in fact encountered already in tracts like *Strict Observations,* they seem to be repeated without any conviction on the part of the poet, as obvious "commonplaces":

should the human Race,
His wicked Master's ART embrace,
Mankind would soon become no more,
Things would be just as heretofore.

(20)

The argument is further subverted by its obviously being no more than a rationalization for simple meanness. Luckily Swinton is able to talk to Bob and persuade him to lie on his behalf. Bob swears that he was bribed by Baker, who subsequently finds himself indicted under the Defamation Act.

A FAITHFUL NARRATIVE: THISTLETHWAYTE

This narrative is indeed "faithful": in its origins in the faithfulness of Baker's friends who were determined to "sift the Affair to the Bottom," in its faithfulness to the truth they discovered, and finally—since the latter tended to justify the former—as a vindication of faithfulness itself. The account can be read, as I for one think it was written, as an affirmation of appropriate male relationships through the affirmation—and denigration— of inappropriate relationships. The text celebrates homosocial relationships in the context of deploring homosexual ones. If Baker had not really dis-covered a homosexual in Swinton, his friends would have had to invent one. The stakes are best described by the author:

[T]ho' he *was not expelled the University* for the enormous Crime re-canted, the Publication of the Form, in which he was made to recant, seemed designed *to expel him from human Society*. . . . (1739, 2)

For Baker to belong to "human Society," Swinton must be cast out of it. The problem is not simply that Baker legally might have *slandered* Swinton, for which he is not even to be expelled from the university, but that the greater damage to homosocial relations requires some sort of expiation— someone must pay. Throughout the pamphlet one senses this terrible dis-crepancy between the legalities of the matter—significant as they some-times are—and the sexual politics. This will also be the issue in *Mr. Bradbury's Case,* to be discussed later, in which Bradbury's accusers simi-larly miscalculate the nature of the charge.

The Robert Thistlethwayte affair begins as an interruption of normal homosocial relations, with Thistlethwayte sending his manciple to conduct Mr. William French, "a young Gentleman of about two Years standing," from a meeting with "Fellow Collegiates" to the warden's lodgings. Some of the nature of that meeting is inferred from its effect on subsequent social gatherings: French is "disordered" during supper, breaks off a meeting with several students in a "Gentleman's Room"—to vomit—and spends the rest of the evening vilifying the Warden:

> *The matter*, said he, *the Murther of one's Father, or whole Family is noth-*
> *ing to it; you can't conceive any thing bad enough.* (3)

On the Monday following the "incident" French invites George Baker and a few others to breakfast with him. An intermediary explains "in what an unaccountable Manner Mr. *French* had behaved ever since he came from the Warden's Lodgings, repeating the Names he called him" (4). Baker recommends prudence, and "all the Company, except one Gentleman, went away" (4).

Later Baker dines alone with the intermediary, and it is to him that "Mr. *Baker* recollected, that, about a Fortnight before, it had been suggested to him, that *the Warden did not love Women*" (4). At that time Baker did not believe the man, partly because the man was at odds with the warden over other business, but mainly because "it was generally believed, that the Warden was over-familiar with a certain Woman in *Oxford*" (5). This "suggestion" and French's innuendos are sufficient to lead Baker and the intermediary to the inference that the warden is "probably" homosexual:

> This, however, coming into his Thoughts on the present Occasion, upon
> comparing Circumstances, the other Gentleman and himself concluded it
> most probable, that the Warden had made a sodomitical Attempt upon
> Mr. *French*. (5)

Baker then resolves to confront French with his suspicion, partly because he "had always been very intimate with Mr. *French*, his Neighbour in the Country, and his professed Friend" (5). Perhaps self-interest would make his duty to protect his fellow from homosexual relations seem greater, the greater his own homosocial relations with that individual. It is not simply a matter of protecting one's relationship, but also of protecting one's self against contamination through it. Again, the emphasis here seems to be on affirming the homosocial by affirming—and decrying—the homosexual. It is Baker who finally utters the charge—"the Thing could be nothing but Sodomy" (6)—and insists that French "make it known, for the good of the College, University, & c. and assuring him, that he should not want Friends to assist him" (6). Ironically, Baker will later be asked to recant for the same reasons. Finally, French signs a "Declaration at large, of which the Particulars are judged too gross and obscene to be repeated, and such as amounted to the most notorious sodomitical Attempt conceivable" (7).

Before prosecuting the warden, French tries to get him to sign a testimonial to his character. The warden agrees to do so, but begs French not to expose him. When he offers to bribe him, French merely denounces him to "Ten or Twelve young Gentlemen" waiting in the college quadrangle.

On Sunday the Rev. Mr. Swinton is asked to testify that he "came to the Warden's Lodgings Yesterday Fortnight in the Afternoon; that [he] found the Parlour Door bolted; that [he] waited some time before the Warden opened it; and that, when [he] came in, [he] found [French and the warden] together" (11). Early Monday morning Swinton sends his "Bed-maker" to ask French's father to join himself and the warden in his lodgings. There the two beg old French to take his son into the country, offering to "provide handsomely for him" (12). Old French refuses to cooperate. At the hearing a few hours later, Swinton cannot be found. About a fortnight later, the Warden himself vanishes.

At the Assizes, various people testify to the warden's practices. The account of one Robert Langford, the butler, reproduced as direct speech, is notable for the way it depicts the latter's almost equal fear of being alone or in company with the warden. Alone, he risks being forced to participate in a homosexual relationship, while in company he risks exposure—by his very uneasiness with the warden—for being involved as much as he is, however unwillingly or one-sidedly, with a homosexual. His predicament partly explains the pressure on French to "out" the warden—even when it is ignored, homosexuality proves inimical to normal homosocial relations. Ironically, Boxley's terror of violating homosocial standards of behavior only forces him into more intimate homosexual relations with the warden:

> the Warden was looking out of his Study Window, and called him: . . . as there were several Gentlemen in the Quadrangle, he did not know what to do, and thought it would appear very odd if he refused to go to the Governor of the College, when he called him: That therefore he went, and as soon as he came into the Room the Warden began his Caresses, trying to kiss him, &c. as before. (17)

A FAITHFUL NARRATIVE: SWINTON

The attack on Swinton begins, according to the author of the *Faithful Narrative,* when Baker receives a letter "from a Gentleman in the Country, a Master of Arts, of *Wadham* College." This "Gentleman" reports that, when he was at Oxford, the "boy" of his servants claimed that "he had lain with Mr. *Swinton*" (1739, 20). Baker interrogates Smith, and finds the report true. Smith recounts that when he found the boy had been in Swinton's rooms he beat him, for fear that he would "fill him full of Lice" (21). Then Swinton intervened on the boy's behalf, explaining that he needed "Bob" to give him medicines.

Baker and company interrogate the boy in a room in a tavern, in a meeting that itself sounds not unlike a homosexual rendezvous as it would be reported in some London magazine:

> At the Sight of so many Strangers the Boy was confounded, and would say nothing: upon which every body left the Room except Mr. *Baker*, *Smith*, and the Boy, to whom one of the Gentlemen, that went out, gave a Penny, which was afterwards alledged to be given by Mr. *Baker*, by way of Bribe. . . . (22)

After the boy describes his homosexual relations with Swinton, Baker returns to his college, and immediately convokes the fellows "to spend the Evening with him at his Room" (24). By the next day, however, Swinton manages to get at the boy. In subsequent testimony before the vice-chancellor, the boy is so confused that the vice-chancellor supports Swinton and asks Baker to sign a recantation.

Baker invokes homosocial duty as reason *not* to sign:

> He added, that his only Motives for what he had done, were for the good of his College, and the Publick in general; and the persuasion, that after the Affair had been made known to him in so clear a manner, it was his Duty, as well as every Man's in the University, as they had all suffered in their Characters upon *Thistle-thwayte's* Account, to have their Eyes about them and not to suffer even the Suspicion of so great a Crime to escape them. (27)

Typically, he delays signing till he can talk to his friends, who advise him "not to sign it in that Form; for it would be much better to be expelled, than to sign a Thing so injurious to his Reputation, and so contrary to Truth, and his real Sentiments" (29). Baker is resolved not to sign, till the vice-chancellor convinces him that the wording of the document, while incriminating, is "*meer matter of Form*" (30). He signs, but when he discovers, to his consternation, that the recantation is to be "inserted in the News Papers" (31), and protests to the vice-chancellor, he finds that the homosocial society of the university has by now united against *him*, and that "some of the

Heads of Houses" would like to punish him further. Baker protests that "[the vice-chancellor] would be much censured for suffering such a Person, as he should appear from that Publication, to continue a Member of the University" (32). He seems to appreciate that he is being punished almost as severely for alleging homosexuality as Swinton would have been for being homosexual.

SOME HYPOTHESES

College Wit Sharpen'd seems technically rather simple, but ideologically complicated. It is never quite clear whether its author's intent is to depict homosexuality as a crime or to use homosexuality as an illustration of other crimes and societal problems—the degradation of preferment, for example, or the partiality of law, or the subjectivity of "art" and "taste," etc. Certainly an equation is established between homosexuality and a number of eighteenth-century commonplaces—attitudes to privilege, to preferment, to taste, to art, and even to certain aspects of neoclassicism. That not all of the equations are negative suggests not only an unusually high degree of sympathy in the writer, but also the disordering capability of homosexuality in eighteenth-century culture.

Baker's mistake in the *Faithful Narrative* is in confounding legality and sexuality, or rather the legal and the homosocial—in thinking that the illegality of homosexuality would not ultimately be subordinated to the homosocial, and (less abstractly) in allowing himself to be duped by the vice-chancellor into believing that a matter of legal form could satisfy the violation of the homosocial by homosexual allegations. Perhaps, concerned as he was with the illicit, he mistook the strength of the licit and put himself in the position of the homosexual. Underlying such a mistake there must have been an even greater mistakenness about the nature of his allegation and of the homosocial relationships that it affected; he must have miscalculated that the allegation would somehow be reversible, that its affect on homosocial society would be reversed without the latter exacting a stiffer penalty than a simple recantation. Baker could not be wrong about homosexuality, could not damage homosocial relationships so seriously yet unsuccessfully, without jeopardizing his own homosocial existence. His mistake is almost symbolized by his victimization in the newspapers, where the niceties of legality are obliterated by a judgment more collective and more primordial.

Finally, I think the *Faithful Narrative* is less satisfying reading than the much cruder *College-Wit Sharpen'd,* because it is an example of rather dull college wit; it is "faithful" in another, more pejorative sense, the way a loyal but unintelligent dog is faithful. For our "narrator" fails to perceive that Baker himself is not very "faithful," either to his own principles, or to the principles of the homosocial game—that you cannot be wrong about something like homosexuality and continue to belong. Evading banishment from his college by admitting his error, Baker is indeed banished from the world, exactly as his friends predicted.

Ironically, while Baker is punished for alleging that Swinton is homosexual, Swinton gets off—even gets Baker's bond for "good behaviour"—while remaining patently homosexual. The implication is that homosexual relationships are not so much inimical as subordinate, or even serviceable, to homosocial ones; when it is easier to preserve homosocial relationships by tolerating than by persecuting homosexuals, homosexuals will be tolerated. The Swinton case demonstrates that homosocial society actually *requires* such toleration and a corollary kind of cooperation on the part of homosexuals themselves, all of which the poet of *College-Wit Sharpen'd* seems to appreciate.

In different ways then, these works indicate what might aptly be called the stubborn inherence of homosexuality in some areas of eighteenth-century life. The poem depicts homosocial arrangements as inherently homosexual; the prose depicts such inherently homosocial arrangements almost inadvertently "arrayed" against their would-be exposer, whose essentially tactical error is his underestimation of the "crime" he is "exposing." Moreover, if what Baker meant to expose was as already obvious as the poet of the Wadhamites suggests, all he really had to expose was himself. As for the homosexual "versus" the homosocial, far from being opposed, the former obviously served the latter in so far as the very accusation of it proved heinous enough to warrant the expulsion and eventual ostracism of Baker, whose accusations seem finally to have posed a greater threat to the order than anything he accused Swinton of.

4

Sporus before Us:
Some Versions of Hervey

In "Sodomy Transformed: Aristocratic Libertinage, Public Reputation and the Gender Revolution of the 18th Century," Randolph Trumbach theorizes that a "third gender"—homosexuality—emerged in eighteenth-century England as men attempted to define themselves heterosexually in the face of increasing equality between men and women:

> The majority of men who knew that men could not desire men, that only women did that, and that the molly was the outcast demonstration that this was so, such a majority, secure in at least one insurmountable difference between men and women, and a difference founded (so it was thought) in human biology and anatomy, could face with greater equanimity in other areas of life the growing equality between the two legitimate genders. (1990, 106)

He illustrates this process with three aristocrats, among whom is Lord Hervey, who (according to Trumbach) "had in his own mind taken on the molly's role; the role of the bisexual rake and libertine was not for him an option." He describes how later satirists even argued that Hervey, who probably was bisexual, only had liaisons with women as a "cover" for homosexual activity (see also Dubro 1976).

In this chapter I wish to consider more carefully how Hervey was depicted by contemporaries besides his more famous enemies like Pope. These depictions indicate a concern about Hervey, and about his homosexuality, that is sufficiently consistent with the above tracts to suggest a growing preoccupation, a deepening anxiety about the meaning of sodomy in eighteenth-century culture. In particular, they indicate a preoccupation with that essential nothingness, that lack of fixity, which characterizes homosexuals in the earlier tracts (*Plain Reasons, Strict Observations,* and *Hell upon Earth)* and which would account for some of the fear of homosexuals exploited by the *Codex* tracts, especially as homosexuals are seen to infiltrate power arrangements or as such arrangements are seen to be almost innately homosexual. The previous tracts indicate, of course, an association of homosexuality with patronage, which would have been aggravated in the case of an obviously powerful patron who was also homosexual.

Most readers will already be familiar with Pope's satire of John, Lord Hervey, in *Epistle to Arbuthnot.* Pope's lines depict the notorious homosexual in a series of contradictions, as essentially "one vile Antithesis" (line 325). While Pope's virtuosic rendering is deservedly the better known, Hervey's character and prominence in Whig politics in the 1730s generated a number of inferior portraits that, if less accomplished, are possibly no less revealing than Pope's of how the age viewed homosexuality, and especially of how the age addressed the problem of homosexuality in a man as prominent and public as Hervey.

The following is simply a review of some of these "versions" of Hervey, an indication of some of the things they reveal. I will summarize these characterizations at the end of the chapter, to suggest what these tracts indicate in common about attitudes to homosexuals, and to aristocratic homosexuals especially. These treatments of Hervey, a figure very much at the center of his culture, will serve as a bridge to a discussion of the more pervasive yet necessarily subtler expression of homosexuality in the 1740s and 1750s in Mark Akenside's *The Pleasures of Imagination* and his *Odes.*

A PROPER REPLY TO A LATE SCURRILOUS LIBEL (1731)

William Pulteney's *A Proper Reply to a Late Scurrilous Libel* was occasioned by Hervey's criticism of his opposition to Walpole in the dedication to *Sedition and Defamation Display'd* (1731).[1] One can imagine those who knew anything about Hervey being especially offended by his insistence in that dedication that he was "a Member of the Community which you are endeavouring to disturb" (1731, i). The thrust of subsequent tracts is either to challenge and control such a claim, or simply to deplore it.

Pulteney's tract is especially important, not only for its almost brutal exploitation of homosexuality for political ends, but for instigating an infamous duel whose "literary consequences . . . were far more enduring than the wounds inflicted" (Halsband 1973, 116). The tract both exploits the conventions of homophobic writing and reinforces their application to contemporary politics. According to Halsband, it "initiated Hervey's career as an object of satire, a career that would outlast his life" (116).

Hervey is depicted throughout as a delicate, perennially immature "schoolboy":

> I thought it beneath any Writer, of Years and Experience, to set his Strength against a young Beginner, and was afraid it would discourage you from pursuing your Studies. . . . Some Persons assured me, that They were the Compositions of a promising young Gentleman of *Eton* School. . . . (4)

This "schoolboy" soon becomes a "school*girl*" or *"Miss,"* whose *"virgin Expressions"* seem to flow from a specifically heterosexual "virginity." Clearly Hervey represents something unique, neither male nor female: "at least such a nice Composition of the two Sexes, that it is difficult to distinguish which is most predominant" (5). Like other writers, Pulteney seems to zero in on a target that is tantamount to "zero" itself, but not nothing.

Thus, like most homosexuals in these tracts, Hervey is marked above all by a "nonessentialism" that in turn facilitates that alarming "amphibiousness" which Pope remarks only slightly later in *Epistle to Arbuthnot*. In consternation, Pulteney demands: "[W]hat will this little Creature come out at last; a *Courtier* or a *Country Gentleman*; a *Gamester*, or a *Patriot*; a *Poet* or a *Pamphleteer*; a *Man* or a *Woman*?" (11). That the list of oppositions that Hervey amphibiously "deconstructs" includes political as well as sexual pairs indicates the nature of the climax to come.

The climax of the two-fronted assault on Hervey's politics and sexuality alike occurs on page 27, where Pulteney answers Hervey's complaint (or the complaint of another writer mistaken for Hervey) that the *Craftsman* has charged Walpole with corruption but never *proved* it. Pulteney balefully observes that such corruption is harder to prove than a much worse form, "a certain, unnatural, reigning Vice," in which "The proof of the Crime hath been generally made by the *Pathick*" (27).

This barbed passage resonates with all sorts of implications. Such comparisons facilitate a degree of "polyvalency," normalizing homosexuality almost as much as they denigrate what homosexuality is supposed to illustrate (even contrastively). While mainly contrasted with more obvious forms of political corruption (bribery, patronage, embezzlement, etc.), it has something in common with them, if only as yet another corruption.

Moreover, it is impossible not to make a comparison of one form of corruption to another, in which one must wonder whether Hervey's "pathick" is not somehow analogous to Walpole's implicitly "pathick" victim, the state—a "pathick" that will never tell, no matter how "a Man [Walpole?] enjoys every Moment the Fruits of his Guilt" (28). The statement is itself a not very veiled accusation of homosexuality, at once both public and private.

Finally, if Pulteney cannot prove *both* public and private corruption, he can at least prove the latter, in which the former, if only by virtue of Hervey's public role, has to be implicated as well.

THE COUNTESS'S SPEECH TO HER SON, RODERIGO (1731)

That the *Countess's Speech,* inspired by another pamphlet depicting Pulteney and Hervey as Cassio and Roderigo (Halsband 1973, 118), seems to have been written by the author in order to ingratiate himself with Pulteney, makes it a good example of the way the homosexual serves the homosocial—the sacrifice that cleanses. The announcement of the author's acceptance and inclusion—through this very work—in Pulteney's society immediately precedes the announcement of the indication of the subject's exclusion and even ostracism:

> As it was presented By the Author, on *Monday* the first Day of *February,* 1731. to the Right Honourable *William Pulteney,* Esq; at his House in *Arlington-street,* near St. *James's,* To which is prefixed, Some curious OBSERVATIONS on BOYS challenging their Betters. (1)

In case we miss his rather clear indication of Hervey's unmanliness, the writer adds a couplet of doggerel in which Hervey's wound, which ought to have betokened his virility, becomes the very "obscure hurt" that denies it:

> Ne'er was a harder Case, pray; let me tell you,
> To have a *SMALL Prick* at Bottom of the Belly.

(1)

A prose introduction suggests that the duel was fought by Hervey in order to prevent his participating in the debate concerning "the continuance of the *Hessian* Forces" (1731, 3) and a comparison to a similar case in the reign of Queen Anne implies that Hervey is a drunkard and a coward— and the tool of Robert Walpole. The poem begins with Hervey's mother's arrival on the scene, at the conclusion of the duel, and her remonstrance:

> What hast thou got by all thy hair-brained Zeal?
> Is *Bob* a Surgeon those curs'd Wounds to heal?

(6)

Of course, Hervey's wounds are sexual as well as physical. The lines could also mean that no amount of power from Walpole could make him a man, or repair the damage to his manhood brought on by such self-exposure. Almost immediately she alludes to Hervey's sexuality, or at least to the effeminacy associated with it:

> He shou'd be damn'd, and all his blund'ring Kin,
> E'er I'd a Pamphlet write, or *spoil that Skin*.
>
> (6)

She chastises both her son, since his death would be a great loss to "*Belles* and *Beaux*," among whom none is "so belov'd" as himself, and Pulteney, for nearly causing it—which the language indicates would not be difficult:

> O! cruel *Pult'ney*, most hard-hearted Man,
> How could'st thou make those Cheeks so pale and Wan?
> Fiercer than Tygers surely thou must be,
> To hurt my Boy, who scarce wou'd hurt a Flea.
>
> (6)

The rest of her speech is laced with praise and deprecation that is all really an attack on Hervey's virility:

> Thou, pretty Youth, was't never made to fight,
> Unless it were with Ladies in the Night,
>
> .   .   .   .
>
> And cou'd you such a Champion hope t'oppose,
> You, who've scarce wip'd the Milk from off your Nose.
>
> .   .   .   .
>
> What tho' thou can'st a *Mattador* command,
> Can'st thou kill *Poultney* with that milk white Hand?
> You wield a Sword, or you State-Pamphlets write,
> You answer *Caleb D'Anvers*, you go sh—te.
>
> (6–7)

The masculine man of *Plain Reasons* was suited for everything; the nonessential Hervey is suited for nothing but, spectacularly, a travesty of the capable "Renaissance Man"—a "Renaissance Failure." The poem implies an identification of writing and fighting, for *both* of which Hervey is equally disqualified by his emblematic, effeminate "white hand." At most he is suited for games, a substitute for the real activities from which he is excluded.

This mother's "anxious Cares," or at least her expressions of them, are terminated by the need to attend a game of her own, ombre. One obvious suggestion of the satire is that Hervey is what at least until recently we termed a "mother's boy," but with the significant difference that the countess of Bristol is not a very good "boy's mother"—at least not in the fostering sense. She clearly hates him, or perhaps it would be truer to the spirit of the piece to write that *he* is obviously incapable of inspiring, even in his mother, any love greater than a china collector's for an especially delicate cup and saucer.

An Epistle from a Nobleman (1733)

Hervey's poem seems to have created almost as much controversy as his "Dedication" to the patrons of the *Craftsman*, though certainly less deliberately, since he had not expected his addressee, one Dr. Sherwood, to show it to others (Halsband 1973, 161). It is written in the persona of a busy courtier, who has forgotten most of the "stuff" he learned at college, so has to respond in "plain native *English*" to the learned "Doctor of Divinity," who had in fact sent him a verse-letter in Latin:

> I'm sure your courteous Rev'rence will forgive
> The homely way, in which you now receive
> These hearty thanks, from an illiterate hand,
> For favours which I barely understand.
>
> (10)

He wants his learning to be judged in relation to that of other lords, to which it is above average:

> And when you see me fairly write my name,
> For *England's sake* wish all could do the same.
>
> (11)

Like the lines above, the following lines seem intended to address charges made against him—here, specifically, the charge of the author of the *Countess's Speech* that he is a (somewhat unloving) mother's boy. He cannot be, Hervey suggests, because he is not even an eldest son:

> Nay, I perhaps could not so much have done,
> Had I been bred and born an eldest son.
> A noble father's heir, spoil'd by his mother,
> Leaves learning always to his younger brother;

> Who at the bar must prate to earn a groat
> While all *our* business is to dress and vote.
>
> (11)

The "our" of the last line anticipates the change upon inheriting the title, described in the next lines. He pretends to be more ignorant than he is, and less a "wit":

> In every company was bold and loud,
> Behav'd myself as rudely as I could,
> And ne'er discours'd of what I understood.
> 'Tis thus among *the great.* . . .
>
> (12)

From this insight, that in some contexts to appear witty it would be foolish, Hervey seems to draw a conclusion that does not clearly follow—that wit is in fact foolish. His argument—from the foolishness of appearing witty to the foolishness of "one" who believes that no wit can be a fool, to a more general critique of wit—is at best hard to follow and tendentious:

> —void of prudence, and too vain of parts,
> How oft good heads have plainer shewn bad hearts?
>
> (12)

An even greater difficulty is Hervey's perverse tendency to implicate himself. He makes his point about wit and the philistinism of the aristocracy with an example of a "witty" exception who illustrates the antithesis of the mistaken belief "that no body with *wit* can be a *fool.*" The foolishness of the example is in maintaining such a belief, or in not having the *common sense* to *not* maintain it.

The important thing, which Hervey typically reveals while missing it himself, is that while we seem to have shifted from the relative value of wit in different circles to its relative value as one of a set of individual characteristics, the problem in both cases remains one of context. Moreover, while the value of wit in different contexts seems uncertain, so does the value of the contexts themselves. Rather than establish any context to support himself and assure the reader, Hervey seems motivated by contradictory desires both "to pass" in contexts for which he feels no strong allegiance and "to out" himself—as he does here, by writing such an autobiographical poem in the first place. Pope usually writes as an "insider" outside the establishment; Hervey writes as an "outsider" inside it.

The object of this attack on wit without common sense or prudence is, of course, Pope himself, whom he criticizes for the very sort of thing he had criticized Hervey for earlier—superficiality:

> Such wits are nought but glittering ignorance:
> What *Monkeys* are to men, they are to sense;
> Imperfect mimicks, ludicrous and mean,
> Who often bite that fool they entertain.
>
> (13)

After this critique of wit and learning, Hervey hardly seems to need to apologize for the "ignorance" that he says characterizes men of his "degree." This is what facilitates the fluency that, he writes, is indicated by the lines of his poem—and that Pope himself acknowledged when he wrote that "His Lordship spins a thousand in a day." But Hervey seems to want to do too many things at once: to turn his "ignorance" into a positive; to accuse Pope of the same "ignorance," only in a negative sense; to claim for himself the status of the aristocratic amateur; and to "share" some of that amateurishness with his middle-class, and more professional, rival. He clearly has difficulty establishing any clear character for himself, and only undermines his ethos when, at the end, he deprecates the court to which he belongs, if he does to anything, and makes damaging admissions:

> Like you we *lounge*, and feast, and play, and chatter;
> In private satirize, in publick flatter.
>
> (16)

Such lines are infelicitous precisely because they are so public. What they admit to is not very different from the "wit's" criticisms, which he cited earlier as worn-out clichés—tired or not, they seem true. Similarly, his positive advice to the poet sounds little different from the exhausted neo-classicism that he continually charges Pope with:

> True wit is reason in her gayest strain;
> That can at once inform and entertain:
> Her lively truths attentive we explore,
> Pleas'd we commend, instructed we adore.
>
> (13)

According to Maynard Mack, Pope could not ignore such an attack from a man as powerful as Hervey (1985, 608). His initial response, *A Letter to a Noble Lord,* was not published in his lifetime, perhaps because (as Mack suggests) he could not find a suitably dignified tone for his reply. Perhaps Mack is slightly partial in his evaluation of the contest between Pope and Hervey, since if Pope found it hard to establish the right tone with which to address a peer of the realm, it seems only fair to acknowledge that Hervey must have been at least as handicapped by being accused of something as indefensible as homosexuality.

TIT FOR TAT (1734)

How puerile are all his lays!
Insatiable his thirst of praise.
Learning "deserts his *John-Trot* head,
"And leaves plain *English* in its stead".
But "he can fairly write his name",
And wishes "all could do the same.
"A noble heir, spoil'd by his mother,
"Leaves learning to his elder brother".
Thus in epitome the Elf
Has foolishly portray'ed himself.

. . . .

Drawn at full length, without a SCREEN,
In proper colours there is seen,
His L . . . . . with a Lady's mein.

(17–19)

The above lines are from *The Review,* the conclusion of the pamphlet called *Tit for Tat,* which also contains the text of Hervey's *Letter* and some introductory criticisms. Though less forgiving, these are not dissimilar to my own.

Understandably, given the nature of Hervey's worn-out advice above, he is criticized for being himself only more wearisomely neoclassical than he accuses Pope of being; worse, the writer refuses to take Hervey's self-deprecation and self-consciousness as in any way an excuse for the place-less and generally unsuited nature he is conscious of, and mercilessly turns the lord's own words against him:

Thy learn'd Epistle well describ'd,
The little rules you first imbib'd;
How happy you! the only ———
Could ever read or write one word.
How smartly you expose the rest
By characters that suit thee best!

(4)

Hervey's criticism of the philistinism of his own class is reversed; it is understood not as an oblique kind of modesty or even self-criticism, but as a libel motivated by his need to look good with only meager accomplishments. Perhaps the criticism of the last two lines is not unjust; Hervey is not the first homosexual to betray himself by language, or by his own mouth. His presentation of elder brothers as "spoiled" is similarly turned against him as a *younger* brother, with at least as much sense as in the earlier presentation, and with more satirical point. The wit or "natural parts" that he cultivates are identified with the sodomitical ass, his penchant for which does not remain "latent" either:

> Being no [lord], you had no patent
> To let your nat'ral parts lie latent;
>
> . . . .
> You quicker learn'd than they could teach,
> And all without one smarting b——ch;
> Fond mamma thought a rod but spoil'd
> The genius of a witty child.

(4)

The implication, reminding one of the emphasis on education or miseducation in *Plain Reasons,* is that the ass that did not smart from the rod smarted from worse things later on; Hervey's mother reverses more than a proverb as, to preserve what she pretty clearly sees as a homosexual orientation, she deliberately "spares" her child and spoils his "rod." Subsequently, the move to the court, which Hervey writes made it necessary for him to interrupt and even disguise his learning, is presented as an easier transition, a part of his education readily undergone, if not in subtler ways undergone already:

> To finish neat the whole that's wanted,
> The stripling was to c—— transplanted;
> But there, alas! the *Greek* and *Latin,*
> Were dropp'd for velvet, paint and satin;

(5)

After describing his taking his seat in the House of Lords, as a "green" youth among "grey-beards," the author of *Tit for Tat* interrupts his animadversions on Hervey's *Letter* to question the fitness of its being addressed to a clergyman, or rather of a clergyman having written him initially. Obvi-

ously the writer suspects that the *Letter* is not a reply, and that the clergyman is just a respectable-seeming excuse. The writer imagines the clergyman and the lord mounting one another "pick-a-pack," a likely allusion to
Hervey's being a sodomite (or at least to his being suspected of being one):

> But when your GOODNESS thought it fit,
> To grace his dulness with your wit,
> You might have mounted pick-a-pack,
> Your raree-show upon your back,
> As *Savoyards* from street to street
> Accost each passenger they meet.
>
> (6)

Our author returns to his critique of Hervey's poem, itself an eighteenth-century *reading* of it, by questioning his judgment in attacking Pope,
who clearly outclasses him. He should have limited his targets to things
within his own "sphere":

> In your own sphere you might have found,
> Some proper mark, for you to wound;
>
> (7)

In this sphere are coxcombs, women like Lady Mary Montagu, writers like
Cibber, and writings like panegyric, "that spurious offspring of *Parnassus*."
This is, essentially, the "sphere" of the homosexual, like the sphere of the
woman, where

> UNRIVAL'D you may talk of fashion,
> And quite new dress the whole she-nation;
>
> (7)

The menacing possibility of a "she-nation," especially menacing given
Hervey's public stature, suggests that Hervey's "sphere" is at least partly
wish fulfillment, something his enemies would have *wanted* to believe in.
Hervey's mistake is in thinking that success inside such a sphere, at the
games that some of the above writers accuse him of playing, implies success outside it, in the "real" world—of men. The writer of *Tit for Tat* might
agree with my statement that Hervey writes as an outsider inside the establishment, but he would almost certainly qualify that "establishment" as
somewhat other than reality. What is striking about his attempt to deny
reality to Hervey's realm is the way he attacks him—again, like one of the

earlier writers, equally as writer and as man of action. Writing would conventionally become the realm of the man not competent in the "real" world,
but that even this shadow-land (which could be nebulous enough) is denied Hervey, underlines the degree of his nonentity. While other incompe-
tents, outcasts, and exiles turn to writing, Hervey must turn to something
even less real, and more fantastic:

> BUT can your arm a weapon lift
> To battle P[ultene]y, P[op]e, or S[wi]ft;
> In an ill hour the task you chose,
> Be——s'd in rhime, be ——— it in prose:
> 'Tis act the second of the farce,
> Just as you duel you write verse.
>
> . . . .
>
> Let *P[o]pe* or *P—[ultene]y* be the man,
> You quit your sword, or drop your pen.
>
> (8)

What Hervey should be, then, is the eighteenth-century homosexual:

> The very essence of perfumes,
> The star of balls and d[rawing] r[oo]ms;
> The wonder of a *Sunday* croud,
> Affected, foppish, vain and loud;
> Poppet all o'er in dress and feature,
> A very linsey-wolsey creature;
> Ne'er made for use, just fit for show,
> Half wit, half fool, half man, half beau:
>
> (9)

The opposition of the first set of items in the last line (wit and fool) is
implied in the second—for "beau" we may read "woman." The suggestion
is confirmed in following lines:

> So finely colour'd, such a grace,
> One takes it for my Lady's face;
> As highly touch'd with nicest care,
> The self-same pert and silly air.
>
> (9)

In such lines one cannot escape the agreement of the homophobe and the
misogynist—women are pert and silly; men are worse than pert and silly

for wanting to resemble them. Finally, Hervey should leave off the "public" entirely, since wisdom and beauty are incompatible:

> Wisdom ill suits a face so pretty,
> Content at most to be thought witty;
> Let dirty patriots hold debate,
> In s[enate]s shine, and mend the s[tate],
> Midst a love speech they surely spoil it,
> And cannot argue at a toilet;
> Sometimes they catch us by the ear,
> Whilst eyes and noses hold you dear.

(9)

One obvious solution for the problem posed by this "inside outsider" is to
put him even further inside, into a sphere that is at once public and restricted—
as opposed to the one he presently occupies, public and unrestricted in terms
of influence and access to the Crown. The newspaper is obviously one means
of such insertion, as is this publication, which inserts Hervey's poem between
two others that tell us how to read it—as the scribble of an effeminate homosexual "insider," as metaphorically contained as he should be literally.

FLAVIA TO FANNY (1733)

The main conceit of *Flavia to Fanny* is Hervey's effeminacy, which
leads Flavia to mistake him for a fellow female scribbler:

> But hold, where is it I am running,
> I may mistake, for all my cunning,
> Faith I forgot that some have said,
> Thou are a Male, and not a Maid. . . .

(3)

Flavia resolves to defend him anyway:

> —if of gender *Epicene*,
> I'll guard thee safe from vulgar spleen

(3)

Hervey's writing resembles women's writing because it is unnatural, though
in a different way. While *Flavia* describes the difference between them in

terms of learning and wit, I think it is really much subtler. Just as the common denominator between them is the unnaturalness of their writing, the difference between them is in the *way* that they are unnatural. Flavia's unnaturalness stems from someone who is otherwise natural, doing something—writing—that for her gender is unnatural. Note that unnatural actions do not make her unnatural. Hervey's unnaturalness is different in kind, since it stems not from any act but from his whole being, the "fact" of his homosexuality, which renders even natural actions unnatural. Natural actions do not make him natural—he makes them unnatural. Thus Flavia, who appears to be genuinely learned, is foolish when she writes, but still no fool; Fanny, who has no learning, appears foolish when he writes, for no other reason than that he is a fool. The woman herself does not perceive the deeper reasons for Hervey's failure and for her own, since she suggests that they simply trade surfaces, supplying one another's weaknesses—she his deficient learning, he her deficient wit. His wit in her will be no better received than her learning in him, because he is a homosexual as she is a woman; "wit" is as incompatible with being a woman as "wisdom" is with being a homosexual. Moreover, each seems to trade what is more appropriate to his or her sexuality for what is less:

> Thus we shall fairly cheat the town,
> While we each other works do own,
> I shine in wit, and you in learning,
> Scarce *Pope* himself, the trick discerning.

(4)

It is probably supposed to be all the more telling, given contemporary notions of women's "softness," that even to this woman Hervey is a "soft hetrogenious thing"—too soft, in fact, to withstand the pillory that awaits him:

> Now ev'ry pretty bard, will scan ye,
> And pelt with satyr, helpless *Fanny*,
> Like rogue on pillory exalted,
> Or drunken wench, by rabble paulted.

(5)

She criticizes Hervey's addressee for not discouraging him from an activity for which he is so ill-suited, makes some unfavorable implications about the nature of their relationship ("A *P[arso]n*, should have delt sincerely, /

With one he seems to love so dearly"), and concludes that they may *both* be fools:

> Yet still he innocent may be,
> Perhaps he knows no more than thee
> What does belong to truth or sense,
> And err'd thro' downright ignorance.

(5)

After a parable of an ass reformed by his mistress's singing (for the reformation of Hervey by Pope, or by his own muse), *Flavia* repeats the identification made earlier by other writers between Hervey's fighting and his writing, at both of which he is equally incompetent:

> Ah Fanny—thou'rt not form'd for *fighting*,
> Prithee forswear both that, and writing. . . .

(6)

The point here is similar to the one above: that Hervey is not *even* a writer. This writer similarly invokes the idea of Hervey's "sphere" as a sort of anti-world of singularly meaningless activity. Again, the issue seems to be Hervey's peculiar role as an outsider inside the establishment; the writer's solution, as usual, is to "control" Hervey by containing him still further, by depicting his "insider" role as a further removal from power (as from potency), when in fact the opposite was almost certainly the case. Note the significant detail of Hervey's "fair" hand, which by now seems almost iconic. It cleverly makes implicit connections between pretty penmanship, pretty (homosexual) writer, pretty (panegyrical) writing, and weak constitution indicated by pallor:

> Thus you may show your hand is fair
> *But* venture not beyond your sphere,
> In politicks you still may dabble
> And forge great Fibs, to please the rabble,
> Your *Patrons* parts, and worth proclaim,
> Or make a *Ballad* on his *Dame*.

(6)

The poem concludes with the example of an honest parson, who refuses to do what is required of him to obtain preferment from his patron, unlike Hervey's presumably dishonest parson-addressee.

A MOST PROPER REPLY (1734)

This seems to be a refinement of the technique of *Tit for Tat*, sandwiching not whole poems but individual lines in an ongoing, negative critique. For the reader unfamiliar with Hervey's *Letter*, footnotes supply quotations. The *Most Proper Reply* is a pastiche of quotations, many from the Bible. Conspicuous among these is a whole series on writing (and not writing):

> [T]his is my Counsel, *Never to open thy Mouth any more. Ez.* xvi. 63. and not to *write*, at least, till you know how to *handle the Pen of the Writer. Judg.* v. 14. For it is said, *Woe to the Writers that write grievously. Isa.* x. 1. In Truth, my good Lord, these Verses are such, as *even a child may write them. Isa.* x. 19. (1734, 8)

The idea of Hervey's childishness, indeed his arrested development, is re-inforced by the (by now) familiar quotation from the *Letter*, given in a footnote at the bottom of the page, in which Hervey's intention was clearly to deflect the charge of being a "mother's boy" from himself onto his brother. Like other satirists, the writer of the *Most Proper Reply* exploits Hervey's tendency to present himself in too many, too varied spheres by suggesting that he is really at home in none:

> You say, you are always imploy'd in *Business*, or *Sport*; but, under Favour, you have no Notion of either. Pray, my Lord, what is your *Business? You have not Business with any Man, Judg.* xviii. 7. (10)

The last is almost certainly a nasty dig at the kind of illicit business that Hervey was believed to have with men. Perhaps also, since (as a footnote indicates) Hervey uses the term "sport," the satirist intends to give it sexual connotations—Hervey has no (legitimate) business with men, only wanton "sport." Other men are not so "sporting" in any sense, but resemble Samson to Hervey's Philistine:

> [T]he silly Lords of the *Philistines*; . . . said, *Call* Sampson, *that he may make us Sport*: And he pulled the WHOLE HOUSE on their head. *Judg.* xvi. 23. (12)

The writer of such stuff reminds me a little of Marvell in his (albeit much more accomplished) animadversions on Samuel Parker's *Ecclesiastical Politie* in *The Rehearsal Transpros'd*. He has the same knack of taking his enemy's words literally and turning them against him. Not surprisingly, he picks up on Hervey's nonchalantly self-deprecating admission of the mendacity of courts (and courtiers):

> But pray, my good Lord, is it not pity you should pass your time, (as you gallantly declare at the End of this glorious Epistle) in Flattering, Slandering, and Lying? *Nay, my Lord, do not lye.* 2 *K.* iv. 6. (16)

Finally, the writer warns him, taunting him for his effeminacy:

> Thou hast need to *tread warily*, though thou seemeth one of the *Daughters of Sion tripping nicely. Isa.* iii. 16. *Thou has made thy Beauty to be abhorred. Ez.* xxv. Verily, verily, *thou art a Nointed Cherub! Ez.* xxviii. 14. And if thou art, as thou sayest, *only to one Point true, [viz. Interest,]* what else can be said of thee, but that *thy* COMELINESS *is turned into* CORRUPTION? *Dan.* x. 8. (19–20)

A quotation from Jonson's *Poetaster* (act 5, final scene) identifies Hervey with Jonson's libeling Fannius, and Pope (of course) with Horace. A generous quotation from Hervey's *Letter* concludes the piece, as if this writer too believed that, for whatever reasons, no one could present Hervey worse than he presented himself.

A TRYAL OF SKILL (1734)

A Tryal of Skill depicts Hervey as the very thing in his *Letter* he wanted to avoid seeming—a "mother's boy," the effeminized son of a woman whose spoiling influence renders futile every effort to educate him. Indeed, she castrates him, first (apparently) by masturbating him:

> WHEN She undress'd the *hopeful Squire*,
> Such was her *Love*, such her *Desire*;
> With Hand, well warm'd she rubb'd his ———
> And swore by all the Demi-Gods,
> That he wou'd prove a *Man of Parts.* . . .
>
> (1734, 3)

Unfortunately, that prophecy seems to have been made in the sense of "some—but not all—parts." Hervey is part of a man, and part man and something else:

> A Play-thing to amuse the *Ladies*,
> Spruce as are Milk-Maids on their *May-Days*.
>
> (4)

While teaching him how to play cards, she instructs him in unusual ways of making love:

> —tho' these Games grow now too common,
> Yet still they will divert a *Woman*.
> Be Master of *My Lady's Hole*,
> If thither 'tis your Lot to strole,
> When once you have began to *Sip*,
> 'Twill be like *Honey* on your Lip.
>
> (5)

A footnote explains that to "sip" is a move in the card game, to "want but one Move to get into *My Lady's Hole*" (5). It also, obviously, has connotations of tonguing, perhaps even of *soixante-neuf*. Hervey's later progress at "gaming" consequently becomes adroitness at illicit sexual practices—all taught him by his mother. When his mother would "make a Third on any Day," the writer does not mean at a card game. When she takes him to the "Doctor" to be further schooled, she warns him that "I'd have him taught but just as much, Man, / As will demonstrate he's no *Dutchman*" (8). While he later fondles women, it is obvious that he wants more, or something—or someone—else:

> But when they stroak'd his blooming Face,
> He on their Breasts his Hand wou'd place;
> And look as fierce as any Lion,
> Yet gently squeez'd those *Hills of* SION;
> Which rais'd in him a *strong Emotion*,
> But brought'em not to his Devotion.
> They guess'd what 'twas he would be at,
> The Valley of *Jehosophat*:
>
> (9–10)

While the last couplet above does not necessarily indicate sodomy, it is obvious from the passage as a whole that Hervey does not especially love or even like women. While he marries a bride his mother provides him, and has a child, he tires of the woman, and only loves the child for its resemblance to himself. He enters politics, fights the duel with Pulteney "to shew his manhood" (12), and takes to writing verses, but remains essentially—like his verses—*nothing*.

AN APOLOGY FOR PRINTING THE NOBLEMAN'S EPISTLE

I believe *An Apology for Printing the Nobleman's Epistle to Dr. Sherwin* (included in *The Tryal of Skill Between Squire Walsingham and Mother Osborne*) comes relatively late in this series of "versions," because it seems to parody *A Tryall of Skill* and summarize other pieces. Halsband describes this as "a mercilessly abusive lampoon" (1973, 165), remarks that Hervey owned it in manuscript, and implies that it was never printed.

An Apology begins by depicting Hervey reciting his verses, at the center of the feminine circle equated with his "sphere":

> As in the gay Circle Lord *Fanny* recited,
> The Nymphs and the Swains of the Court were delighted.
> He audibly read'em his late famous Letter,
> Which he, to dear Doctor, had sent for a better.
>
> (*The Tryall* 1734, 22)

The success of his poem in this "sphere" leads to his typical error—his failure to realize what his proper "sphere" is—and subsequent attempt to assume a role outside that sphere, first by having the poem printed:

> The whole so compleat—to his lordship they hinted,
> A Poem so sprightly deserv'd to be printed.
>
> (22)

Print is, curiously, the medium where the unsuitability of Hervey for the "straight" world becomes apparent. The idea of Hervey playing a part in that world strikes the writer as absurd, for reasons implicit in his identification of Hervey with a whole series of homosexual prototypes:

> O thou! whate'er Title best please thee, Lord *Fanny*,
> Or *Hebe*, or *Iris*, *Narcissus*, or *Ganny*;
> Or fragrant *Adonis* or fair Maid of *Dian*,
> Who can'st rouze the proud Patriot, or chase the fierce
>   Lyon;
>
> (22–23)

His verse is no more his own than his cosmetic complexion. The remainder summarizes and condenses points made against him elsewhere. His being of doubtful manhood, his never "knowing" women, despite always being in women's company, and his erratic desertion of such company for politics are all typical of the strain of criticism that depicts him not just as an outsider, but as one who is especially problematic because he seems to have no "inside," who must first, therefore, somehow be contained in order to be controlled:

> When your Beard first appear'd, —if your Beard ever
>   grew;
> As *Achilles* rough *Chiron's*, you shook off *Friend's*
>   Tramel,
> And, a Female in Beauty, were counted a Female;
> . . . .
> 'Till the Dangers, that threaten'd thy Country, call'd
>   forth
> Thy Vigour, and Courage, and masculine Worth.
>
> (23–24)

LOCAL HYPOTHESES

There is clearly something chameleon-like about Hervey, with the difference that he tends to resemble not his protection but his enemy, as if assimilation were ultimately the best defense. Indeed, what we surmise about Hervey suggests that in everyday and political life it probably was. The trouble begins with art, especially the formulaic and rhetorical art of formal verse satire, where one cannot resemble the enemy and not lose the audience. Hervey exhibits a kind of Keatsian negative capability, although it was never fashionable or even prudent to do so. If at best he simply has no character of his own, this ultimately achieves the same effect as his negative persona; his enemies consistently either identify him with the negatives that (by his own admission) he resembles, or supply the lacunae in his character with what he writes about *them*.

I think the common denominator among these presentations is not simply Hervey's being an outsider, but rather his being an outsider dangerously inside a society to which he himself fails to express clear allegiances and which criticizes him for failing to express them. Perhaps because his outsideness moves them most, many of these satirists argue, not that he should be further cast out, but that he should be further contained—even integrated. Most of them argue not that his sphere is wrong, but that he has no sphere, is in the wrong sphere for him. His homosexuality is principally a kind of cosmic unsuitability, the universality of which is implied by the series of antitheses that usually accompanies him: public and private life, writing and fighting, peace and war. With some ambivalence these writers, if only from a desire to somehow control Hervey, make a not insignificant start at finding a role for it.

It is arguable that the way Hervey's own writings are handled in the writing of his contemporaries—in quotations and ample footnotes, sometimes in complete interleaved reprintings—is consistent with this desire not so much to banish as to surround and contain the homosexual paradoxically at the center of a homophobic world. These textual practices amount to an admission that homosexuality itself is an ineradicable part of society, which must therefore be contained.

Finally, perhaps in their very partisan nonliterariness, these versions depart from Pope's more famous depiction. This latter seems to address more directly what it was about Hervey that bothered the lesser writers— his uncontainable "amphibiousness":

> Amphibious Thing! that acting either Part,
> The trifling Head, or the corrupted Heart!
> Fop at the Toilet, Flatt'rer at the Board,
> Now Trips a lady, and now struts a Lord.
>> (*Epistle to Arbuthnot,* lines 326–29)

What is frightening about this Hervey, and consequently more convincing, is the very thing that lesser writers, perhaps "protesting too much," want to deny in *their* versions—that Hervey, dangerously unallegianced as he is, without a proper sphere, can still succeed in *many* spheres. Perhaps *because* they are inferior writers, they trivialize their subject matter, or possibly vice versa. My point is that Pope's version and theirs are complementary; his version is the threat that theirs is the reaction to, and moreover the *denial* of.

Maynard Mack's idea of what mattered about Hervey is perhaps a bit too idealized, not only for Pope but for many of his late-twentieth-century readers as well:

[W]hat mattered about Hervey was not what might have been offensive about his treatment of a certain A. Pope at this or that time or place (however much that particular poet might hate him on that account!), but what would be found representatively offensive about such a figure, always, everywhere, and by all. (1985, 610)

If this is really so, then Pope has failed of his aim, since in characterizing Hervey as Sporus, partly by refashioning some of the earlier commonplaces of homophobic "literature," Pope created something new and unique: the soulless amphibian, the outsider within, the nonessential essence of a whole society increasingly conscious of its own nonessentialism. Later, in analyzing Sporus's character in *Epistle to Arbuthnot,* Mack similarly understates the evidence of "Sporus's" homosexuality and even androgyny, allowing only that "he looks like a girl" (644). Some "girl"! Subsequently he cannot appreciate how significantly yet specifically Sporus's sexuality, which seems anything but girlish, is metaphorically related to the very thing he mainly allows him: "doubleness and duplicity that all power systems spawn" (644). Mack's criticism is "universalizing," but what "universality" the portrait has is almost entirely on the level of a stereotype, or a racist slur, which of course is not really universality at all.

SOME GENERAL HYPOTHESES

We have not really come so far from our initial tract of the 1720s, where the writer defined masculinity in terms of both a suitability for many roles and guises and a hard essentialism that failed to be affected by any of its roles, certainly resisted identification with them, and consequently did nothing to disturb them. Almost paradoxically it was the homosexual's soft pliability and his obsession with appearances—with roles—that incapacitated him for playing any role at all. Hervey is depicted in nearly the same terms as the sodomite of *Plain Reasons,* but with an anxiety that belies the stereotype.

Other tracts suggest that this version of the sodomite as definitely hapless amphibian was merely wishful thinking. Homosexuality, or at least sodomy, could stand for arrangements and institutions that themselves have come to be nearly identified with eighteenth-century culture. The fact that these identifications were being made in newspapers and cheap pamphlets suggests how pervasive they must have been. A lot was known in areas of which we still know only a little.

At the same time, the writers of this material seem to have imperfectly understood how disruptive homosexuality was, even as it disrupted their own work. Perhaps they were helpless to do anything else but risk complicity with the very "sins" they exposed. To give them their due, they were bravely willing to do so, as they themselves appeared in turn misogynous, obsessive about mere appearances or dress, subversive of the very conventions whose violation they decried, or just confused. Ultimately their accusations and insinuations proved uncontrollable, as if they really were just parts of some early sort of Foucauldian mechanism or "power/knowledge" operation. Thus, the serious consequences of asserting homosexuality in print (even to retract it) seem (in *A Faithful Narrative*) to have recoiled on Baker with unexpected social (or homosocial) violence. Similarly, Pulteney accused Hervey of being an ungrateful client, at the same time he depicted patronage in general as corrupt and even (thanks to patrons like Hervey) homosexualized. As a political associate of Hervey, Pulteney could scarcely escape stigmatization himself. Worse, Hervey was on much more intimate terms with no less an important social figure than Frederick, Prince of Wales. Reactions to Pulteney's tract, like Chesterfield's quoted in Halsband (1973, 111), indicate that contemporaries deplored the "homosexualizing" effects of Pulteney's tract, not because he had lied, but because he had told the truth in print. It is as if one important aspect of homosexuality that was a function of print was its *criminality*, its *heinousness*; its being printed made it evil, and its being evil got it printed more and more.

Many things here, like the shrill assertions of masculinity or domesticity that accompany depictions of sodomy and homosexuality, tend to confirm other hypotheses that homosexuality emerged simultaneously with concepts of masculinity and femininity, an essential element in a system of "difference" that is still largely intact. In this system homosexuality must be tantamount to the mathematicians' discovery of zero, a quintessential nothingness. Perhaps this is why it principally manifests itself as the middle term in equations without which the others cannot make sense, something that either must elide or be elided.

Never, however, does sodomy signify *only* a physical act. It is always accompanied by something else—a style of dress, a mode of speech, a kind of politics, a manner of procreation, etc. That these tracts indicate considerable consensus about these things suggests that it was never *not* an orientation; in these tracts, at least, it is synonymous with "homosexual."

5

Mr. Bradbury's Case Truly Stated:
A Polyvalent Text

I have chosen to discuss *Mr. Bradbury's Case* because it illustrates some of what Michel Foucault means, or at least what I take him to mean, by a "polyvalent discourse." It also serves to illustrate the complex role of sexuality, specifically sodomy, in the life of an eighteenth-century congregation, in a text, and before the law; moreover, the text suggests some of the *interrelationship* among all of these, as the textual role of sodomy (for one example) would subsequently affect the congregational role, and that the legal role, and so on. Just what the role is, in every case, is often the very opposite of what must logically have been the writer's intention. Such reversal is part of what Foucault means by "polyvalency," but by no means all.

I have chosen to treat this text *here*, at the end of this section of tracts, not just because those other pieces chronologically preceded it (so should in a book), but because, to a degree difficult to determine but probably significant, such earlier texts must have prepared the ground for *this* text, and even for the kind of "polyvalent" reading of it that I do. The audience that read *Mr. Bradbury's Case* would also have read *The Parson and his Clerk, College-Wit Sharpen'd,* and many other, similar discourses, the tendency of most of which, I think I have demonstrated, is not to prohibit homosexuality but to promote it.

In vol. 1 of *The History of Sexuality,* Foucault lists a series of four rules to observe, or procedures to follow, as we "immerse . . . discourses on sex in the field of multiple and mobile power relations" (1978, 98). Even the ability to imagine a "free sphere" of sexuality denotes the presence of power ("rule of immanence"). Such power is permanently possessed by no one ("rule of continual variations"), and at any given point is capable of both realizing local tactics and fulfilling global strategies ("rule of double conditioning"). Finally, perhaps as a function of all the preceding, discourse itself must be seen as unstable and unpredictable ("rule of the tactical polyvalence of discourses"):

> Discourses are not once and for all subservient to power or raised up against it, any more than silences are. We must make allowance for the complex and unstable process whereby discourse can be both an instrument and an effect of power, but also a hindrance, a stumbling-block, a point of resistance and a starting point for an opposing strategy. Discourse transmits and produces power; it reinforces it, but also undermines and exposes it, renders it fragile and makes it possible to thwart it. (101)

In effect these "rules" amount to guidelines for a special kind of interpretation, one that is not ethical in focus but rhetorical or what Foucault calls "strategic." Generally, in keeping with this kind of interpretation, discourses on sex are not to be regarded as true or false but as more or less effective strategies of a kind of power that is also new, also "strategic" in that it is no longer perceived as essentially negative but as a set of strategic relationships, not a *possession* but an *exercise*. A discourse on sex could not be so "polyvalent" unless power were immanent in sex and vice versa, in continual variation, as tactic and as strategy. Thus, as the most inclusive and perhaps the most explicitly textual of Foucault's "rules" or "guidelines," "polyvalency" seems to be the most important one to observe, the one capable of yielding the richest discoveries.

David Halperin illustrates part of how he understands the rule of polyvalency with a gay magazine's parody of a notorious issue of *Newsweek*. The latter asked the obviously loaded questions: "Lesbians: What are the limits of tolerance?" The gay magazine "reversed" the discourse by asking the very same question, only of heterosexuals. Fundamental to his understanding of polyvalency is some such subject/object reversal, which is obviously facilitated by earlier "arrangements" that can be exploited as part of "resistance." Halperin describes some such *overall* reversal as the cumulative effect of many kinds of sexual discourse, by virtue of which homosexuality ultimately becomes "a legitimate *condition* of knowledge" (1995, 61).

I think *Mr. Bradbury's Case* makes a small contribution to such a shift, interesting for its historical earliness. It raises too many questions, and suggests too many possibilities, simply to expose the sodomitical Hearne and vindicate the heterosexual Bradbury, as it was meant to do. This text itself becomes "a hindrance, a stumbling-block, a point of resistance and a starting point for an opposing strategy" (Foucault 1978, 101).

THE PREFACE

The title page of *Mr. Bradbury's Case* draws attention to two related circumstances: the unreliability and even "false witness" of "other people" concerning Mr. Bradbury, and the tract's having been authored by Bradbury himself. Various passages from the title page and the preface assert the transparency of the text that follows, its being a plain and forthright statement of the truth, "A Genuine and undisguised Narrative of the whole Affair."

However, the text is everywhere marked by the author's appreciation of its peculiarity, which he exploits to excuse techniques that would normally never be resorted to, if only because they would fail. Thus, its being written by himself would normally be a liability as an indication of bias, but here is justified in terms of truth and candor, and by the nature of the accusation:

> [T]he severe Necessity I am under of vindicating my Character, notwithstanding my honourable Acquittal in a Court of Judicature, will, I presume, excuse this Appeal to all candid and dispassionate Persons. (Bradbury 1755, preface, n.p.)

Here and elsewhere the author indicates his understanding that, apart from his reflection on that very probability, he is not apt to be believed. And it is painfully obvious to Bradbury himself that the way his "Concern . . . to preserve his Character" expresses itself is apt to achieve an effect directly opposite to the desired "vindication." But this concern necessarily seems to take a different, if clearly more hazardous, form, when the "Heap of Obliquy [*sic*] and Scandal" it is intended to remove is the charge of sodomy. Again and again, Bradbury underlines the failure of conventional means, reminding us that he is, after all, defending himself against a charge of which he has already, technically, been cleared: "'Tis true," he writes, "I have been honourably acquitted, by an impartial Jury, of the horrible Crime with which I was charged" (1). But just as some stories seem true because of the improbability their writers would have avoided if it had been false, Bradbury's story seems true because of the risk he deliberately takes of appearing false, but which he presumably only takes because he is innocent and even virtuous. Bad strategies are redeemed partly by their own badness, and partly by the badness of the charge.

The desperateness of the struggle, the likelihood that he will lose and even *worsen* his reputation, suggests that his motives *must* be "truth at all costs"; suggests, indeed, a dedication to the truth above any merely self-interested defense. Since he cannot expect belief, he writes entirely from a spirit of conviction. Here anticipated failure, in the face of what he remains convicted of, faced out of equally stubborn conviction in his own inno- cence and his vindication before posterity and ultimately God, guarantees a measure of success. But these strategies would never work were it not for the nature of the thing he is convicted of.

This appeal to ultimates, worth risking everything else for, would not be so effective, would not work at all, unless it were widely believed that the charge of sodomy had already risked, perhaps even "lost," everything. A defense that must have the same effect as self-indictment is a *religious* act, a *testimony* required not so that *God* would know, but so that *men* would know, that *he* (Bradbury) knew God would know. And like all acts of witness, this one must especially be made when and as it is most apt to be misconstrued, if for nothing else than an affirmation, the costlier the better, of the judgment that matters the most.

Nothing better indicates the nature of the charge than the fact that Bradbury is defending himself publicly against it, "outing" himself in ef- fect, *after* having been found innocent by a court of law. This public de- fense he calls his "second trial":

> As I had no Favour or Indulgence shewn me by the Court (as indeed it was not proper I should in a Charge of so high a Nature) more than is allowed to the worst of Criminals that stand at the Bar; so neither do I now, in the *Second Trial* (if I may so call it) by the public Voice, desire or expect any one to judge more favourably of my Cause, than he is con- vinced that Truth and Justice are on my Side. (preface, n.p.)

Simultaneously, he argues that he has suffered excessively and unjustly from the nature of the charge, and that such "extra-legal" suffering is appropri- ate. He almost seems to be in collusion with his own accusers, especially considering that most of the pamphlet describes these accusers' truly perverse ability to exploit the "heinousness" of the charge to their own advantage.

Finally, in the case of an accusation of sodomy, silence, even when it would normally be the least incriminating strategy, is simply not allowed. Bradbury realizes, painfully, that "Should I make no Reply . . . I should afford them a new handle for their Insults, and to boast, that my Silence is a plain Confession of my Guilt" (preface, n.p.); at the same time, to "speak" is not necessarily to be believed:

> [I]f I speak for myself, I am told, I am too much interested to deserve Credit. So that which Way soever I turn myself, whether I speak, or am silent, such is their inveterate malice, they will give me no Quarter; but I

> must still be guilty, because they have no other Way to clear themselves
> of the odious Imputation of combining and confederating together in a
> Scheme to take away my Life, in a Manner the most ignominious. (pref-
> ace, n.p.)

Perhaps the "extralegality," even stubbornness, of the charge sheds some
light on the Thistlethwayte affair, at the same time that the consequences of
that affair for Baker indicate why Bradbury's accusers remain determined
to convict him.[1] Such *extra*legality is no doubt aggravated by print, if not
created by it too. Such proliferation of discourse seems to occasion Bradbury's greatest indignation, and eloquence, all the more ironic in the context of the impossibility of his own silence:

> Great is my Affliction, that the Sentence of the Law has not been able to
> stop the Mouths of my Enemies, who still continue to load me with In-
> famy. (preface, n.p.)

In fact, no one seems capable of shutting up about it, Bradbury included.
And the law can do nothing about it, except, as we shall see, contribute
more "facts" to the discussion. And print only broadcasts an accusation
already serious enough that it *must* adhere to *someone*, if not the accused
then the accuser. In an accusation of sodomy, someone is always, and always extremely, guilty. But *who*?

The Initial Narrative

The Beginning in October 1754

The narrative begins on page 2, "Some Time in *October*, in the Year
1754," when, as Charles Bradbury puts it, "I unhappily became acquainted
with *James Hearne*, the Prosecutor, a Youth then about fourteen Years of
Age." Hearne had been coming to hear his preaching at "Glovers Hall."
Bradbury notices Hearne in the congregation, and makes inquiries. He asks
a member of his congregation who he is, and is informed that he "lived
with his Master Mr. *Nokes*, Watch-maker, in *Charterhouse Square*, and
that he had been brought up at *Douay* in *France*, with an Intent to make
him a priest in the *Romish* Church" (2). James Hearne continues to attend
meetings at "*Glovers-Hall* in *Beech Lane*," and at the chapel in "*Chandler-
Street, Grosvenor Square*" (3).

Bradbury must have been flattered by the information that hearing his sermons had convinced Hearne of the errors of Catholicism. Perhaps that is why he asks to speak to the young man. He only does so, however, in the presence of other members of the congregation, whom he specifically names. This seems such a fastidious point, one wonders whether it were not entirely retroactive, and wonders too perhaps, if it were *not*, *why* then he was so careful not to talk to Hearne alone. Did eighteenth-century preachers live in such fear of being associated with sodomites that they avoided talking to male parishioners alone?

First Doubts: Hearne's Loss of Employment

Bradbury's doubts seem, initially at least, entirely nonsexual, entirely commercial in origin, as he himself states that he has "all the Reason in the World to entertain a good Opinion" of Hearne, till one morning, on his way to breakfast at one Mrs. Carter's, he meets Hearne ostensibly on his way to receive some money for his master. When Bradbury meets Hearne again, sitting in the vestry later that day, he suspects that the young man has stolen the money and run off with it.

After preaching, Bradbury meets the distraught James at a parishioner's house and insists on his going back to his master, Mr. Nokes,[2] a watchmaker in Charterhouse Square. Nokes will take the money, but not Hearne. And his father will no longer support him, after his conversion. Temporarily, Hearne is taken in by one Mr. Stephenson.

Throughout the narrative and the proceedings surrounding it, one notes the constant intercourse, the checking and counter-checking, among numerous permutations of the following elements: business, religion, sex, denomination, gender.

Hearne is "Taken-In" by the Whitakers and Bradbury Himself for Two Nights

One "Mr. *Whitaker*, of the *Minories*," who, Bradbury writes, with an almost novelistic anticipation of the treason he thereby alerts us will follow, "professed great Friendship to me" (5), offers to take in Hearne. There follow some obvious signs of duplicity, as if the Whitakers were already planning to trap Bradbury by inviting him over at James's bedtime:

> [T]hey repeating their Invitations with great Earnestness, I, to avoid the Imputation of too much Stiffness, and lest they should think I refus'd their Offer because their House was but mean, at length consented to

> their Request. A little before Bed-time, they told me, that having but two Beds, they must entreat me to lie with *James*, but it should be in their own Bed, and they would lie in James's. (5–6)

Note the length to which Bradbury goes to explain that he stayed at the Whitakers in order to avoid insulting them, to reassure them that their house was not "mean" (5). He stays at the Whitakers two nights this way. At other points in the narrative Bradbury invokes Christianity, or more specifically "pastoral duty," as a reason for associating with people whose characters might be questionable. Surely such considerations would have sufficiently overborne any considerations of *class*. Bradbury must have even *promiscuously* associated with the Whitakers, and worse. For now, it is interesting how one kind of promiscuity seems, at least implicitly, to be identified with another, and how Bradbury's defense actually exposes him all the more to the accusation of one, if not the other too.

Bradbury Learns of Hearne's having Committed Sodomy

Shortly after his "lying at Whitaker's," Bradbury learns that *James Hearne* had forcibly committed *Sodomy* on the Body" (6) of a fellow apprentice, son of one Mrs. D——. When Bradbury interrogates him, Hearne denies having committed "that beastly Act" (6).

Now Bradbury becomes *self-conscious*, despite the above implications of self-consciousness *all along*. Now that it appears possible that Hearne is a sodomite, he declines not only to sleep in the same bed with him, but even in the same house.

Hearne Loses another Job but Gets a Bed in the Chapel

Shortly after Bradbury's "discovery," Hearne gets a job, thanks to one Mr. Brown and the Register Office, "at Mr. *Mayne*'s, Haberdasher, in the *Strand*" (7). Almost immediately, he loses it for "laying out of Master's House." He goes looking for Bradbury, and finds him. Women living in Bradbury's house, members of the congregation, plead with Bradbury to let the boy sleep in the "spare Bed in the Chapel in *Chandler's Street*" (7).

A few nights after the boy's return, Bradbury interrogates him about his leaving his second place; fastidious as ever, he wants us to note that he does so "in Presence of another Person" (8). To him, Hearne relates what appears to have been a sodomitical "date" with a "short, bluff-fac'd, pock-fretten Man" who picked him up while he was out delivering a message. After staying away all night, Hearne is fired by his master.

Mrs. Shore Finds Hearne a Job, which Bradbury Loses for Him:
Bradbury "Outs" Hearne and Hearne Attacks Bradbury

The women—Mrs. Shore and Mrs. Pickering—find Hearne another
position, but when Bradbury is not enthusiastic about their efforts, they de-
mand to know why. He tells them what Hearne told him. Hearne confronts
Bradbury for exposing him, and speaks "very saucy Language" (9). Bradbury threatens to turn him out of doors, he leaves, and returns to the Whitakers.

Mrs. Whitaker supports him, accuses Bradbury of venality, and encourages Hearne to accuse him of "indecent Actions" (10). Their plan is
for Hearne to threaten Bradbury with exposure if he won't take him back.
With another couple, the Browns, they confront the clergyman when he
visits the Browns on the next night, Tuesday, 15 April 1755. When Mr.
Brown and his wife "accost" him, the real issue appears to be something
other than plain sodomy: "I ought to maintain the Boy," is how Bradbury
describes a main thrust of their argument. Apparently the issue is that, for
having sodomized the boy, he ought now to support him. It seems at least
possible that the adults have concocted a scheme to help the boy, using the
clergyman's alleged wealth and greed as an excuse. Remember that Mrs.
Whitaker's response to the boy's story after leaving Bradbury's house is
that "she thought [Bradbury] only preached for gain" (10).

As Bradbury describes Hearne's accusations, it appears at least slightly
possible that some of their inconsistency is due to Hearne's ignorance, his
not knowing the meaning of "sodomy": "Is it *Sodomy* you accuse me of?
He answer'd, No!" (10). But this becomes increasingly unlikely, as we
learn more about Hearne's experiences and background.

According to Bradbury, the Browns vocally encouraged Hearne in his
attack, in an atmosphere that seems almost carnivalesque: "[B]oth *Brown* and
his Wife encouraged him to speak up freely and boldly, which he, finding
himself so well back'd, did with an uncommon Assurance, and continued
so to do upon their spiriting him on with—*Well done*, James, laughing all
the while" (11). Bradbury stops arguing, and simply asserts his innocence:

> When I found myself thus audaciously attack'd, and that no Arguments I
> could sue would convince them of my innocence, I solemnly declared I
> was entirely guiltless of any indecent Action; but finding they were posi-
> tively determin'd, right or wrong, to be on his Side, I thought proper to
> take my Leave. (11)

As Bradbury leaves, Brown sends James after him. Apparently right at
the door, Hearne relents, maybe even repents. Perhaps Brown too has repented,
or decided that this scheme had gone too far.

Bradbury advises Hearne "to come to the Chapel the next Night" (11). It is curious that Bradbury himself believes his reputation is already ruined at this point; at least his resolve to "consult with my Friends about it" seems certain to ruin it if it were not ruined already.

The Recantation

The next day, Hearne signs a recantation in the presence of Mrs. Pickering and others. Hearne himself desires "for the Satisfaction of the Public, a paper might be drawn up, and he would very readily sign it; which being done accordingly, he, in the Presence of Mr. *Cook*, (who was since come in) did actually sign it; in which paper he declared, that all he had said against me was false" (12). This recantation stresses its voluntariness, its being motivated entirely by Hearne's sense of his wrong against Bradbury and even against God, and his hope that by recanting in such a fashion he will avoid legal proceedings against himself.

After the recantation, Mrs. Pickering wants Bradbury to "let the Boy lie in the Bed at the Chapel" (13). This too suggests that part of the motive for the accusations in the first place might have been to compel Bradbury to support the boy. At first, Hearne refuses, "declaring he should never lie under my Roof any more" (14). He relents enough, however, to allow Hearne to stay there for a few days before returning to France. When Bradbury suggests that Hearne return to live with his former master, Mr. North, Hearne explains that he is afraid "Mr. D——, his Fellow-prentice's Father, would take him up and hang him, for what he had done to his Son, a Lad about fourteen Years of Age" (14). Bradbury's note maintains that the boy "was an old Practitioner at this foul Game before he came from *France*" (14).

Hearne Returns from France to England and Glovers Hall

Mrs. Pickering, out of compassion, persuades her mother, Mrs. Shore, to supply the boy with the means of going to France. A mutual acquaintance sees Hearne safe onboard a ship bound there. Bradbury emphasizes that he played no role in such assistance. From 18 April to Friday, 6 June, Bradbury sees nothing of the boy. But on that day, "going across the Field behind *Warburton's* Timber-Yard, *Tottenham-Court-Road*, I observ'd him sitting on a Log of Wood with a Basket of Pictures" (15). Bradbury passes him without speaking, but informs his household.

Meanwhile, Whitaker and Brown continue to attack Bradbury's character. Two of Bradbury's friends, Milward and Hopkins, want to talk to the boy themselves. On 12 June, they find him in Leicester Fields. He affirms that Bradbury "had been guilty of *some Indecencies* with him" (16). Milward and Hopkins bring the boy to speak to Bradbury. Again, the boy admits to having falsely accused the clergyman. He agrees to accompany him to "*Glovers-Hall*," to "publickly declare the Truth" (17).

The Examination in the Vestry on 12 June 1755

The "examination" begins with Bradbury declaring to a group of watchmakers, weavers, spinsters, and wives that "this is the wicked Boy that had said such Things of him that his very Soul abhorr'd; and that he was come there to declare his Guilt or Innocence" (18).

Hearne is asked to speak the truth. Bradbury then opens the recantation that he had with him (signed on 18 April 1755). Hearne is asked to confirm that the contents of the recantation were true, that he had signed it, and that he had not been compelled. He does so. When asked what had induced him to lie, he first answers, "[T]he Devil" (19), but then, with a little encouragement from someone in the group, admits that "*Brown* and *Whitaker* had drawn him in to say such Things. And said, *James*, you must first threaten *Bradbury*, and if he will not maintain you, you must swear the Fact against him, for your Oath will be taken before his, and we will hang him, and provide for you" (19). Hearne then begs Bradbury's pardon and hopes he will forgive him. Bradbury does.

Brown and Whitaker Take Alarm

After searching hard for him, Brown and Whitaker find Hearne on 13 June, one day after his public examination, working for an Italian maker of weather-glasses in "*Newtoner's-Lane*" (20). They take him to Brown's house, where Hearne is confined for six weeks, "during which Time he was *properly* instructed to lay two Informations against me" (20). They have difficulty finding a justice who can believe Hearne, but mysteriously one Justice Fielding "was pleased to grant a Warrant against me for an assault with an intent to commit *Sodomy*" (21). Bradbury remains quite perplexed why Justice Fielding was willing to grant the warrant, when so many other justices refused:

> What the Reasons were, which induced this Gentleman to give more Credit
> to the Testimony of a Wretch that had all the Appearance of a Vagabond,
> than the other Justices did, are best known to himself. (21)

Bradbury gives bail "to the Warrant before Justice *St. Lawrence*" (21).

Brown and Whitaker continue to "plague" Bradbury. On 29 June, a crowd led by Brown and Whitaker disrupts Bradbury's preaching in Grosvenor Square. One Mrs. Stone, a baker's wife, pointing at him from the door, exclaims, "There is a *Sodomite*" (21). When Bradbury goes to court he discovers that the charge has been increased: "[N]othing less than my Life could gratify their Malice, which they could not accomplish upon this Information, and therefore they laid their Indictment against me, for actually committing that most detestable Sin of SODOMY" (22). Bradbury again obtains his liberty, this time by giving bail to not one but two justices, because of the seriousness of the charge against him. Now the justices who take his security are Wright and Trent.

While it is not perfectly clear from Bradbury's initial narrative, from the attached depositions it is apparent that on 16 July Bradbury's friends manage to find Hearne, arrest him, and bring him before Justice Wright, to whom he declares Bradbury's innocence. Such successful intervention may explain why, as Bradbury does report in his narrative, he is hounded the next day by a mob consisting of Brown, Whitaker, the Mrs. Stone who had called him a sodomite before his congregation, and Hearne's father, who "declar'd I had murder'd his Son" (22). These are possibly the desperate measures of a now losing side, or possibly the angry reprisals of people frightened by what they might have regarded as the evil machinations of an archsodomite who looked like he was going to get away. At least some of the crowd must have been severely appalled and disgusted by the occurrence of the very sort of thing they were trying to avoid—a sexual criminal's successful exploitation and corruption of innocent prey. This time Bradbury barely saves himself by showing his "Supersedeas," but the next day his persecutors have him brought before Justice Fielding, who claims that this "Supersedeas" is "of no use" and has him "committed to *New-Prison*, where I lay eight Weeks, wanting but two Days" (23).

Bradbury in Prison Receives Hearne's Letters

Bradbury preaches in prison one Sunday, but is stopped from doing so regularly by order of his enemies. He tries to be admitted to bail once more, this time by Lord Chief Justice Ryder, but is denied, since "his Lordship said, the Crime I was charged with was not bailable by law; and if the whole Court of *King's Bench* were then sitting, such a Thing could not be granted. So I was remanded back to Prison" (14).

Soon however, James Hearne sends Bradbury a letter, in which (incidentally) he complains of being eaten up by lice, and asks Bradbury to help him leave the vicinity, because of his fear of reprisals from Brown and Whitaker. Bradbury asks his friend, Mr. Fullylove, to write Hearne to discover whether Hearne or his friends had employed an attorney against Bradbury. Hearne replies that he himself had never employed the lawyer, Pepper, but that Pepper had been brought to Brown's house by Mrs. Stone.

Hearne sends a third letter to Fullylove, which is interesting for the way it recounts events that Bradbury has already related:

1. his being at Brown's house, and accusation of Bradbury when he visited there;

2. Hearne's relenting, apparently because Bradbury said he would take him before a justice;

3. his "Recantation";

4. his going to France, which he calls his "escape";

5. his return, and false accusation of Bradbury to his friends;

6. his declaration at Glovers Hall;

7. Whitaker and Browns' visiting him in Newtoner's Lane on Friday and bringing Hearne to Brown's house;

8. Mrs. Stone's coming to Brown's, and taking Hearne to Hawkins, and then to Hughes and Justice Fielding, where she gets a warrant;

9. Bradbury's superseding the warrant and Mrs. Stone threatening Hearne that he could be "listed";

10. Hughes and Pepper coming the next day and arguing that he should "put it to the Fact (or the jury will laugh at you,) *and hang the Dog out of the Way*";

11. his being kept for 6 weeks at Browns's house;

12. his finally coming before Judge Wright where, "it pleased God, I was taken up, and . . . I declared the Truth, that Mr. *Bradbury* was not guilty of what I charg'd him with before, for he *never did commit* or *offer to commit any thing indecent to me,* nor I did not know that Nature of an Oath" (28).

THE TRIAL PROPER

The Start of the Trial: Thursday, 11 September 1755

Bradbury begins this, the second part of his narrative, with a strange appeal to the first, the real trial. Such a final appeal renders all the preceding unnecessary: Why go to such lengths for a second trial, if at the end of it your principal defense remains the *first?* Nonetheless, Bradbury concludes his introduction of this part of the "case" with the oddly self-defeating admission:

> [A]t Nine my Trial came on; a *Review* of which, with Remarks upon it, I shall presently give, for the Satisfaction of the Reader; by comparing of which, with what I have here related, and shall afterwards insert, he will be enabled to form some tolerable Judgment of the Reality of my Case, and whether, upon due Consideration of the Facts, as I have stated them, and which are confirmed by the Testimonies upon Oath, of such a Number of creditable Witnesses, he believes in his Conscience, I am guilty of the horrid Crime, of which I was accus'd, indicted, tried for, and of which I was Acquitted in the most honourable Manner, by an impartial Jury, and even in the Opinion of the Judge himself. (29)

Here he confronts again the apparently poor strategy, the only defense of which is its very obviousness, which indicates some motivation beyond simple expediency, an "ultimacy" befitting the nature of the charge. Of the risks he is manifestly aware, but it is essential to his strategy, such as it is, to make that manifest to *us* as well:

> [W]hen malice is resolved to ruin a Character; the most Innocent will find it almost impossible to escape the Mischief intended; for such is the Depravity of Human Nature, that Scandal always meets with a better Reception, and a more ready Belief, than the best attested Evidence, in Vindication of injur'd Virtue. . . . How difficult is it to combate Wickedness, when sharpen'd with the Malevolence of invenom'd Tongues. (29)

The difficulty of persuasion seems to justify unusual earnestness, and an unusually circumstantial relation:

> [L]et any one take a serious unprejudic'd View of the Case as I have already stated it, which I can truly affirm, I have not disguised with any false Colourings, sophistical Arguments, or mental Reserves, but told the plain Truth in an artless Manner. (29)

The very inconsistency of such details, becomes a part of the narrative's overall cogency, an *inconsistency* related to that improbability that *has* to be true; the *text* is true in spite of itself, or rather in spite of its author, true *regardless.*

[L]et any impartial Man weigh, and compare the Circumstances, and Incidents here related, one with another, and I dare venture to submit the Decision of my Guilt or Innocence, to his Determination. (29)

What he inadvertently does, however, by adding such a plethora of details, and even *versions*, is create his own kind of "polyvalent" text. He opens his text to totally different interpretations, and through it opens to us an aspect of his society that we seldom get.

Before relating the trial in detail, Bradbury attempts to answer what he considers the strongest objection to his conduct. This answer only illustrates the "problem":

> that I went to lay with him at *Whitaker's*. In Answer to which it should be consider'd, that at that Time I had no Reason to entertain an ill Opinion of the Boy, otherwise than that he had been guilty of some Faults, such as are incident to those of his Age. (31)

Obviously, his answer to this, the strongest objection, is the most incriminating; the good appearance of the boy, as well as the time, and the distance from home, all of which could equally have worked to the advantage of a sodomitical, sexual "affair":

> [N]either had he then the Dress or Appearance of a Vagrant or a Vagabond, but such as became the Apprentice of a Tradesman, and which could not render him disagreeable, as a Bed-fellow, (upon a Case of Emergency) I not being inform'd, where I was to lie, 'till between Eleven and Twelve o'Clock, and I then near four Miles from my Lodging. (31)

Where do the "proprieties" of class end and the attractions of sex begin? Excusing himself for sleeping with the boy he actually provides himself with a motive for buggering him. What justifies sleeping equally, or perhaps even more so, justifies sodomizing. It is curious that Bradbury himself does not guard against such self-exposure.

In answer to the charge that he is socially promiscuous—the implication that with social irregularities go sexual ones—he defends himself with a similar appeal to alleged universals like Christianity and Humanity:

> But who ever considers my Station, and the Duties of my Function, will not wonder that I endeavour to render myself agreeable to all, that so I may, some Way or other, become useful to all. . . . If my Discourse or Conversation can be of any Use in promoting the Service and Honour of

> my *Great Master*, I should think it a Breach of my Duty to refrain from
> the Company of those who desire it. (31–32)

Again, a reason for innocently sleeping in a strange bed with a boy could
also be a reason for "going to bed" with him: "[W]here was the Fault, if, at
their urgent Instances, I lay in their Bed, since it would be no Disappointment at Home, because I had no Wife or Family to expect me" (32). If there
would be "no disappointment" at home, there could still be, or might even
more probably be, "satisfaction" abroad.

It is part of Bradbury's retroactive strategy to show the Whitakers "press-
ing" him to sleep with the boy, "framing" him in fact, again at the risk of
making us wonder why he was not more cautious at the time, especially
when he had previously been cautious enough to avoid speaking to the boy
alone. He is a strange mixture of prudence and rashness.

> Twice I lay at their House, *and not oftner*, and both Times with the Boy,
> tho' frequently press'd to it afterwards both by *Whitaker* and his Wife.
> (32)

At about this time, he writes, Mrs. D—— tells him why Hearne had been
fired the first time (32). He confronts Whitaker with this story from the
mother of the buggered apprentice; Whitaker informs Bradbury that Hearne
"lay with his Cousin at his House, who had come from, or near *West
Chester*." Bradbury asks to talk to this cousin, but Whitaker seems convinced that Hearne never sodomized him. However, Mrs. D——'s story is
corroborated by Hearne's admission to having lost his second place for
sleeping around. It is Bradbury's use of this information, to frustrate Hearne's
getting a third position, that leads directly to the trouble:

> [T]he true Reason of *Hearne's* Spite and Malice against me, as I have the
> greatest Reason to believe, was this: Mrs. *Shore*, as before observ'd, pity-
> ing his forlorn Condition, was going to put him out Apprentice to Mr.
> *North*, Peruke-maker, in *Thames Street*; and on her and her Daughter
> Mrs. *Pickering* asking my Opinion about it, I apprehending the Inconve-
> niencies that would probably follow on his being placed in a sober Fam-
> ily, and the Scandal that might arise to them for recommending him,
> thought this a proper Opportunity to inform them of what *Hearne* had
> related to me the *Friday* before, in the Presence of another Person, which
> was, that he had committed beastly Actions with a man with whom he lay
> one Night at a House in a Court opposite *Somerset-House* in the *Strand*.
> (32–33)

To many modern judgments it would appear that Bradbury is at least partially guilty himself of violating the young man's confidence, of "outing" him, and of seriously harming his potential for employment. It is pretty obvious that what follows is an attempt, masterminded by parishioners like the Whitakers and the Browns, to turn the tables on the accuser, to deflect the charge back onto the charger, and ultimately to alleviate Hearne's punishment, effectively the loss of his livelihood if not of his life, by threatening Bradbury with the same.

The circumstances of the case must themselves have appeared somewhat "polyvalent," susceptible to reinterpretation and even reversal, for them ever to have attempted such a strategy. In practical terms, Bradbury should simply have played along with them; that would have been, at least in terms of practicality, the better strategy. But it is already apparent, from the text so far, that the "better strategy" is not applicable to this charge, at least not for Bradbury, for whom there is more at stake than "earning potential" or even *public* reputation—at stake is something like final judgment. The Whitakers and the Browns fatally miscalculate, by calculating too much, or on a different scale than Bradbury's.

Let us consider some more of these circumstances, related in the course of the trial.

The Alleged Assault at Meredith's Funeral

Hearne goes to hear Bradbury "at *Glovers-Hall*, the same night Mr. *Meredith* was buried from the *Tabernacle*" (38). Bradbury dismisses Mrs. Hall, telling her, "he would stay with *James*, for he wanted to speak with him" (38). It is then, at about nine o'clock, that Bradbury assaults the boy:

> [A]s he stood leaning his head against the chimney-piece, Mr. *Bradbury* pull'd him down upon his knee, and kiss'd him, put his hand thro' a torn hole of his breeches, put out the candle, and unbuttoning his own breeches, bid him do what modesty here forbids us to mention. (38)

When Hearne fears being late at his master's and having a "noise" with him, Bradbury bids him "not be afraid, for if they should scold him, he should come away, and he would get him another place" (38).

Bradbury admits to having conversed with Hearne "several times" (38) before Meredith's funeral, but not to ever having desired him to come to hear him at "Glovers Hall." He does not desire people to leave him alone while they bury Meredith but, because Mrs. Hall wants very much to go to the funeral, he "(tells) her, as she had such a desire to go, she might have all the doors open, and need not stay on that account" (38). After taking care of the fire, he goes home. Evidently Mrs. Pickering calls at about eight-thirty, and Bradbury has already gone home.

One Mrs. Hall testifies that she is at Glovers Hall the night of 23 January 1755, the night of Meredith's funeral. She denies that Bradbury says anything about the door closing itself with a spring-lock. Generally, she insists, Bradbury does not try to be alone that night. She confirms that in February she hears Mrs. Whitaker and Hearne press Bradbury to go home and spend the night at her house, but Bradbury refuses.

The Loss of the First Job: Meeting Hearne in the Street

About a week later, Hearne meets Bradbury in the street: "[B]eing sent of an errand to receive some money for his master, as he was going up *Tyburn-Road* he met Mr. *Bradbury*, who asked him if he had breakfasted? and talked about his religion" (38). Bradbury asks him to take some books to Brown. When Hearne learns at Brown's that it was already noon, he does not want to go home, so he "wander[s] about the streets till night, and then [goes] to Mr. *Bradbury*" (39).

Then Bradbury, Hearne, and one Mr. Cook go to hear Bradbury preaching in Chandler Street. Bradbury asks Cook to tell Hearne's master that Hearne cannot deliver the money till the next day. When Cook returns, Bradbury asks him if it is true that Hearne had not been at home the night before. Discovering that he had not, Bradbury decides to go back with Cook to Hearne's house, adding, "[I]f his master refused to take him in, he would." Though Hearne's father will not let him in, the landlord lets him sleep in the house.

In the morning Hearne wanders around Charterhouse Square, and his master briefly takes him in again in the afternoon. After a brief stop at his sister's in St. John Street, Hearne goes to one Newton in Bartholomew's Hospital. From Newton's he goes to Mrs. Brown's in St. John Street, where he meets Bradbury again. There Bradbury speaks sweetly to James: "Said he, *James*, what made you in such a hurry to come away? you should have staid till I had got you a place" (40).

William Cooke (spelled "Cook" in the narrative and "Cooke" in his deposition; such inconsistencies are part of the reality of the piece) has much to say about these early meetings, starting with Bradbury's first acquaintance with Hearne, sometime in November 1754:

> [H]e, this Deponent, heard *Hearne* say, he had been brought up in *France* for a *Roman* Catholic Priest; Mr. *Bradbury* then asked to see some of his Books, and accordingly *Hearne* brought some Books about a Week after, and in the Presence of this Deponent, first tore one, and afterwards burnt it. (66)

One might wonder if ripping up the boy's books is really decent. It at least suggests a rather *intense* relationship, although Cooke insists "he *never saw any* Indecency in Word or in Action, pass between them, but at all Times, when he was present, their Discourse was about religious Matters" (66).

He also insists, in reply to Hearne's insinuations of an illicit relationship between himself and Bradbury, that Hearne was never in his house, and that Bradbury and Hearne were certainly not together there when Hearne said they were. He recounts in detail the night in the chapel in Chandler Street, when he heard Bradbury reprimand Hearne for "staying" on an errand. Bradbury asks him to take Hearne home, but Hearne, perhaps understandably, does not want to go, and stops at Brown's, where Bradbury joins them a little later. Bradbury insists, with all the others, that he go back to his master. Cooke then accompanies him "into the Court where Mr. *Noakes*, his Master, lived" (66–67). Hearne sends in the money he had received, but is refused admittance. He then goes back to Bradbury at Brown's, who advises him to go to his father's. Cooke and Hearne part at Garden Square.

The reason for Hearne's dismissal, which Cooke says Bradbury finally extracts from him, is Hearne's having sodomitical relations with another man, an expression of a "habit" that Hearne says he learned from an evidently largely sodomitical Catholic clergy. Cooke dismisses the idea that Hearne did not know what sodomy was:

> [T]his Deponent declareth, that he heard *Hearne* say, (on Mr. *Bradbury's* insisting to know the Reason of his leaving his Place crying, if Mr. *Bradbury* would not be angry with him, he would tell him the Truth, which was, that he had lain with a Man, and had committed Sodomy, and that he had been taught such Practices, ever since he was eleven Years of Age, by the Priests of *France*. (67)

Mrs. Pickering adds some details of his own, on the subject of Hearne's corruption by the clergy of France, starting at Hearne's coming to live in the chapel:

[F]rom that time he had the Run of her Kitchen, and behaved in an or-
derly manner, but was always exclaiming against the Falcy of the *Romish*
Priests, representing them as being guilty of all manner of Wickedness,
under the Mask of Religion; and further said, as they were debarred the
Company of Women, they practised and taught their Pupils the Sin of
Sodomy, and [the Priests] had practised it on him at eleven Years of Age.
(69)

The Nights at Whitaker's

Mr. Stephens, as Bradbury requests, finds Hearne a lodging in St. John
Street, and "desires" Whitaker to let Hearne "lie at his house, till he could
get him another master" (40). Bradbury sleeps at Whitaker's that Sunday
night, and again on Thursday night. Mrs. Whitaker tries to dissuade him
from sleeping with James, because his bed "was but small" (40). This conversation happens at Glovers Hall. Later, "between 9 and 10, the same
night, we went to Mr. *Whitaker's*, and lay together; and the candle being
put out, he perpetrated the fact charged in the indictment: *(but with such
particulars as are not fit to be repeated, and too gross and foul for a modest
ear to hear, as may be seen in the trial)"* (40–41).

According to the prosecution, "in all about four or five times [he slept
with him]]; and every time perpetrated the same fact as he did the first
night" (41). He stays at Whitaker's six weeks, at Bradbury's expense, till
he gets a job at Mr. Mayne's in the Strand. He soon loses this place too, for
"staying too long on his errands." Finally, he boards at Mrs. Shore's, and
lives at the chapel, Bradbury having got Mrs. Shore's sympathy for him by
telling her that Hearne "was a poor lad."

The Garret and the Candle

According to "the evidence," one night after Hearne retires to his garret, Mrs. Shore wants to send the maid to fetch the candle, but Bradbury
volunteers to get it himself. Upstairs, he tells Hearne to come down "when
every body was a-bed" (42). Hearne meets him where he is "reading in a
large book" (42); he tells him to get back into bed "and he would come to
him, as he did immediately" (42). The whole seems a little involved, perhaps
contrived, or perhaps Bradbury could not speak openly to him in the garret.

Mrs. Pickering's version is radically different:

When the Family were going to-bed, this Deponent desired Mr. *Bradbury*
to take the boy's Candle, which she had ordered him to set on the top of

the Stairs, as there was Linnen laying about the Room. . . . to the best of her Knowledge, Mr. *Bradbury* did not enter the Garret, but took the Candle off the upper Stair, for she was talking to him as he went up, so if *Bradbury* had spoken to *James*, this Deponent verily believes she should have heard him, were it ever so softly, besides the Bed is about six Yards from the Stairs. (69)

She talks to Bradbury, following behind him, as he ascends. Her mother tries to get Hearne up early in the morning to avoid having to listen to Mr. Bradbury's "huffings" (69).

Later, again according to the "evidence" of the prosecution, at Mrs. Brown's, after his departure from the chapel (not, in this version, for having been "outed"), Hearne is in the process of telling on Bradbury, just as Bradbury enters. Hearne then accuses Bradbury to his face. The reasons for Hearne's telling are curiously accidental. Part of the problem is that, having tolerated such liaisons for some time, he has no obvious motive for exposing Bradbury. He does so in the course of explaining other phenomena, such as Bradbury's hitherto inexplicable interest in someone else (43), or Hearne's remaining awake so long whenever he sleeps in Bradbury's bed (43). Curiously, they sleep together the very night of the accusation.

Mrs. Whitaker's testimony substantiates such explanations. She says that Bradbury "never wanted to lie at their house before the boy came there; and that she had never spoke to him before that time" (46). When Bradbury comes to the house and starts fondling a visitor's baby, calling it "dear *Billy* boy," Hearne remarks, "You don't know what has passed in this house between *Billy Cook* and Mr. *Bradbury*" (46). She repeats Hearne's charge that Bradbury preached against sodomy "and about half an hour before had been acting the same thing" (46).

The Stronger Charge: From Attempt to Assault

One of the most telling aspects of the case is the way the initial charge of "indecencies" is altered to actual sodomitical assault, a capital crime. The reason for this seems to be the need to get Bradbury out of the way, having maligned him, or rather his reputation, more seriously than they intended to. Perhaps more than anything else, this "upping of the ante" indicates the nature of the thing they had accused Bradbury of, a nature that Whitaker and Brown had almost certainly underestimated.

It is part of the nature of the thing charged, or at least of the charge itself, that Bradbury's friends feel an especially compelling need to verify and prove it. Thus, one Mr. Milward explains, "[O]n the 12th Day of *June* last, hearing of the scandalous Defamation *James Hearne* reported of Mr. *Charles Bradbury*, and desirous to know the Truth of the matter, [he] resolved, if possible, to find out the said *Hearne*" (55). He finds him in the vicinity of Leicester Fields. He "happened to see *Hearne* selling Weather-Glasses, asked him how he did, and where he had been?" (56). More to the point, he asks him "if Mr. *Bradbury* was guilty; of what he had reported of him? *Hearne* replied, he was guilty of some Indecencies" (56). Milward leaves Hearne and goes to inform Bradbury, who asks him to bring Hearne there. Once in his company, Bradbury interrogates Hearne:

> I now ask you, did I ever commit Sodomy with you? *Hearne* replied, No; whoever said so? And Mr. *Bradbury* further asked him, Did I ever attempt to commit it? *Hearne* replied, No, you never did. Mr. *Bradbury* asked him, and said, In the Presence of God, did I ever offer any Indecency to you whatsoever? *Hearne* then began to cry;, and wring his hands, and tore his Hair, and said, O! what have I done, in accusing an innocent Man! And said, O that I had taken Mr. *Bradbury's* Advice, then I had never known the Troubles and Hardships I have gone through! and that Mr. *Bradbury* had given him better Advice than ever his Father gave him. And this Deponent farther saith, that he heard *James Hearne* acknowledge that he had been guilty of Sodomy from Eleven Years of Age with the Priests of *France*. (56)

Whitaker and Brown catch up to Hearne and make him change his story yet again. One Mr. Righ is "providentially" present at one of their training sessions:

> [H]e, this Deponent, on or about the thirtieth Day of *June* happened to be providentially at Mr. *Brown's* House, situate in Saint *John's-Street*, in the Parish of Saint *Sepulchre's* without, *Middlesex*, in the Presence and hearing of Mr. *Pepper*, Attorney or Sollicitor at Law, Mr. *Brown* and others on the Examination of *James Hearne*, who was then the Prosecutor on the scandalous Defamation of Mr. *Charles Bradbury*. (51)

It is the lawyer's idea to increase the charge:

> Mr. *Pepper* asked the Prosecutor whether Mr. *Bradbury* did ever enter his Body, *Hearne* answered, he attempted but never could; Mr. *Pepper* made this Reply, I don't know how he could, and said he would lay it as bad as he could, the one is Death, and the other is not. (51)

Part of the justification is overheard by one Mr. John Bond:

[He] heard the said *Whittaker* declare it was Mr. *Bradbury's* own Fault that he was prosecuted, for they had appointed to meet Mr. *Bradbury* at one Mr. *Brown's* House, situate in Saint *John-Street*, in the Parish of Saint *Sepulchre* without, in order to accomodate the Affair relating to the scandalous defamatory Words spoken by *James Hearne* against Mr. *Bradbury*. ... Mr *Whittaker* further declared, the Boy *James Hearne* would or should swear the Fact against Mr. *Bradbury*, and they would prove Circumstances, and that must hang him. (52)

Whitaker seems to feel that Bradbury has it coming to him, if only for refusing to be reasonable:

And this Deponent saith, that *Whittaker* told him, the Boy's Father had been to Mr. *Bradbury*, and if Mrs. *Pickering* had given ten Pounds it had been all hushed up and no one would have known any thing of the Matter but themselves. (52)

The whole transaction, for all its venality (and worse), seems to have been marked by an air of piety that suggests that the Whitakers and the Browns believed in what they were doing, absurd as it seems:

And this Deponent further saith, that on the *Monday* following he was at said Mr. *Brown's* House, in Company with Mr. *Brown* and Wife, *Whittaker* and one *John Bailey*; and this Deponent after being there about ten Minutes, *Brown* ordered the Shop to be shut up, and the Doors lockt; then *James Hearne* was called down, and after *Bailey* had sung an Hymn and prayed, that *Hearne* might overcome *Bradbury*, there was a written Paper pulled out of the Table Drawer for this Deponent to subscribe one Guinea towards carrying on the Prosecution against Mr. *Bradbury*. (52)

Finally, nearly six weeks later, Bradbury catches up with his now well-rehearsed detractors:

[O]n *Wednesday* the sixteenth of *July* last this Deponent went in Company with Mr. *Thomas Brown* an Officer, to the House of *Henry Brown*, and desired the Boy, *Hearne*, might be called down Stairs, which *Frances Higden* did, and Hearne coming into the Room, this Deponent said, here is the Coat I promised you; then the Officer said to *Hearne*, I have got a Warrant for you, and you must go along with me. (53)

It is extremely interesting how the language of seduction applies to what the (apparent) conspirators do as well as it does to what they allege Bradbury did. They go to Justice Wright, where

Hearne hanging down his Head, wept, and said, Mr. *Bradbury* was innocent, and never had offered any Indecency to him, but that he was insti-
gated by *Brown* and *Whittaker* who seduced him to swear against Mr.
Bradbury, and in case Mr. *Bradbury* would not maintain him, he must
swear against Mr. *Bradbury*, and then they would take him up and hang
him, and afterwards provide for *Hearne*. (53)

Such statements tend to reinforce the suspicion that the charge really
got away from Brown and Whitaker, who originally only intended to use it
to get some support for Hearne, whom they felt Bradbury had harmed; all
of this tends to confirm that sodomy is the sort of charge that cannot be
"used" this way. Mrs. Brown's "real" reasons for so much prejudice against
someone "she knew no Harm of" (73) are actually quite mundane—a combination of greed and self-destructive obstinacy, at least on Bradbury's part:

[H]e was covetous, and put more Persons into the Pew than she approved
of, and that she had entertained a bad opinion of him ever since, and that
if Mr. *Bradbury* had not told the Story to Mrs. *Shore*, and this Deponent,
it would have been all hushed up amongst themselves, but, now, *(Brown)*
would tell it wherever she went. (73)

SOME CONCLUSIONS

One thing that emerges out of Bradbury's own anxiety is how easily,
even in the supposedly less self-conscious middle of the eighteenth century, religious interest could be mistaken for sexual, the spiritual care of a
convert to Protestantism for sodomitical interest in a potential initiate into
homosexual or at least sodomitical sex. The felt intensity of the problem is
indicated by Bradbury's defensiveness:

[W]hat was I to do as a Minister and Preacher of the Gospel? Was it not
my Duty to examine into the Truth of his Conversion, and encourage him
to persevere in it? (30)

Obviously, and therefore alarmingly, Bradbury's "Christian" efforts on
Hearne's behalf to get him a new job could be reinterpreted, or perhaps just
"misunderstood," as one stage in an attempt to alienate the boy from respectable employments and to take control of his life for his own sodomitical purpose. As the prosecution puts it neatly: "*Bradbury* desired him to
come away, and he would get him another master" (39).

If he was deceived, then, as he writes himself, "so were many others, who were equally persuaded of his Sincerity" (30). But it was his duty as a Christian, and moreover a Christian pastor, to be involved: "If Excess of Compassion to a poor Creature in Distress, be a Fault, I must own myself blame-worthy" (30). Thus, he cannot avoid the implication, however slight, that doing one's Christian duty and dabbling in illicit sexuality could, at least initially, bear some resemblance. Part of his problem is finding an identifiable role for himself vis-à-vis Hearne that is socially acceptable. His difficulty only underlines the absence of such a role, as he acts partly as spiritual advisor, partly as much more worldly "father," and, indeed, partly as friend:

> [B]efore I gave him any Tokens of my Kindness, I used my best Endeavours to make up the Difference between his Master and him; and that I offer'd him no Assistance or Encouragement, till I found his Master was irreconcilable, his Father had deserted him for turning Protestant, and he was in Danger of perishing for want of Bread and Lodging. (30)

Finally, he appeals to humanity: "Could Humanity do less than I did?" Would inhumanity then be the only way to avoid running the risk of being falsely accused of sodomy? The fact remains, or even is made to appear a little more obvious, that most people would have done less. Such an appeal seems at least slightly ironic, at least as an explanation of "benevolent interest," considering his own diatribe against humanity only slightly later:

> Is it not amazing that men, to whom I never did any wrong, should conspire to ruin my reputation and take away my life? What a deplorable instance is this of the depravity of human nature, that is capable of cherishing such a diabolical spirit against a person who never willingly gave offence to any, but on all occasions has shewn his readiness to do offices of kindness to all, as well in temporals as spirituals? (49)

I think most readers would have to agree that Bradbury fails of his primary object, by means of this casebook,

> to wipe off every Stain injuriously thrown on my Character, and efface every Impression which this malicious Prosecution may have made on the Minds of my Friends, to my Disadvantage. (2)

Besides whatever suspicions his enemies create, he creates many more by his own discourse, not just of himself but of what we might generally call "eighteenth-century" arrangements. Retroactively, because of his own increasingly self-conscious retroactive rethinkings and even *reworkings* of such arrangements, he *sexualizes* them and, moreover, part of the society to which they belong. His casebook depicts an early example of the deployment of sexuality through some of the power mechanisms Foucault describes, "pedagogization" especially, and around such recognizably Foucauldian "saturation-points" as home, church, and school.

Such institutional places have obviously been sexualized for Bradbury by his experience to a degree that they almost certainly never were before; what intrigues me most is the way they must have been sexualized for his readers too. In ways impossible to measure but possibly significant, this "casebook" contributes to the processes by which power and sexuality grew together.

Let the last word, a passage really (typical for all the questions it raises and that never get addressed, let alone answered), be Hearne's:

> [After losing his second job, at Mr. Mayne's, haberdasher in the Strand] He said, he had lain the first Night after he came away with a young Man near *Strand Bridge*; the next Day he went to his Aunt's, who lives near *Covent Garden*, who late at Night, turn'd him out, and he lay on the Stones at her Door, where, while he was asleep, somebody stole his Shirt; and on *Sunday*-night he had lain with Mr. *Gillyman*, a Schoolmaster at *Kensington*, where he had formerly been at School. (7)

Part II:
Akenside's *Pleasures:*
A Midcentury Poetics of Elision

6

Narcissism and Homoeroticism in Mark Akenside's *The Pleasures of Imagination*

Akenside's *The Pleasures of Imagination* attempts to distinguish aesthetic from other pleasures, physical and spiritual, but at the same time endeavors to situate them in a larger moral scheme. Unfortunately, however, all his "pleasures" have a tendency to look the same, to appear physical or erotic, or even homoerotic. His scheme, based on a mimetic aesthetic to begin with, in which physical things are allowed to stand for spiritual, facilitates other elisions. His frustrated homosexuality, his "real" pleasure, eventually displaces every other, ultimately subverting the didacticism of this extremely didactic poem.

In the other works we have read, where homosexuality has appeared as a target, or as an illustration for other targets that are supposed to be almost as bad, it has paradoxically appeared only to immediately disappear again, underneath a pile of signifiers, puns, and allegories as exaggerated as the sodomite himself is alleged to be. "He" is a nothing, a negation, a nonessential who announces his nonentity the only way he can, by drawing attention to his "joke" hats or some other kind of "language" that, as we all know, works through absence anyway. I think of Ellison's "invisible man," but in a different context or with a different, sartorial emphasis: all those conspicuous bandages, so at odds with the "nothing" underneath.

In those other texts homosexuality is elided; here, perhaps for the first time, or at least for the most important time so far, it actually elides something else. And "here" is, incidentally, arguably one of the most important, certainly one of the most popular, poems from the middle of the century, an appropriate place for elision to occur. It is significant that on such an important occasion homosexuality is not what is elided but what elides; if this poem, in its endeavor to harmonize beauty and truth, philosophy and poetry,

115

the many and the one, is as central to the period as its contemporaries and at least some of ours believed, its aesthetic and poetic as well as chronological heart, then that heart is profoundly homosexual.

Akenside's poem is in three books. Book 1 describes his basic scheme, in which the arts imitate nature imitating god. The arts arise vicariously, from the desire for "delightful perceptions . . . independent of the objects which originally produced them" (Akenside 1845, 1). Book 2 allegorizes the right relationship of truth and beauty in Harmodius's tale of how the "first man" subordinated beauty to wisdom as the price of enjoying beauty at all. The book indicates more clearly Akenside's political agenda by anticipating a kind of eighteenth-century renaissance of truth and beauty, virtue and the arts, and (of course) philosophy and poetry. Finally, in book 3 Akenside considers those pleasures arising from the ridiculous in nature. He concludes with a section on taste and what appears to be a rather flattering self-portrait.

Two major problems soon become apparent. The first is vicariousness. While in book 1 Akenside attempts to organize beauty according to Addison's scheme (greatness, novelty, and beauty) and his own hierarchy of "colour, shape, natural concretes, vegetables, animals, the mind" (5), his remains a system based on absence—of solid matter, on one hand, and of pure abstraction, on the other. His defense of "delightful perceptions . . . independent of the objects which originally produced them" makes such perceptions seem faintly pornographic at times, like secondhand "pleasures" at an unhealthy remove from their object. Teetering precariously between spiritual and physical, Akenside's pleasures dip down even as (perhaps conveniently) he looks up.

The second problem is the great discrepancy between what we feel we are supposed to take pleasure in and what we really take pleasure in. While the "nature" of Akenside's poem is a displacement, it is itself displaced by the real "object" of Akenside's imagination, his ephebe, usually himself. Ultimately, I hope to show, these two "problems" of vicariousness and narcissism are just two aspects of the same problem of displacement: an evasion of the essentially feminine thing to be displaced and a (necessarily self-)revelation in the essentially masculine thing that takes its place. This evasion is itself evaded, or at least disguised, in Akenside's subsequent revisions of his poem, some of which appear to have been undertaken in response to Smollett's satire of him and of his whole philosophy in *Peregrine Pickle*. I want to consider the problems of the original, Smollett's criticisms, and Akenside's reaction to them and to his own work.[1]

More generally Akenside's neoclassical system of mediation and substitution lends itself to sexual subversion, since it makes no immediately obvious difference whether the "exquisite pleasures" of "men of warm and sensible tempers" are aesthetic or sexual, aroused over the re-creation of an absent mountain that would certainly be missed, or over the subtler reconstruction of a female whose absence seems almost convenient. The interstices in his neoclassicism are all too readily penetrated by the masculine. Similarly, the development of the arts that he describes in his prose introduction and subsequently in the poem proper is essentially a process of subordination. Nature retreats as an older Socratic figure reconciles a fresh-faced if tearful ephebe to its loss. Nature literally gets "philosophized over"—except, of course, for the ephebe himself, whose own "natural beauties" are curiously exempt from such austerity, the only asphodel in Akenside's otherwise asphalt poem.

HOMOEROTIC LANDSCAPE

Early in book 1 nature is presented as a seductress charming "the consenting hearts / Of mortal men" (lines 2–3), but the seduced is more seductive, in an invocation ostensibly of a kind of diffused nature but really, I think, addressed to the ephebe himself (albeit somewhat fetishized):

> Be present all ye Genii, who conduct
> The wandering footsteps of the youthful bard,
> New to your springs and shades, who touch his ear
> With finer sounds; who heighten to his eye
> The bloom of Nature, and before him turn
> The gayest, happiest attitudes of things.
>
> (lines 25–30)

You never read of a path, a sight, a sound in Akenside without being immediately distracted to the foot, the eye, the ear of some young male. What attracts him makes *him* attractive, till *he* becomes the object—the pleased the *pleasing*. It is one thing to make a painting of a mountain, another to make a man, as Akenside does here and throughout *The Pleasures of Imagination*.

Consequently, while the poem is meant to show the spiritual pleasures derived from perceived objects, it does so over the more or less dead and fetishized body of someone else. Akenside's objects are less things on the way to people, than people on the way to things. Moreover, as subjects like the perceiving ephebe become objects, Akenside, identified with them to the extent that he is necessarily the poem's first and most important reader (who presumably wrote it, since it is a didactic poem, on the premise that we would all read it the same way), to some degree objectifies himself as *reader*. Of course, in the revisions that I consider below, Akenside reads his poem again but in a different and totally destructive way, responding in part to contemporaries who seem to have noticed—rather disapprovingly—some of the same things remarked here. For now, however, it is curiously possible for the ephebi of the poem to be objects and subjects simultaneously, and so to all be Akenside. In other words, the text becomes a zone of constant transaction between homoeroticism and narcissism that is, not surprisingly, redeeming, since the contents are never entirely matter (as happens in some kinds of pornography), if only because they are never entirely *not* Akenside.

The homoerotic and indeed narcissistic qualities of the poem are not reduced by its didacticism, the poet's attempt to situate these pleasures in a larger moral scheme, to "dispose the minds of men to a similar taste and habit of thinking in religion, morals, and civil life" (4). For one thing, while these "objects" arouse pleasures in us because they bring us nearer to God,

> the sire Omnipotent unfolds
> The world's harmonious volume, there to read
> The transcript of Himself.
>
> (lines 99–101)

this is a distinctly *male* deity, whose gendered beauty, later in book 2, actually opposes and competes with female beauty. For another, the alleged goal of such pleasures, "to breathe at large / Aethereal air, with bards and sages old" (lines 41–42), is less distinctly social than *homosocial*. In our enjoyment of nature there is a kind of divine agreement where we will find ourselves at one (physically as well as spiritually) with Socrates and a lot of attractive Greek boys. For all his rant about Liberty, he is not with men to be free, but free to be with men. The "Genius of ancient Greece," which he invokes towards the end of book 1," with its "heroic youth / Warm form the schools of glory" and invocation of the *Phaedrus*,

> Guide my way
> Through fair Lyceum's walk, the green retreates
> Of Academus, and the thymy vale,
> Where, oft enchanted with Socratic sound,
> Illisus pure devolved his tuneful stream
> In gentler murmurs.
>
> (lines 590–95)

probably makes this as explicit as it can probably be in the 1740s. One has
to wonder what hothouse flower he has in mind, when he writes

> From the blooming store
> Of these auspicious fields, may I, unblamed,
> Transplant some living blossoms to adorn
> My native clime. . . .

(lines 595–98)

Akenside's difficulty is that by "inspiration" he means Socratic instruction, from older bards and sages to younger, prettier ephebi, usually in
some kind of Illisus-like setting:

> there to breathe at large
> Aethereal air, with bards and sages old—
> Immortal sons of praise. These flattering scenes,
> To this neglected labour court my song.

(lines 41–44)

If this is his love of nature, what then is the nature of his love? Following
lines suggest an interesting combination of homosocial if not homoerotic
motifs with conventional ideas of retreat and retirement, all the more pleasing for their air of mystery if not forbiddenness (a kind of superhybrid
homoeroticized Neoplatonic georgic):

> the love
> Of nature and the Muses bids explore,
> Through secret paths erewhile untrod by man,
> The fair poetic region, to detect
> Untasted springs, to drink inspiring draughts. . . .

(lines 48–52)

When women do appear, they are almost immediately obliterated again
by the men who desire them—if not also by that man Akenside's desire for
the men who desire them. Thus, in a list of preponderantly male pursuers
of Truth, a woman who appears to pursue Truth in a novel immediately
disappears as herself the object of pursuit by a pursuer who is himself pursued:

> The virgin follows, with enchanted step,
> The mazes of some wild and wondrous tale,
> From morn to eve; unmindful of her form,

> Unmindful of the happy dress that stole
> The wishes of the youth, when every maid
> With envy pined.

(lines 250–55)

I cannot help thinking that Akenside, like Keynes, would have "inculcated himself between them." Similarly, Akenside's invitation to his ephebe to unite Truth and Beauty is coupled with an invitation to reject a "false Beauty," which he calls "lavish Fancy":

> Oh! wherefore, with a rash, imperfect aim,
> Seek you those flowery joys with which the hand
> Of lavish Fancy paints each flattering scene
> Where beauty seems to dwell, nor once inquire
> Where is the sanction of eternal Truth. . . .

(lines 378–82)

This false Beauty or Fancy appears all the more feminine when contrasted with the distinctly masculine Truth of the following lines:

> From the grove
> Where Wisdom talked with her Athenian sons,
> Could my ambitious hand entwine a wreath
> Of Plato's olive with the Mantuan bay,
> Then should my powerful voice at once dispel
> These monkish horrors. . . .

(lines 402–7)

I do not think it is forcing things to find in such lines a telling identification of "true" Beauty with the beautiful, homoerotic relationships of the *Phaedrus*, or perhaps of Greek culture generally, here curiously opposed to the alleged effeminacy (and homosexuality?) of Gothic. (I wonder what he thought of likely homosexuals like Thomas Gray. Does he protest too much?) Later, he allows a degree of false Beauty or Fancy, but typically subordinated to masculine Truth:

> the benignant Sire,
> To deck the honoured paths of just and good,
> Has added bright Imagination's rays:
> Where Virtue, rising from the awful depth
> Of Truth's mysterious bosom, doth forsake
> The unadorned condition of her birth;

> And, dressed by Fancy in ten thousand hues,
> Assumes a various feature, to attract,
> With charms responsive to each gazer's eye,
> The hearts of men. Amid his rural walk,
> The ingenuous youth, whom solitude inspires
> With purest wishes, from the pensive shade
> Beholds her moving, like a virgin muse. . . .

(lines 545–57)

This, I think it is fair to say, is male Virtue in female drag, and the "ingenuous youth" ("purest wishes" notwithstanding) is in imminent peril of becoming just another statistic.

Finally, while the noble agenda Akenside has in mind appears to be homosexual, that mind itself, on which so much of his system—its spirituality, its nobility, its beauty, its virtue—is based, is at times even ludicrously self-regarding, a Neoplatonic Belinda at the toilet of nature:

> Not so [unaffecting to the heart] the moral species, nor the
>   powers
> Of genius and design; the ambitious mind
> There sees herself: by these congenial forms
> Touched and awakened, with intenser act
> She bends each nerve, and meditates, well pleased,
> Her features in the mirror.

(lines 532–37)

The harmony and agreement that Akenside's system strives for, indeed requires, are achieved at the cost of difference—of anything to harmonize. Ironically, the only mind we really get is his own highly idiosyncratic one, the strangeness of which becomes apparent in the same book 1 when he tries to illustrate his argument with examples of "spiritual" beauty, which seem not only grossly physical but morally rather dubious as well. Thus the scene of Caesar's assassination is offered as a "spiritual" or "moral" beauty higher than any natural scene, yet is as bloody-minded as anything by David. Similarly, after this grotesquely inept attempt at "beauty," a classic example of friendship betrayed, Akenside seems perversely determined to betray *himself* still further, by immediately asking whether "In Nature's fairest form, is aught so fair / As virtuous friendship?" (lines 503–4). Akenside almost seems to *dare* us to say that *his* pleasures are not *ours*, an appearance that is surely at variance with his avowed public, didactic aims.

An Allegory: The Marriage of Philosophy
and the Divorce of Women

While book 3 concerns itself with what Akenside calls "the ridiculous," it
contains some striking passages of self-depiction and one of the poem's
few references to female beauty. Curiously, but not inconsistently, the one
is subsumed under the other. In the poet's "attempered bosom," he tells us,

> the virgin's radiant eye,
> Superior to disease, to grief, and time
> Shines with unbating lustre.
>
> (lines 371–73)

Akenside could mean merely that natural female beauty is eternal, never-
fading for the poet, but he probably also means that the poet himself, vicariously, gives off such eternal, never-fading beauty—nature is beautiful
and eternal for the poet, who subsequently becomes beautiful and eternal
too (just as desirable women, like the novel reader above, are subsumed by
desire for the men who desire them). Typically, female nature becomes
male. Consequently the universal pronoun is here, I think, at its most devious, since it enables Akenside to deflect women's due onto other males, to
disguise homosexual as heterosexual admiration. The poet's attempered
bosom guarantees not just her radiant eye but her virginity too—alas, perhaps. Significantly, *he* is the one who gets pregnant, as he "in silence bends
/ O'er these mixt treasures of his pregnant breast, / With conscious pride."

I have chosen to deal with Harmodius's "tale" last, though it occurs in
the middle of book 2, because it is at the heart of the poem, physically and
spiritually; it condenses in itself all the poem's cruxes, which the second
and third book respectively approach and evade. Significantly, the tale, the
heart of the story, appears embedded at the highest level of fiction, an appropriate place for Akenside to divulge his truth. The "Spirit of Human
Kind" teaches Harmodius, a "spotless youth" (line 188), who in turn instructs young Akenside, presumably spotless too. It is really a tale of aborted
marriage, or more precisely aborted heterosexual fulfillment, which is related first to Harmodius when his marriage is aborted by the death of his
sweetheart, and second to Akenside at a time of unusual turmoil in his
"afflicted bosom." It is studded, incidentally, with homoerotic details, like
the "Spirit of Human Kind" himself, who arrives like some kind of masker
in a purple cloud, dressed in suitably Grecian drag—see-through robe and
"radiant zone of gold / Aetherial" (lines 234–35) and even a name tag:

"Genius of Human Kind." Adam himself is "a smiling youth / Whose tender cheeks displayed the vernal flower / Of beauty" (lines 400–402).

This spirit grants Harmodius a vision of our "first parent" (really *non*-parent), a kind of Adamic ephebe awaiting Socratic instruction in an Illisus-side Eden. Adam is more attracted to Beauty than to Wisdom, so God sends Nemesis to help him *straighten* out his priorities. Adam is allowed to "keep" beauty, provided he subordinate her to wisdom. Besides its relevance to the theme, the most interesting thing about the tale of strife between beauty and wisdom, beauty and truth, is its manipulation of different gender-related kinds of beauty. Akenside's ostensibly female beauty, Euphrosyne, is not more female—certainly not more a blushing "rosy" maid—than Akenside's Adamic ephebe. Wisdom, which ultimately wins, presents an essentially *male* beauty—God himself calls her "Best image of thy Author" (472)—and in this case one has to think of that lesser male author, Akenside himself. Wisdom and Beauty are *both* beautiful, only Beauty's beauty is chastised because it is more overtly *female*.

The meaning of the story, and indeed the meaning of Akenside's "beauty and truth," becomes clear when one considers that the hour of philosophical ravishment is the hour of heterosexual "abortion." The marriage of truth and beauty that Akenside longs for so badly is achieved here in this embedded tale—pun intended—at the cost of heterosexual marriage specifically. Rather, it is displaced by Socratic linkings, pseudomarriages, and discipleships between wise old males and pretty young ones. For Akenside at least, the marriage of truth and beauty is a distinctly *homosexual* union, the closest to which he dare come is a heterosexual divorce.

AKENSIDE AND SHAFTESBURY

Akenside's allegories probably can be better understood if one reads them generically, as particular instances and indeed developments of a kind of writing for which he is especially indebted to Shaftesbury's allegorizing in *Characteristics*. Consider, for example, Shaftesbury's allegory of "the most beautiful princess," in section 2 of *Soliloquy, or Advice to an Author*. Tho most beautiful princess in the world is taken captive by a heroic young prince, who never visits the princess himself but commits her to the care of a virtuous young nobleman, his favorite. While the heroic prince declines to visit the princess out of a prudent sense of own weakness, his susceptibility to female beauty, his friend believes the prince's and his own virtue are proof against it:

> They who are honest and just, can admire and love whatever is beautiful, without offering at anything beyond what is allowed. How then is it possible, sire, that one of your virtue should be in pain on any such account, or fear such a temptation? (Cooper 1963, 1:119)

Of course, the friend, finally alone with the princess, gradually falls madly in love. Learning the lesson of his own weakness, he acknowledges it to the prince, who offers to forgive and even to reinstate him, provided he "retire only for a while" and "quit the charming princess." The princess herself is not consulted in the matter, but since she initially alerted the prince to his friend's passion for her, she is presumably against it too; nevertheless, she seems surprisingly ancillary to the action. To the prince's question, "Can you, then . . . resolve to quit the charming princess?" (121), he responds with an all too pat-sounding philosophical gush:

> "Oh sir!" replied the youth, "well am I now satisfied that I have in reality within me two distinct separate souls. This lesson of philosophy I have learnt from that villainous sophister Love. For 'tis impossible to believe that, having one and the same soul, it should be actually both good and bad, passionate for virtue and vice, desirous of contraries. No. There must of necessity be two: and when the good prevails, 'tis then we act handsomely; when the ill, then basely and villainously. Such was my case. For lately the ill soul was wholly master. But now the good prevails by our assistance, and I am plainly a new creature, with quite another apprehension, another reason, another will. (121)

Thus, the beauty of even this "most beautiful" princess seems to exist entirely for the sake of a philosophical lesson, after the learning of which the beautiful woman herself disappears. And while the soul of the noble friend is now more divided, or rather the noble friend is at least now conscious of its dividedness, he is more united with the noble prince than ever, if only in terms of philosophical agreement. When the moral is finally stated for us, in the unlikely event that we might have missed it, it seems to be for a different lesson than the one the prince's friend has just learned: "Thus it may appear how far a lover by his own natural strength may reach the chief principle of philosophy, and understand our doctrine of two persons in one individual self" (121). The lesson appears to shift from beauty to love, or perhaps the alteration is merely a matter of emphasis. Either way, it is apparent that all the beauty was between the noble friend and the princess, and all the love—as much or as little as there is—and certainly all the truth are between the two young men. Evidently more than the noble friend's soul is divided; beauty and love, and indeed beauty and truth, themselves are divided. It is as if, while arguing for a kind of Platonic "divided soul," Shaftesbury has inadvertently divided Plato, perhaps out of conformity to contemporary morals. Elsewhere, indeed almost anywhere else, he would argue vigorously for the union of the very things he leaves divided here, but not *here,* because to unite them he would have to let the noble friend fall in love with the beauty, not of some strangely abstract and inconsequential "most beautiful princess in the world," but of the noble prince. Then, and only then, would he learn not only that his soul was divided, but that such division was manageable and highly productive. But to do so he would have to remain in the presence of that beautiful, homosexual lover who, in Shaftesbury's version, is oddly and awkwardly transmogrified into a "princess" to whose femaleness Shaftesbury, in censoring or editing away Plato's homosexuality, has done a similar or even greater disservice.

Consider the allegory of the "lady-fancies" in section 2 of part 3. Here is the same subordination of female beauty to male, as mere "fancy," that one finds above in Akenside. It is these distinctly "lady" fancies that men must learn to examine by means of a Neoplatonic "inward colloquy": instead of an older man and an ephebe doing it to each other, each man does it to himself, or rather, discovers both older man and ephebe in himself, who together are able to withstand the "ladies":

> [T]hus it appears that the method of examining our ideas is no pedantic practice. Nor is there anything ungallant in the manner of thus questioning the lady fancies, which present themselves as charmingly dressed as possible to solicit their cause and obtain a judgment by favour of that worse part and corrupt self to whom they make their application. (202)

The lady fancies resemble artful whores, seductresses, or "solicitresses" as Shaftesbury calls them, among other expressions with similar connotations:

> It may be justly said of these, that they are very powerful solicitresses. They never seem to importune us, though they are ever in our eye, and meet us whichever way we turn. They understand better how to manage their appearance than by always throwing up their veil and showing their faces openly in a broad light, to run the danger of cloying our sight, or exposing their features to a strict examination. So far are they from such forwardness, that they often stand as at a distance, suffering us to make the first advance, and contenting themselves with discovering a side-face, or bestowing now and then a glance in a mysterious manner, as if they endeavoured to conceal their persons. (202)

His language is laced with unflattering, potentially misogynistic innuendo. Among these "solicitresses" is one who, while not seductive or charming in herself, contributes enormously (if contrastively)) to the seductiveness of her "sisters" by impersonating Death:

> And if by her tragic aspect and melancholy looks she can persuade us that Death (whom she represents) is such a hideous form, she conquers in behalf of the whole fantastic tribe of wanton, gay, and fond desires. Effeminacy and cowardice instantly prevail. . . . The ideas of sordid pleasure are advanced. Worth, manhood, generosity, and all the nobler opinions and sentiments of honest, good, and virtuous pleasure disappear and fly before this Queen of Terrors. (203)

This death-impersonating "lady fancy" takes after Melpomene, but to counter her and the "unmanning" fear she inspires, appears a rival "lady fancy" who takes after Calliope:

> But see! A lovely form advances to our assistance, introduced by the prime Muse, the beauteous Calliope! She shows us what real beauty is, and what those numbers are which make life perfect and bestow the chief enjoyment. She sets virtue before our eyes, and teaches us how to rate life from the experience of the most heroic spirits. She brings her sisters Clio and Urania to support her [representing, of course, history and philosophy]. (204)

Such exhaustive use, or rather exploitation, of distinctly female beauty to stand for different kinds of polarized abstraction obviously anticipates Akenside's similar (if worse, because more "gendered") exploitation of it later. Female beauty is literally exhausted, ransacked, as an illustration for something else, something that (one cannot help but notice) does not happen to male beauty, at least not so totally. In Shaftesbury female beauty, while clearly subordinate, continues to exist, even if it resembles a kind of neoclassical cheerleader:

> Thus we retain on virtue's side the noblest party of the Muses. Whatever is august among those sisters, appears readily in our behalf. Nor are the more jocund ladies wanting in their assistance when they act in the perfection of their art, and inspire some better geniuses in this kind of poetry. Such were the nobler lyrics, and those of the later and more refined comedy of the ancients. The Thalias, the Polyhymnias, the Terpsychores, the Euterpes willingly join their parts, and being alike interested in the cause of numbers, are with regret employed another way, in favour of disorder. (205)

In Akenside such beauty eventually disappears, at least as a positive.

Finally, in discussing the third order of beauty, after lifeless forms and forms that form, the Theocles and Philocles of *The Moralists* demonstrate a colloquy in action. Their diction, and their imagery for the processes they describe even as they undergo them, amounts to another allegory, this time for the creative processes. But as in the other allegories, the female, while persisting for its illustrative value, has lost all reality. This almost certainly provided Akenside with a precedent for his use of biological processes, essentially female, as a metaphor for spiritual processes that are essentially male:

> Do you not see then, replied Theocles, that you have established three degrees or orders of beauty? As how? Why first, the dead forms, as you properly have called them, which bear a fashion, and are formed, whether by man or Nature, but have no forming power, no action, or intelligence. Right. Next, and as the second kind, the forms which form, that is, which have intelligence, action, and operation. Right still. Here therefore is double beauty. For here is both the form (the effect of mind) and mind itself. The first kind is low and despicable in respect of this other, from whence the dead form receives its lustre and force of beauty. For what is a mere body, though a human one, and ever so exactly fashioned, if inward form be wanting, and the mind be monstrous or imperfect, as in an idiot or savage? This too I can apprehend, said I, but where is the third order? (Cooper 1963, 2:132)

Theocles asks Philocles if there is some even higher order of forms, and the latter answers that yes, indeed, there is such an order, comprised of the forms capable of "producing other living forms like themselves" (133). Theocles congratulates his "pupil":

> [H]ere you have unawares discovered that third order of beauty, which forms not only such as we call mere forms but even the forms which form. . . . [T]hat which fashions even minds themselves, contains in itself all the beauties fashioned by those minds, and is consequently the principle, source, and fountain of all beauty. (133)

Note that the answer Theocles seeks, as to what comprises this third and highest order, will itself belong to it—a thought, an idea, though in this case the thought must be of thought itself. That this process which brings this thought about, paradigmatic in that it brings about thought itself (though it could bring about any thought), is analogous to the birthing process is conveyed by the diction of the passage. As Philocles struggles to arrive at the thought that thought is the highest beauty, he protests "I am barren" and asks for Theocles' help to make him "conceive." When Philocles success-fully answers that he must mean his "sentiments," Theocles refers to his friend's "parent-mind" as "that fertile part," his "pregnant genius" and to his thoughts as his "offspring." The relationship is only analogical, how-ever, since unlike the female womb Philocles' mind is "never spent or ex-hausted, but gains strength and vigour by producing." Philocles deliber-ately carries the analogy a bit too far, thereby turning it into a joke at this point. He compares Philocles to the midwife without whom his "labouring mind" would "prove abortive." This seems intended to relief the stress of the implication, rather strong to this point, that as Philocles is to the woman, Theocles is to the man. The "man" of the relationship proves in fact to be God, as Theocles subsequently explains, or even reassures:

> You do well, replied he, to give me the midwife's part only; for the mind conceiving of itself, can only be, as you say, assisted in the birth. Its pregnancy is from its nature. Nor could it ever have been thus impreg-nated by any other mind than that which formed it at the beginning; and which, as we have already proved, is original to all mental as well as other beauty. (135)

By supplanting heterosexual procreative processes with a homosexual dialectical one, Shaftesbury comes rather close to the erotic processes described in the *Phaedrus*. The looseness of the analogy, which Shaftesbury takes some pains to expose, seems intended to downplay its homosexuality.

What these allegories have in common, Shaftesbury's and Akenside's alike, is a tendency to reproduce something like a Platonic dialectic be-tween truth and beauty, but one that is oddly nondynamic, deprived as it is of a continual interchange between lover and beloved, between beauty and truth. That beauty is usually feminine (at least ostensibly) and truth mascu-line appears to be part of the reason. This would not be a sufficient cause however, unless both Shaftesbury and Akenside found it difficult to con-ceive of such a dialectic between a man and a woman, at the same time they found it impossible (for obvious reasons) to depict it between one man and another.

HOMOSEXUAL REPUBLICANS

Significantly, Harmodius bears the name of the classical Athenian who, with his lover Aristogeiton, murdered the tyrant Hippias's brother Hipparchus for his unwanted advances—and from mistaken fear that his hurt feelings would lead him to use his brother's power against them. Here the combination of homosexual love and republicanism proved disastrous, since it led to the (probably unnecessary) murder of the wrong ephebe, death for the lovers at the hand of an angry mob, and harsher measures for the rest under what had been a benign regime (Thucydides, *Peloponnesian Wars* bk. 6).

While Akenside might have wanted us (or at least *some* of us) to see homosexual solidarity as a strength or even a basis for the republicanism for which he was later to be as notorious as he was for sodomy,[2] his allusion (if it really *is* one, and one cannot be sure) is only too typically self-betraying. Among all the other displacements, that of public by private may not be the least.

Indeed, it is hard not to see a parallel between Harmodius and his lover Aristogeiton and Akenside and his patron and probable lover Jeremiah Dyson, between the weakness of Athenian republicanism to some degree cemented and motivated by a love relationship and even jealousy,[3] and the weakness of a form of eighteenth-century republicanism similarly compromised by being based too much on passionate relationships, not enough on principle. Houpt (1944, 156) notes, for example, the strange conversion of Akenside to the Tory Ministry of Lord Bute under the newly crowned George III—following, no doubt, his patron. While I cannot resist paraphrasing against him, Pope's lines to Akenside's own old enemy, William Pulteney, earl of Bath,

> Thro' clouds of passion *Akenside's* views are clear
> He foams a Patriot to subside a *Queer*.

for me his "pleasures" become a cautionary tale about the perils awaiting those of us who have no alternative but to fight their private battles publicly.

VERSIONS OF AKENSIDE

Howard Buck (1932, 10–26) argues quite convincingly that Smollett caricatured Mark Akenside in the second volume of *Peregrine Pickle* because of Akenside's abuse of Scotland in his recently published *Ode to the Earl of Huntingdon*. Buck also argues that the identification was well known at the time, exploiting characteristics for which Akenside was already famous (or infamous): overzealous republicanism, pedantry, abstract theorizing, and what Buck characterizes rather euphemistically as "chilly impersonal-ness" (13). Smollett's caricature seems to exploit other characteristics as well, which lead to a conclusion that must have been unavoidable, and that the language of even later critics like Buck seems at once to indicate and to evade:

> Despite Akenside's long and devoted intimacy with his friend and liberal patron, "dear Dyson," it is impossible to believe that he was not rather exceptionally devoid of human warmth. He never married, nor, despite one or two conventional plaints in his poems, is there any evidence that he was ever in love; nor (of more significance) does any human being besides Dyson appear in his biography on terms of intimacy. (14)

Peregrine Pickle's adventures with the doctor and Pallet comprise a kind of last fling in France before returning to England. Having received news that "the commodore" is declining, and that his sister is interested in marrying a "young gentleman," Peregrine decides to return after a stay in France of about fifteen months; he remains, however, another week or two in Paris, before making the tour of Flanders and Holland on his way home, seeking "some agreeable companion disposed for the same journey." At the Palais Royal he encounters two gentlemen getting out of their fiacre, one of whom is believed to represent Akenside: "a young man, in whose air and countenance appeared all the uncouth gravity and supercilious self-conceit of a physician piping hot from his studies." His companion, a painter named Pallet, is taken by some for a caricature of Hogarth: "a strange com-position of levity and assurance" (Smollett 1964, 224).

This doctor and Pallet are meaningfully coupled, the former a young man trying to be old, the latter an old man trying to be young:

> [T]heir characters, dress and address were strongly contrasted; the doctor wore a suit of black, and a huge tye-wig, neither suitable to his own age, nor the fashion of the country where he then lived; whereas the other, though seemingly turned of fifty, strutted in a gay summer dress of the Parisian cut, with a bag to his own grey hair, and a red feather in his hat, which he carried under his arm. (224)

Pallet explains that "his fellow traveller was a man of vast learning, and beyond all doubt, the greatest poet of the age" (224). Observing one painting, he complains that "the fore-shortening of that arm is monstrous" and appeals to the doctor's anatomical knowledge: "[D]octor, you under-stand anatomy, don't you think that muscle evidently misplaced?" (224–25). When Pallet blunders, mistaking the Swiss's exclamation, "sans prix," for the name of the artist, "Sangpree," the doctor sententiously corrects him with a quotation from Horace, which is utterly lost on Pallet, who is "rather more ignorant of Latin that of French" (225). When the doctor rebukes Pallet with a quotation from Homer, Pickle defends the painter with another quotation. Challenged not just in terms of knowledge but of gravity by "such a repartee from a youth of Peregrine's appearance" (225), the doctor bombards them with quotations that he "must have been at infinite pains in conning" (226).

Pickle responds with amusement and scorn, and something else more predatory. He has been hunting for an interesting companion and he finds one, and in tandem with a natural sidekick or alter ego. Smollett's diction at times suggests that the doctor is like the host body to Pickle's parasite, from which "an infinite fund of diversion" might be "extracted." On the other hand, Pickle "cultivates" the doctor rather like a farm animal, a cow or a pig perhaps. The implication is that the doctor is not an autonomous being, not even as a source of amusement. He is not even a good fool without Pallett.

In the course of the next half-dozen chapters the painter probably fares the better of the two, at least in the reader's esteem; he is essentially a foil for the doctor's character. That character is cowardly, hypocritical, chauvinistic, and vain. Most of these traits are reflected in the doctor's republican politics, where they appear at their socially most dangerous. It may be for this reason—a concern over what the doctor represents for the state— that Smollett lavishes so much attention on his views. Whether or not the doctor is homosexual is never made explicit, but remains a strong probability, implied by the presence of homosexuals at his feast, by the homoeroticism associated with his Platonizing, by his fervor for homosexual republicans like Harmodius and Aristogeiton, and by his strong misogyny.

In chapter 47 the doctor's "rank republicanism" is exposed for the first time at a dinner-table clash with Jolter, a high churchman:

> It was an article of the governor's creed, that the people could not be happy, nor the earth yield its fruits in abundance, under a restricted clergy and limited government: whereas, in the doctor's opinion, it was an eternal truth, that no constitution was so perfect as the democracy, and that no country could flourish, but under the administration of the mob. (229)

Naturally, Pickle encourages their debate, which begins with the doctor's assertion that English partridges are inferior to French because the latter "are not so well fed. The iron hand of oppression is extended to all animals within the French dominions, even to the beasts of the field and the fowls of the air" (230). Pallet seconds him, observing that Frenchmen have been hungrily eying their well-fed-looking English complexions, and that even French horses have sniffed at them "as a couple of delicious morsels" (231). When Jolter reprimands the doctor for his chauvinism, for having spoken like a "true Englishman," the doctor asserts the universality of his beliefs, a universality that Smollett sees as a disguise for misanthropy: "his affections and ideas being confined to no particular country; for he considered himself as a citizen of the world" (230). His affection for England is based on democratic principles: "[T]he British constitution approached nearer than any other, to that perfection of government, the democracy of Athens, which he hoped one day to see revived" (230). He gloats over the execution of Charles I, and concludes with "forty or fifty lines from one of the Philippicks of Demosthenes" (231).

Jolter, the high churchman, responds by attacking Athenian democracy as a source of "anarchy and disbelief," and by defending monarchy for its "divine institution," its stability, and its generous patronage of the arts. Pickle is swayed most by Jolter, and even the doctor's sidekick begins to waver, till the doctor responds that such power to reward amounts to arbitrary license. Pallet applauds but Jolter counters by asserting that "supreme power" stops short of tyranny and that it must always be adapted to the "genius of the people," which, if not accommodated, has the right to revolt. Pallet wavers again, suggesting that his champion has "got into the wrong box," but "this son of Paean" offers to refute Jolter's sophistry "by argument and facts" and even "with his own words." Jolter snobbishly accuses the doctor of ill breeding, while the doctor insolently accuses Jolter of dilettantism. After Jolter departs in a huff, Pickle congratulates the doctor on his victory, and Pallet reveres him more than ever.

The doctor then waxes rhapsodic on topics that tend to confirm his identification with Akenside: "the whole scheme of Plato's republic, with many quotations from that ideal author; touching the 'beautiful, the fair'; the moral sense of Shaftesbury" (232), whom Smollett denigrates as a "frothy writer" (232). As Pickle urges him on, the doctor hints that he himself is no less than Pindar reincarnate, although Smollett indicates that his odes and Pindar's are "as different as the Odes of Horace and our present laureat" (233).

Perhaps the most important point illustrated by this exchange, at least for our purposes, is the shakiness of the doctor's ostensibly principled politics. His claim to objectivity is undermined by his intensely subjective vanity. In mentally leaping from French fowl to French politics, he indicates a total want of discretion in particulars that makes one doubt his ability to distinguish public from private, or universal from particular. Finally, despite his claim to universality, he is intensely chauvinistic.

The potential ruthlessness of his confounding of public and private, his subordination of private things including friendship to a *res publica* that turns out to be private again, is revealed by his disappointment at Pallet's later release from the Bastille. Through Pickle's fault he is arrested for insulting a French aristocrat and impersonating a woman. The doctor, when informed of their arrest, sees it as confirmation of French oppression and everything he ever said about arbitrary power: "Such a calamity as this could never have happened under the Athenian democracy: nay, even when the tyrant Pisistratus got possession of that common-wealth, he durst not venture to rule with such absolute and unjust dominion" (248). He proceeds to argue that they should not try to get the prisoners released, since the injustice of their captivity will inflame a popular revolt.

Like the Brutus whom Akenside praises, the doctor asserts that he would "rejoice" to see even the blood of his own father spilled, "provided such a victim would furnish me with the opportunity of dissolving the chains of slavery, and vindicating that liberty which is the birth-right of man" (248). His motive, however, is obviously vanity, specifically a desire to find his name immortalized with the names of Harmodius and Aristogeiton, whom Akenside praises too, and fervently, in *The Pleasures of Imagination*.

When Pallet finally safely returns to his apartment, the doctor is visibly disappointed, since "he hoped to have heard that he and Mr. Pickle had acted the glorious part of Cato; an event which would have laid the foundation of such noble struggles"; worse, "he had already made some progress in an ode that would have immortalized their names" (255). Pallet's reaction is hardly surprising: he "could not brook the doctor's reflexions, which he thought savoured a little too much of indifference and deficiency in point of private friendship" (256). After Pallet compares the doctor's favorite metaphor (his own) to something by Bayes in *The Rehearsal*, the doctor turns on his old friend, justifying himself by comparison to Manlius and Brutus, "who shut their ears against the cries of nature, and resisted all the dictates of gratitude and humanity" (256). Not unlike Akenside at times in the *Pleasures*, the doctor seems a bit too eager to subordinate private things like friendship to a public thing that itself seems at least as private and arbitrary.

Precisely *why* he is this way is never made explicit, perhaps because Smollett's caricature was so recognizably Akenside, and potentially actionable. One of the earliest consequences of Pickle's encouragement of the doctor, his "insinuating behaviour" as Smollett calls it at the start of chapter 48, is the doctor's increased affection for him. The doctor expresses his "friendship" by inviting Pickle to "an entertainment in the manner of the Ancients." For more fun, Pickle invites as well a number of foreigners whom he knows to be "egregious coxcombs" (234). The guests recline on couches, like the guests at a classical feast. Among them is an Italian count. After a series of inedible "classical" dishes, the guests satisfy themselves with wine and olives, the doctor entertains his drunk or sleeping guests with "odes of Anacreon to a tune of his own composing," and finally, "seized with such a qualm," he asks Pickle to conduct him to his chamber. The count then takes the opportunity to fondle the sleeping German baron, whom he approaches singing an air from *Il Pastor Fido*, kisses, and tickles under the ribs "with such expressions of tenderness, as scandalized the virtuous painter" (242). The lines describe a lover's "amorous thirst" for "forbidden liquor"; significantly, a middle passage has been deleted stating that it would be better to die than to quench such a thirst. Alerted by Pallet, who in his vanity is "alarmed for his person," Pickle observes that the baron is not "averse to the addresses of the count" (242). To punish the two male lovers he sends in the landlady, a woman with a temper. Angered at the "mutual endearments of the two lovers," she scolds them and beats them with the baron's cane. They are in some danger of being beaten by the "populace" who gather at the door, but are rescued by their lackeys. Pickle congratulates the landlady, and invites Pallet to a masquerade, which he attends in drag and at which he is arrested.

While the doctor is not overtly homosexual, unless his "qualm" and his asking Pickle to lead him to bed indicate a tacit invitation, he does at least offer a feast at which the main attraction seems to be a homosexual "liaison." His inability to give a "decent" supper may stand as a metaphor for the dysfunctionality of his politics, or for an elaborately organized system that not only fails to work but also degenerates into private depredation, from feast to sexual foray. That the foray assumes the most heinously antisocial shape of homosexual assault, suggests that Smollett not only discerned something unworkable—unfeastlike, private, predatory —about Akenside's politics, but also identified it with something analogous (at least to Smollett) about his sexuality.

At several points Smollett indicates that the doctor is a misogynist, almost always in conjunction with his republicanism. When a couple of French officers refuse to pay the landlord, Jolter and the doctor debate again the relative merit of absolutism and democracy:

> [T]he doctor with great warmth alledged, that those officers ought to suf-
> fer death, or banishment at least, for having plundered the people in this
> manner. . . . and as for the little affronts to which a man may be subject,
> from the petulance of the multitude, he looked upon them as glorious
> indications of liberty, which ought not to be repressed, and would at any

time rejoice to find himself overthrown in a kennel by the insolence of a
son of freedom . . . adding, by way of illustration, that the greatest pleasure he ever enjoyed, was in seeing a dustman wilfully overturn a
gentleman's couch, in which two ladies were bruised, even to the danger
of their lives. (269)

On another occasion, when Pallet remarks that he would have grown a
beard so as to resemble Rubens, whom he admired, the doctor observes
that "a man who is not proof against the solicitations of a woman, can
never expect to make a great figure in life; that painters and poets ought to
cultivate no wives but the muses; or if they are, by the accidents of fortune,
incumbered with families, they should carefully guard against that pernicious weakness, falsely honoured with the appellation of *natural affection*,
and pay no manner of regard to the impertinent customs of the world"
(332). Anyone familiar with Akenside's poetry knows how fond he is of
marriages with flesh-and-blood women that get aborted for marriages with
abstract masculine virtue. His scorn for heterosexual marriage is nearly
allied to his political scorn for the private realm, indicating his own confusion of public and private. At least some of the considerable violence of his
republicanism seems to derive from hatred of women.

Thus, as caricatured by Smollett, Akenside is marked by a tendency to
mistake public things for private and vice versa, conveniently overlooking
his own selfish interest in his public schemes. Worse, his private self is
especially equivocal, motivated at times less by fervid love than by hate.
This in turn is directed especially at women in a way that emphasizes the
uncertainty of his sexual orientation, already undermined by the context:
his almost sexual passion for types of male virtue like Aristogeiton and
Harmodius (both homosexuals), his Platonizing, his parodic love feast, his
obviously symmetrical opposition to the flagrant womanizing of Pallet,
etc. Akenside becomes the type of a homosexual aesthete turned politician,
his republicanism motivated entirely by misogyny, his ostensibly public-
minded love of man really a private love of a different sort (according to
his enemies at least, little more than unusually virulent narcissism) and,
finally, his social program hijacked by a conveniently abstract transcen-
dental agenda.

Versions and Revisions

Several critics have commented on the character of Akenside's revisions of his poem after 1744. According to Jeffrey Hart the revisions span

a number of years: "The revised version of Book I was printed in 1757 for circulation among Akenside's friends; Book II of the later version appeared in a similar fashion in 1765" (1959, 67). Hart attributes some of these changes to Akenside's growing conservatism: "By 1761 . . . it was clear to their outraged friends that both Dyson and Akenside had abandoned their earlier Whig, or even republican, principles, and now enthusiastically supported the efforts of George III to strengthen the powers of the crown" (68). More recently, Michael Meehan agrees with him, while arguing for the close association of Akenside's politics with his aesthetics:

> [I]t's clear that the later revisions didn't involve simply the dropping of a few patriotic effusions, something that might have supported the idea that they were merely a gloss on the surface of a substantially independent aesthetic scheme. In the later versions, not only was the political restraint associated with changes in the aesthetic doctrine, but the new theory reflected new political interests. (1986, 52)

For Hart these changes are generally positive, in the direction of increased "powers of observation" and "sensitivity to fact and detail." However, his own examples, besides mine below, indicate that revision was also towards diminished physicality, which, given that most of the people in his poem are men, means diminished homoeroticism. Akenside's revisions can therefore also be seen as a form of self-censorship reflecting his reaction to Smollett's virtual "outing" of him above. They might even be taken as an oblique admission.

BOOK 1

Compare the opening of the 1744 version to that of 1757. The 1744 edition reads:

> With what attractive charms this goodly frame
> Of nature touches the consenting hearts
> Of mortal men, and what the pleasing stores
> Which beauteous Imitation thence derives
> To deck the poet's, or the painter's toil,
> My verse unfolds.

(lines 1–6)

The 1757 edition says:

> With what enchantment Nature's goodly scene
> Attracts the sense of mortals; how the mind,
> For its own eye, doth objects nobler still
> Prepare; how men, by various lessons, learn
> To judge of Beauty's praise; what raptures fill
> The breast with fancy's native arts endowed,
> And what true culture guides it to renown;
> My verse unfolds.
>
> (lines 1–8)

In the first, "nature" is essentially a warehouse of images to be used by poets and painters. Since "consenting" to its "attractive charms" suggests an affinity stemming from their mutual Creator, the associations of these warehouse images do not seem entirely arbitrary. The second version, however, emphasizes precisely this arbitrariness, the mental operations and "various lessons" that artists learn themselves and teach others in order to associate these images properly. The subject of the later version is more idealizing, and its treatment more abstract.

The second version has obviously been masculinized, as in the lines immediately following. Compare one of the prettier, more homoerotic passages of the 1740s version to the corresponding passage in the revision of 1757. The 1748 version:

> Attend, ye gentle powers
> Of musical delight! and, while I sing
> Your gifts, your honours, dance around my strain.
>
> . . . .
>
> Be present all ye Genii, who conduct
> The wandering footsteps of the youthful bard,
> New to your springs and shades, who touch his ear
> With finer sounds; who heighten to his eye
> The bloom of Nature, and before him turn
> The gayest, happiest attitudes of things.
>
> (lines 6–30)

The 1757 revision:

> Ye gods, or godlike powers,
> Ye guardians of the sacred task, attend,
> Propitious. Hand in hand, around your bard
> Move in majestic measures. . . .
>
> . . . .

> Be present all ye Genii, who conduct
> Of youthful bards, the lonely-wandering step,
> New to your springs and shades; who touch their ear
> With finer sounds, and heighten to their eye
> The pomp of nature, and before them place
> The fairest, loftiest countenance of things.

(lines 8–47)

I think it is fair to remark that his "godlike powers" now do not "dance" but (rather laboriously) "move in majestic measures." Akenside seems to have tried to disguise the natural body of the youthful bard by contorting it with unnatural "poetic" syntax, with enjambment that artfully (or fussily) gets in the way of the object.[4] Pluralized, the bard seems less concrete and the nature he focalizes less vivid: "pomp" instead of "bloom," static "placing" instead of constant "turning," "lofty countenances" instead of "happy attitudes." Whereas previously nature was apposite, now it is opposite to youth, shorn of the fetishistic attributes of an eroticized male.

That what was formerly an invocation of "nature's kindly breath" as well as a rhetorical *excusatio propter infirmitatem* ("Yet not unconscious what a doubtful task / To paint the finest features of the mind" [lines 45–46]) is now an address to Dyson suggests some of the fervor of their relationship. Moreover what Dyson has done in the text is precisely what Akenside says he has done in his life; he has supplanted Nature and all its doubtful pleasures, helped the poet straighten out his priorities. That Dyson replaces an overtly and dangerously sensuous Nature does not necessarily mean that his relationship with Akenside must be sensual. What seems clearer is that the bachelor invokes their relationship as a virtuous friendship in order to disinfect this version of the *Pleasures* of images that he seems to admit were beautiful and that, since they also were male, probably were homoerotic. Perhaps the bachelor poet had no alternative but to employ such a strategy, pitting the homosocial against the homosexual, reasonably confident that given the sacredness of the former, the latter must lose. We have all seen examples of this before.

The passage in the original where he compares the human mind to "Memnon's marble harp" (line 109) is probably improved by including Milton and Homer in the dream of Fancy (lines 162–73), inspired by the God-given affinity of mind and nature. Typically, however, the original apostrophe to the youth who enjoys such affinities is toned down, the youth himself subdued from one "Whose candid bosom the refining love / Of Nature warms" to another, rather paler being "Whom Nature's aspect, Nature's simple garb / Can thus command." Akenside's revision of young men is almost never an improvement, and often more like a guilty after-thought.

Small verbal revisions remove the suggestion of sexuality and even gender. Thus in the next passage introducing the "orders" to which Fancy refers Nature's forms, "inflame / The powers of Fancy" (lines 141–42) becomes "inspire / Attentive Fancy" (lines 182–83), "pregnant stores" (line 139) becomes "ancient store" (line 180), etc. Perhaps significantly, Akenside reduces the original trio of "the sublime, / The wonderful, the fair" (lines 145–46) to just the "sublime, or fair" (line 188). Similarly, in a passage describing man's ascent through Nature to "The applauding smile of Heaven," the physicality of "wherefore darts the mind / With such resist-less ardour to embrace / Majestic forms, impatient to be free" (lines 169–71) gets muted to "Why departs the soul / Wide from the track and journey of her times, / To grasp the good she knows not?" (lines 213–15).

The most important section of the original version of book 1 is that devoted to Beauty (lines 271–407). This conveniently can be broken into sections. A brief invocation (lines 271–80) quickly blends into an apostro-phe to his own song (lines 281–87), and then a kind of (homo)eroticized pastoral (lines 287–95), as the "song" conducts us through a series of beau-tiful, natural settings:

> Wilt thou fly
> With laughing Autumn to the Atlantic isles
> And range with him the Hesperian field, and see
> Where'er his fingers touch the fruitful grove,
> The branches shoot with gold; where'er his step
> Marks the glad soil, the tender clusters glow
> With purple ripeness, and invest each hill
> As with the blushes of an evening sky?
>
> (lines 287–94)

The poet addresses his song again, urging it to bring Tempe's "flowery store" and Hydra's "Hesperian fruits" to Dione (lines 305–22), a personifi-cation of moralized beauty. From this singular abstraction he next imag-ines himself singing of all beautiful women to all young men, and possibly vice versa (lines 302–35):

> Then the pleasing force
> Of Nature and her kind parental care,
> Worthier, I'd sing: then all the enamoured youth,
> With each admiring virgin, to my lyre
> Should throng attentive, while I point on high

> Where Beauty's living image, like the morn
> That wakes in Zephyrs arms the blushing May,
> Moves onward
>
> (lines 322–29)

At line 335 he shifts his addressee to the "youths and virgins" whom he promises not to depress (or bore?) with gloomy "Superstition dressed in Wisdom's garb." He argues that beauty and morality are not incompatible, that Nature "sanctifies" man's choice, and illustrates his point with another passage of homoerotic landscape (one of his specialties), "whose bosom smiles with verdure" (line 365), as if a hairy breast were beautiful because of its association with grass, or verdure attractive because of its resemblance to a hairy breast (lines 349–72).[5] He attacks the false beauty of Fancy (lines 377–91), attacks Gothic poetry for moralizing too morbidly (lines 391–401), and recommends his own more attractive beauty, with himself as a kind of synthesis of Plato and Virgil (lines 401–17). He seems zealous, even jealous to make himself true Beauty's true spokesman to Youth, the Socrates of his day.

In the 1757 version Dione is replaced by a more personalized "Melissa." Subsequently, the movement from singular to plural abstraction is aborted as Akenside addresses her only, instead of the mixed throng. Here he seems altogether more respectable, more heterosexual in fact, which was probably his object. Instead of assuring the throng that he won't depress them with gloomy moralizing, he assures Melissa, in a long and rather coy passage, of his admiration:

> While my tongue
> Prolongs the tale, Melissa, thou may'st feign
> To wonder whence my rapture is inspired;
> But soon the smile which dawns upon thy lip
> Shall tell it, and the tenderer bloom o'er all
> That soft cheek springing to the marble neck,
> Which bends aside in vain, revealing more
> What it would thus keep silent, and in vain
> The sense of praise dissembling.
>
> (lines 366–74)

Only after having more vigorously asserted his heterosexuality does he address a mixed throng of men as well as women (lines 387–99). Lines arguing (as in the original) that beauty and goodness are naturally one conclude with a passage similarly pastoral but less homoerotic (lines 415–31):

> Yon flowery bank
> Clothed in the soft magnificence of Spring,
> Will not the flocks approve it? will they ask
> The reedy fen for pasture?
>
> (lines 415–18)

The passage of anti-Gothic diatribe (Akenside seems to hate Young with the passion of a rival in love) is preserved, but the passage depicting himself as a modern Socrates, like such passages generally, is toned down, the lines describing the "steps / Of those whom Nature charms, through blooming walks" replaced by more austere ones about "conducting" young minds "By ruling Heaven's decree, through various walks / And prospects various" (lines 483–84)—a curiously flat revision.

In the remainder of the original book 1 Akenside concludes the hierarchy of beauty with the (to him) incomparably beautiful assassination scene of Julius Caesar (lines 487–98):

> Look then abroad through nature, to the range
> Of planets, suns, and adamantine sphere,
> Wheeling unshaken through the void immense;
> And speak, O man! does this capacious scene
> With half that kindling majesty dilate
> Thy strong conception, as when Brutus rose
> Refulgent from the stroke of Caesar's fate,
> Amid the crowd of patriots; and, his arm
> Aloft extending, like eternal Jove
> When guilt brings down the thunder, called aloud
> On Tully's name, and shook his crimson steel,
> And bade the father of his country, hail!
>
> (lines 487–98)

This is entirely deleted in the revision (though it will later reappear in the revised book 2), replaced with a long discussion of abstract beauty, the "universal Venus" enthroned with God but meted out in more racially specific incarnations (lines 565–649). Gone is the intense republicanism of the original; gone too are most of the intense republicans like "The ingenious youth, whom solitude inspires / With purest wishes" (lines 555–56). Of the rest, like the "heroic youth / Warm from the schools of glory" (lines 589–90) replaced by a more temperate "unconquered youth, / After some glorious day rejoicing" (lines 713–14), the intensity at least has gone. The same might be said of the whole poem.

BOOK 2

The second book almost describes a kind of *translatio stultii* as in the *Dunciad*, as Akenside recounts how Beauty and Truth or "Each Muse and each fair Science" (line 15) were separated after the barbarians destroyed classical culture. It is part of Akenside's poetic task to facilitate the reunion of truth and beauty by first showing how pleasures and even pain complement the effect of "objects grand or beauteous" (line 72). Just as Akenside harmonizes other dualities like pleasure and truth, so he does passion and delight, illustrating how even grief becomes a source of pleasure with the tale of Harmodius (lines 187–770), with which he concludes this book.

As already discussed, in the name of the teller he almost certainly alludes to the fourth-century Athenian tyrant slayer, who must have represented to Akenside a union of a different sort, since he is known in Thucydides for having killed the tyrant's brother from mixed motives, but partly to preserve a homosexual relationship.[6] He would have represented a union of republicanism and the kind of sexuality to which Akenside was attracted, and which he probably shared. Harmodius recounts, as he recounted to the poet earlier, how his grief for Parthenia was allayed by the visionary lesson of the very beautiful Spirit of Human Kind. The allegory suggests that while our priorities might not be God's, we can continue to enjoy as second what we would prefer to be *first*, provided we can tolerate God's arrangement. The allegory is complicated by the way it depicts a series of divorces entirely from the perspective of the "remarrier" (marrying philosophy): some minds "grow up and flourish" and, indeed, seem to batten on others that do not. Unfairly, the mind that flourishes is always male, and what it flourishes on, or in the absence of, female.

The most striking thing about Akenside's 1765 revision of book 2 is the deletion of the allegory, Harmodius's tale. More precisely, he retains and amplifies the content of the Spirit's speeches, but banishes the Spirit of Human Kind himself, along with all the other pretty personifications. Again, he seems to do to his original version what he advocates generally, viewing "In matter's mouldering structures, the pure forms / Of triangle or circle" (lines 137–38), or abstracting truth from matter and "falsehood," but in ways that indicate his own (harsh) second thoughts about the homoerotic content of the original, as well as a degree of incompatibility between virtue and what seems to have constituted his own "pleasures," once upon a time. Akenside restores the assassination scene here, making it the last in a series of illustrations of the beauty of virtue, instead of a more isolated and therefore glaring illustration of the superiority of mind, as it had been in the original book 1. I note that "virtuous friendship" now precedes this illustration, as if Akenside had been embarrassed by the way it had somewhat anticlimactically and inconsistently followed it in the original; now friendship seems as subordinated to politics as Akenside's illustration suggests it always really was. The scene is less out of place, and so less shocking.

Book 3

Akenside's argument that pleasure can even be derived from the observations of "vicious or absurd" behavior is perhaps consistent with his abstract, idealizing tendency; however, readers must continually remind themselves of this thesis, not to feel that in the pleasures derived from the imagination of negative things Akenside finds their partial justification. Perhaps some such leap is unavoidable, exposing Akenside to the obvious charge of facile complacency.

Lines 1–14 describe our pleasure in studying human characters. As is consistent with his unifying approach, he attributes this pleasure to the perception of one underlying "common nature" (line 4), varied by circumstances. Men are united to men by their passions, Akenside perhaps by his passion for men themselves. This process depends on a sort of neutral Fancy that can "paint in all / Their genuine hues, the feature which they wore / In Nature" (lines 20–22). Opinion depends on such depictions, and Action on Opinion:

> For Action treads the path
> In which Opinion says he follows good,
> Or flies from evil, as the scene
> Was drawn by Fancy, lovely or deformed
>
> (lines 23–26)

After "true" Fancy he depicts the effects of false Fancy, which aggravates the youth's fear of death, and makes him less susceptible to things like "the pomp / Of sacred senates . . . the guardian voice / Of Justice on her throne, nor aught that wakes / The conscious bosom with a patriot's flame" (lines 38–41) and consequently less patriotic (lines 31–62). Fancy is countermanded, however, by Folly, which exposes the former to Ridicule, in a long procession of caricatures of academics, soldiers, priests, politicians, vain beauties, virtuosi, etc. (lines 78–258). Ridicule is generously provided us by "benignant Heaven" to prevent Folly from causing inordinate "public evil" (line 269); moreover, the sense of ridicule is instinctive, something the "passing clown" can enjoy without the benefit of education.

This instinct leads him to another: man's capacity for metaphor, which essentially seems to be a capacity to see himself in lifeless matter, but "himself" in an idealized sense: "to behold in lifeless things, / The inexpressive semblance of himself, / Of thought and passion" (lines 284–86). From metaphor generally Akenside seems to move to specific kinds of it, such as that which works through association, metonymy, or synecdoche (lines 312–47). He recounts the role of memory in such processes (lines 348–73), describes the process whereby the poet fashions his material (lines 373–409), and how the product of this process, an imitation, becomes in its turn a source of pleasure and imagination (lines 410–36). After praising God for connecting our pleasures to things in nature, and a passage on taste, Akenside concludes with a kind of hymn to the liberty that follows from cultivating such affinities.

What is most striking about the book's central section on the creating process is the way its depiction suggests birthing and femininity, at the same time it obviously must be sterile and entirely masculine, unless the creating male is supposed to be androgynous. The actual creating process is tellingly prefaced with a passage describing how a beautiful woman is kept perpetually beautiful *and* virginal in memory, as if to separate what follows heterosexual, physiological processes, or perhaps on the other hand to identify artistic creative processes with homosexual sterility: "the virgin's radiant eye, / Superior to disease, to grief, and time, / Shines with unbating lustre" (lines 371–73). The "child of Fancy" is femininely "pregnant . . . / With conscious pride" (lines 376–77). In the throes of something like labor, "blind emotions heave / His bosom" (lines 382–83), and not from his womb (since he cannot have one) but "the womb of earth" (line 387) come "ten thousand shapes" (line 385), the raw images of his composition. The product, the "lively child of Art" (line 421), seems now to compete with "Nature's great original" (line 420) for admiration. Beauty's indecision over which is most beautiful suggests not just cooperation but competition between creative processes, between one that the birthing metaphor tends to identify as physiological and heterosexual and another that is spiritual and implicitly homosexual. Typically, after this Akenside finds it necessary to anticipate the criticism of "some cold, fastidious judge" (line 444), and in the subsequent revision of his poem becomes that judge himself.

In the revised version book 3 consists almost entirely of an unfinished tale told by Solon to console four patriots who have come to him during the tyranny of Pisistratus. More generally the tale is supposed to address the problem of evil:

> why bade he
> The viper Evil, creeping in, pollute
> The goodly scene, and with insidious rage,
> While the poor inmate looks around and smiles,
> Dart her fell sting with poison to his soul?
>
> (lines 9–13)

Old Solon, returning to an Athens that has lost its democratic spirit, is fondly, physically described:

> His bright helm,
> Even while the traitor's impious act is told,
> He buckles on his hoary head: he girds
> With mail his stooping breast
>
> (lines 105–8)

When the Athenians fail to rouse themselves, "his big bosom heaved" (132). Later, in retirement, Megacles, Clisthenes, Miltiades, and Cimon visit him. Young Clisthenes in particular, with heaving chest and fresh face, seems homoerotically depicted:

> thro' the illustrious band
> Was none who might with Megacles compare,
> In all the honours of unblemished youth.
> His was the beauteous bride: and new their son
> Young Clisthenes, betimes, at Solon's gate
> Stood, anxious; leaning forward on the arm
> Of his great sire, with earnest eyes that asked
> When the slow hinge would turn, with restless fee,
> And cheeks now pale, now glowing: for his heart
> Throbbed, full of bursting passions, anger, grief
> With scorn imbittered, by the generous boy
> Scarce understood, but which, like noble seeds,
> Are destined, for his country and himself,
> In riper years, to bring forth fruits divine
> Of liberty and glory.
>
> (lines 209–22)

Clisthenes' burgeoning political passion is indistinguishable from an adolescent sexual initiation. His first visit to the republican's house or to a brothel might be described in nearly the same terms, with the same anticipation of yet unexperienced pleasures, which readers are supposed to flatter themselves that they already know. The tale stops after Solon recounts how he heard of the Athenian tyranny at Crete, but it obviously is intended by its own example to illustrate the role of the arts in maintaining and even restoring political virtue.

The 1770 fragment of a fourth book preserves some of the creating process depicted in the original book 3, but now more personalized, with Akenside's own memories of his youth in Newcastle on Tyne included in what previously was a more general discussion of memory (lines 31–45). Throughout the tone is more elegiac, as in the beginning with its ritualistic repetition self-consciously repeating prior attempts. Akenside depicts himself rising early in the morning in order to meditate before a busy day:

> From sleep I rescue the clear hours of morn
> And, while the world around lies overwhelmed
> In idle darkness, am alive to thoughts
> Of honourable fame, of truth divine
> Or moral, and of minds to virtue won
> By the sweet magic of harmonious verse

(lines 52–57)

SOME HYPOTHESES

While generally less vivid than the original, Akenside's revisions are also thematically incorrect, since in terms of the theory of associations that he is expounding, his youths and nature really *should* be apposite. Nature's "bloom" becomes beautiful by association with the youth's, not by opposition; that is the whole point. Indeed, it may be that homoeroticism is consequently at the very core of Akenside's aesthetic system, since without this "given" beauty, Akenside's real equivalent of the Shaftesburyan "implantation," there is nothing beautiful by association. Unfortunately, deleting it as he does, especially from the 1757 revision, effectively reduces that poem to something like an enthymeme or less, an argument whose major premise is not only missing but denied.

It is the beautiful young men who, by association, establish the all-important connection between expressive mind and inexpressive matter by virtue of which the latter is enabled to produce the "higher pleasure" of mind itself. Association stimulates inanimate nature or enables it to stimulate us: at the same time association homoeroticizes it, with the beauty that ultimately elides it. The principle of association that Robert Marsh sees as Akenside's solution to the central problem of his system, namely "to establish a positive connection—or, as Akenside called it, to learn 'that secret harmony'—between the actual expression of mind and scenes of inexpressive matter" (Marsh 1965, 62), proves to be, more precisely, *homoerotic* association.

Significantly, in a passage in book 1 (lines 48–97) replacing lines 31–55 of the original, Akenside seems to refer to that earlier version as the "adventurous lay" that "serious Truth" later purges of "Falsehood's evil brook / Vice and deceitful Pleasure." The earlier version has itself become one of the physical pleasures from which the mind abstracts purer ones by virtuous association, here Akenside's virtuous friendship with Dyson. The editing process itself facilitates a kind of dialectic between truth and beauty, in which the kinds of prettiness indicated above get weeded out and—as Akenside himself puts it—"excluded." Indeed, Akenside seems to be aware of the character of the first version's beauty; perhaps that is why he is so hard on it.

7

Invoking Present Absence:
Women in Akenside's Odes

What Robert Marsh says of the *Pleasures* could equally be said of many of the odes:

> [T]he task which Akenside set for himself does demand a "harmonizing" method of thought and discourse in which key ideas and terms may readily and swiftly shift, through more or less obvious analogies, from one realm of being to another. (1965, 50)

These shifts, as Akenside moves to the new meaning of a term, require the elision of what was signified by the old. Since these elided meanings are consistently feminine, together they amount to the virtual elimination of women; consequently, Akenside's "harmony" proves false and dangerously misleading in its claim to unity. Not surprisingly, key terms or "pivots" around which these elisions occur include nature and beauty and, with a particular appropriateness given Akenside's emphasis on unity, marriage.

Divorced Women

In *Ode on the Winter Solstice,* for example, women are identified with the absent spring; however, both absences contribute to rather than detract from male conviviality:

> Each dictates to the god of wine
> Her name whom all his hopes obey,
> What flattering dreams each bosom warm,
> While absence, heightening every charm,
> Invokes the slow-returning May!

(stanza 8)

The slower the better. Masculine conviviality is created in the name of or even disguised as an invoked femininity, the very summoning of which underlines the absence. Even more individualized women are usually invoked in Akenside's odes as absences, the more loved the more removed, as if the conventional abstraction of the genre, its rhetorical summoning of some absent principle or ideal, were suited to his attitude to his ostensible subject. In a typical political ode, like most of Dryden's panegyrics for example, the absence of the ideal (the *optimus princeps*) would be felt as a negative that ought to be restored by a deficient reality. Significantly, in this poem, the general absence of women is made all the more positive by the only woman really present at all being an unattractive "village Dame" pathetically yearning for her husband (stanza 3); if not absent in body, she is certainly distracted in mind. Subsequently her unhappy domesticity provides an essentially negative contrast, or becomes merely a *foil*, for the poet's mainly masculine society.

Akenside is at his most disingenuous in the final stanzas where he promises, provided that "Eudora" is present and willing, to sing "with sweeter sound" his "free Horatian song" (stanza 10), despite the fact that his song has hitherto only been sweetened by a feminine absence that has been quite the opposite of a "pang." It is worth noting that both the "village Dame" and "Eudora" were entirely absent from the original version of the poem, as if Akenside self-consciously "feminized" his revision the only way he knew how, by dramatizing his identification of them with absence.

Similarly, but more thoroughly, a feminine nature is elided by its masculine imitation in *Ode 1.13: On Lyric Poetry*. In the first stanza Akenside represents lyric inspiration as admission to a mainly masculine company of Greek lyric poets: "O parent of the Grecian lyre, / Admit me to thy powerful strain" (stanza 1.1). Although this company includes some females like Sappho, it is much more strongly characterized by males. Anacreon, for example, homoeroticizes the landscape by indicating its beauty through an arousal that elides what arouses it. As with Akenside's men generally, his beauty is authenticated by the naturalness it imitates even as it replaces it. Akenside steals nature's endorsement for the beautiful in men without indicating any sense of obligation or capacity to sustain what he steals it from:

> I see Anacreon smile and sing,
> His silver tresses breathe perfume;
> His cheek displays a second spring
> Of roses taught by wine to bloom.

(stanza 2)

The maleness of such beauty is reasserted by the conclusion of the first trio with Alcaeus, famous for the scholia celebrating Harmodius, the violent content of which Akenside seems to allude to:

> Broke from the fetters of his native land,
> Devoting shame and vengeance to her lords,
> With louder impulse and a threatening hand
> The Lesbian patriot smites the sounding chords:
>
> (stanza 3)

Alcaeus and, through him, Harmodius displace the femininity of Anacreon, in a way that parallels the way that his namesake in the *Pleasures* subordinates feminine beauty through the allegory. Given the homosexual motivation of Harmodius's act, it is arguable that the first trio of stanzas describes a movement away from female toward greater male and ultimately homosexual beauty, feminized figures like Anacreon functioning as bridges, themselves rather like pivotal terms, toward not less but greater homoeroticism. Just as Anacreon is displaced by Alcaeus, the Sappho of the second trio is displaced by Pindar; just as the former is essentially a vehicle for Harmodius, the latter becomes a vehicle for Akenside, the modern Pindar (as Smollett and others accused him of wanting to be). Significantly, in terms of homosexual implications, Akenside is in the second trio what Harmodius is in the first.

The third trio similarly presents poets, "Pleasure's lawless throng," only to have them displaced by Akenside himself. In the final trio Akenside displaces some of his *own* austerity, displaces the displacement as it were, with the figure of Olympia:

> O! seek with me the happy bowers
> That hear Olympia's gentle tongue;
> To beauty link'd with virtue's train,
> To love devoid of jealous pain,
> There let the Sapphic lute be strung.
>
> (stanza 4.3)

The poem begins to describe a circle, as Akenside reintroduces with Olympia what he expelled with Sappho; ultimately, however, he banishes her too, as he becomes more emphatically the modern Alcaeus/Pindar that the structure of the poem indicated that he really already was:

> Nor Theban voice nor Lesbian lyre
> From thee, O Muse, do I require;

> While my presaging mind,
> Conscious of power she never knew,
> Astonished grasps at things beyond her view
>
> (stanza 4.3)

Thus, the poem's unity is in the series of displacements by which the poet equals and exceeds his predecessors, Alcaeus especially. These involve the displacement of soft, feminine beauty with a harder, masculine variety that is implicitly homosexual. The displacements intensify until the fourth trio, when what is displaced, perhaps because it is an attribute of the poet himself, is displaced more violently and emphatically; finally even the concession itself is conceded. Almost imperceptibly, the origins of beauty in feminine nature are lost.

In *Ode 14: To the Honourable Charles Townshend; From the Country* the absent feminine dramatizes the absence of Akenside's friend, but is not restored by his presence. The poem begins as a very conventional invitation to Townshend to leave unhealthy London for spring in the country. Akenside first challenges him to state what advantages London has to compensate for its unhealthiness, unpleasantness, noisy courts, raging factions, and so forth. He suggests that if Townshend only knew about the power of "the balmy air, / The sun, the azure heavens" (stanza 2), he would immediately leave London for the country.

However, his own stay in the country almost immediately proves highly problematic. It is even doubtful that he is really *there* in mind as well as body: "Oft I look'd forth, and oft admire'd; Till with the studious volume tir'd" (stanza 3). When, heeding his own advice, he actually goes outside, the distance remains as a feminine absence of nymphs and naiads: "Nor Naiad by her fountain laid, / Nor Wood-nymph tripping through her glade, / Did now their rites unfold" (stanza 4).

This general feminine absence is due, of course, to another, more specific absence—that of his beloved: "offended with their guest, / Since grief of love my soul oppress'd, / They hide their toils divine" (stanza 6). Again, as in *Ode on the Winter Solstice,* nature is a an absent female, or a female whose absence the poet, perhaps all too readily, reconciles himself to through male companionship, but more subtly and profoundly through poetry itself with its tradition of neoclassical imitation. This replaces the feminine with a "nobler" masculine in stanza 7:

> soon shall thy enlivening tongue
> This heart, by dear affliction wrung,
> With noble hope inspire:
> Then will the sylvan powers again

Receive me in their genial train,
And listen to my lyre.

(stanza 7)

Thus, the poem is imitative in another sense, alluding as it does to Horace's
invitation to Maecenas, suggesting that Townshend and Akenside have many
precursors, invoking what amounts to a veritable male continuity of female displacement. Neoclassicism facilitates the reconstruction of a non-
female nature, which is not necessarily nonfeminine; moreover, it finds a
precedent for it in a long, masculine past.

In the very next poem, *Ode 15: To the Evening Star,* Akenside announces his intention to sing a "suppliant song" to Hesperus. He bids her to
shine on young, marrying couples but indicates his own grief for Olympia
on the way to Philomela's bower, and asks Hesperus to guide him there.
Like *To Townshend,* this poem initially depicts nature as a feminine absence, but instead of recreating it in a masculine image, revises it in reflection. When the poet reaches the moment in stanzas 11 and 12 when he must
discuss "her," precisely who or what is absent, instead he asks the "wan-
derer" to "think . . . What ruin waits on kingly rage: / How often virtue
dwells with woe" (stanza 12). Significantly, given how this poem in particular supplants Olympia in more ways than one, Philomela's "talking" in
stanza 6 makes her seem more like a potential female rival than a bird; of
course, she is neither. Philomela is poetry itself.

RE: MARRIAGE

It is surprising how many of Akenside's poems are about marriage,
considering that Akenside remained a bachelor all his life, but not so surprising considering the unifying effort of his system. Marriage for him is
principally a metaphor; moreover, it facilitates elision, because a marriage
to one thing can so easily disguise a divorce from something else. The prominence of marriage here, as in the *Pleasures,* indicates that it stands for
something central to Akenside's system; that upon even slight examination
every marriage proves to be a *divorce* must also, therefore, be significant.
Akenside's ostensibly unifying, harmonizing system is anything but.

As in Harmodius's *Tale* in the second book of the *Pleasures,* in *Ode 3:
To a Friend Unsuccessful in Love,* a young man achieves wisdom at the
price of his beloved, who in this case has married an older man for money.
The original ending to *Ode to a Friend Unsuccessful in Love* (originally *To
a Gentleman, whose Mistress had Married an Old Man*) goes like this:

O just escap'd the faithless main,
Though driven unwilling on the land,
To guide your favour'd steps again,
Behold your better Genius stand!
Where Plato's olive courts your eye,
Where Hamden's laurel blooms on high,
He lifts his heaven-directed hand.

Where these are blended on your brow,
The willow will be nam'd no more;
Or if that love-deserted bough
The pitying, laughing girls deplore,
Yet still shall I most freely swear
Your dress has much a better air
Than all that ever bride-groom wore.

One of the elements toned down in the final version is its homoeroticism: in the revision the youth's Genius is surrounded by abstract Truth, Virtue, and Honour, while we are merely invited to behold him lifting his "awful hand"; in the original the Genius more actively lifts his hand, "heaven-directed," in the flesh-and-blood company of Hampden, in a suggestively Platonic setting: "Where Plato's olive courts your eye." The original is more active, more concrete, but at the same time it is also more redolent of Platonic philosophy. That the revision represents mainly or solely a gain in abstraction and schematic organization (the "status inconsistency" of virtue and honor being one of Akenside's preoccupations) suggests that the motive for excision was the connection of Platonizing with homosexuality, and the connection (made by Smollett and others) of Akenside with both.

The final stanza reinforces this suspicion, since the original is even more explicitly homoerotic, with the poet remarking how good olive and laurel look on the young man's forehead, and that even if the "laughing girls" cannot admire his new patriotic and philosophical uniform, it looks good to Akenside. So many passages like this one, slighting or critical of marriage, indicate that almost *anything* looked better to Akenside than a bridegroom's attire.

The fleshly marriage of a man and a woman, aborted for the spiritual marriage of one principle and another (truth and beauty or virtue and honor, etc.), is the great commonplace of his poetry, perhaps its principal theme. At the same time it is its most revelatory aspect, since the substitute marriage involves enough physicality to suggest that it is not simply matter that Akenside is averse to, but specifically *female* matter.

Ode XI: On Love, to a Friend is yet another poem addressed to a youth warning him, if he would be virtuous and famous, to beware of Love's "enchanting snare" (stanza 1). The only right way to do so is "by thought, by danger, and by toils" (stanza 2), which, opposed as they are to the feminizing effects of love, are implicitly masculine:

> But Love unbends the force of thought;
> By Love unmanly fears are taught;
> And Love's reward with gaudy sloth is bought.
>
> (stanza 2)

Love ostensibly is masculine, but just as Akenside's positive goddesses generally prove gods, his negative gods tend to prove goddesses, at least in their effects.

In stanza 3 Akenside introduces beauty, which, like subordinated and ultimately elided female beauty of the *Pleasures*, exists in some sort of problematic, oppositional relationship to wisdom. This beauty also requires subordination, which here takes the form of imperviousness to "Love's deceit" (stanza 4). By implication beauty can be either one of Love's snares or Wisdom's. The only way to guarantee that it will be the latter is, it seems, to renounce sexual love for virtuous friendship, virtually impossible with a woman:

> In vain with friendship's flattering name
> Thy passion veils its inward shame;
> Friendship, the treacherous fuel of thy flame!
>
> (stanza 7)

The poem's configuration of love, beauty, and wisdom, each subordinated to the other in a way that prevents sexual love, resembles the central allegory of the original *Pleasures*; the philosophical marriage of beauty and wisdom is achieved at the price of divorcing beauty from love. As usual the configuration is triangular, the difference being that beauty is itself more obviously divided, and that the poet seems less confident here of his ability to maintain clear distinctions between beauty's kinds.

Even allowing for the fact that the friendship here is between a man and a woman, Akenside's severity on friendship for the way it enables us to deceive ourselves about which kind of beauty attracts us is surprising, given the importance of almost exclusively male friendship in his own life. His severity is incriminating too, given that it purports to be based on hard experience and given that the only really intense experience of friendship he is known to have enjoyed is with another man, Jeremiah Dyson. The ostensibly autobiographical passage, illustrating the difficulty of maintaining a virtuous friendship with his own misadventure with a woman, reads like a decoy.

Finally, some of the odes turn out to be about a more abstract kind of marriage, though they begin as something else. *Ode 8: On Leaving Holland,* begins as an insult to the Dutch, who are depicted as heavy louts, drunk on everything except poetic inspiration. The next set of stanzas begins with an address to England, some of the fervor of which is attributable to the probability that the addressee is equally Jeremiah Dyson, from whom (his letters indicate) he also wished "to part no more." The Dutch nymphs he insulted appear to have been Dutch women, but the "Nymphs" he anticipates at home are the idealized *genii* of streams and rural retreats, the effect of a shift towards abstraction that probably suited his sexuality at least as much as it flattered England; however, the comparison remains unequal, suggesting that Dutch women may be inferior because they are Dutch, or simply because they are women. The ode concludes with an address to Freedom, "protectress of my lays." Freedom follows Akenside's "Daughters of Albion," whose praises he sings in the preceding stanza, a political ideal where a human one might equally have been. Akenside's enthusiasm for the feminine typically short-circuits or elides into the political, and a political that contains little of what we normally signify by politics, but that is rather a misogynistically driven retreat from the human and the concrete into the abstract.

In the first stanza of the final trio Akenside sees himself doing what the political poet traditionally does, honoring force and wisdom equally, thereby achieving their reunification. This is also, of course, a kind of marriage, but here of essentially male qualities represented by Somers and Hampden. Akenside's marriages typically follow his elisions, are typically abstract, and are typically all male.

Given the above, it is hardly surprising that some of Akenside's poems celebrate intense male friendship more overtly, and perhaps more successfully too. Two of these—*Ode 5: Against Suspicion,* and *Ode 6: Hymn to Cheerfulness,* both from book 1—illustrate Akenside's characteristic procedure more positively. In the latter the feminine is elided by a masculine female personification. (I think one has to note even in poems like this, celebrating warmth and geniality, the solitariness of the poet.) Cheerfulness is begotten on feminine Health by masculine Love, but biology has little to do with it. "Health majestic" could just as easily be another man, while Love cannot be anything else. "She" is depicted first in a typical domestic scene, its formality and artificiality all the more frigid for having been intended to convey warmth:

> Nor sullen lip, nor taunting eye
> Deforms the scene where thou art by:
> No sickening husband damns the hour
> Which bound his joys to female power;

(163)

While ostensibly feminine, Cheerfulness *seems* masculine, opposed to feminine wiles and their "feminization" of the characteristic youth "whose anxious heart / Labours with love's unpitied smart." Undone by a woman, the youth is restored by Cheerfulness, whose effects, at least, are masculine:

> thou, auspicious power, with ease
> Canst yield him happier arts to please,
> Inform his mien with manlier charms,
> Instruct his tongue with nobler arms,
> With more commanding passion move
> And teach the dignity of love.

(163)

Akenside opposes all but "masculine" love; insofar as they are benign, his goddesses are gods.

In the final verses Akenside seems to allude again to his relationship with Dyson, "Sophron," when he asks Cheerfulness to bless their times together and apart, but especially the latter:

> But, if by fortune's stubborn sway
> From him and friendship torn away,
> I court the Muse's healing spell
> For griefs that still with absence dwell,
> Do thou conduct my fancy's dreams
> To such indulgent placid themes,
> As just the struggling breast may cheer,
> And just suspend the starting tear,
> Yet leave that sacred sense of woe
> Which none but friends and lovers know.

(165)

Ode V: Against Suspicion also deals with this relationship. In the beginning it is unclear whether Akenside wishes to cast off his suspicions of others, or theirs of him. Throughout stanza 7 use of a vague second person suggests the former, but after a shift to address "What God, in whispers from the wood, / Bids every thought be kind," the poet introduces himself and Dyson in a way that suggests the latter possibility:

> If far from Dyson and from me
> Suspicion took, by thy decree,
>   Her everlasting flight;
> If firm on virtue's ample base
> Thy parent hand has deign'd to raise
>   Our friendship's honoured height;

(stanza 10)

Finally, the emphasis is less on indicating that they are above suspecting than that they are above suspicion. Of course, Akenside never indicates clearly what suspicion he, by writing this stanza in a presentation copy (so a footnote tells us), seems to have wanted to defend himself against. It is less likely that he is presenting himself and Dyson as examples of a friendship based on suspecting nobody (which would be meaningless) than that he is responding, however obliquely, to suspicions cast on the nature of that relationship. This is one of Akenside's most personal poems and, as one would expect by now, evasive as it attempts to ward off suspicion by offering not to suspect.

THE ELISION OF THE HUMAN

From the above, it would appear that the only *marriage* Akenside really cared about was an abstract elision. That his favorite or at least most frequently treated "marriage" was the union of poetry and power suggests a disturbing potential for the elision of the concrete, the particular, and the human from the political domain, as if the political were not an extension of human relationships but their substitute or even their "annulment." Some such cancellation also characterizes, or rather problematizes, Akenside's homosexuality, or at least what we find of it in his poetry; his politics can no more be separated from sexuality (or vice versa) than can the politics of Harmodius, the original homosexual republican whom he admired so much. Akenside's politics remain, for this reader at least, whatever apparently "wise" myrtle dresses them publicly, dangerously different.

A number of poems describe this elision of the human from the political. *Ode VII: On the Use of Poetry* initially suggests the complementary subordination of poetry to power, then proceeds to suggest that poetry actually transcends the latter:

> Lycurgus fashion'd Sparta's fame,
> And Pompey to the Roman name
>   Gave universal sway:

> Where are they?—Homer's reverend page
> Holds empire to the thirtieth age,
>   And tongues and climes obey.

(stanza 5)

Similarly, in stanzas 1 and 2, poetry seems to be the corrective of arbitrary political fortune, if only by its power to recollect greatness as Akenside does there; however, the emphasis shifts in stanza 3 from poetry as cure or corrective to poetry as itself another victim of arbitrariness. Now poetry and politics seem like rivals:

> Who train'd by laws the future age,
> Who rescu'd nations from the rage
>   Of partial, factious power,
> My heart with distant homage views;
> Content if thou, celestial Muse,
>   Didst rule my natal hour.

(stanza 3)

The poet stands conspicuously apart from the politicians and heroes, and while "Not far beneath the hero's feet" perhaps not really subordinate at all: "Though not with public terrors crown'd, / Yet wider shall his rule be found, / More lasting his award."

It is finally unclear whether it is even appropriate to speak of the "use" of poetry, since if poetry asserts "Freedom's, Glory's, Virtue's cause" it does so in self-perpetuating abstraction, married to power at last but divorced from the world, in a sphere where a term like "useful" is either meaningless or ironic.

Curiously, considering the above, in *Ode X: To the Muse,* Akenside asserts his identification with the republican Milton, a potentially happier metaphor for the union of poetry and power or poetry and politics, and for less abstract marriages too. This ode seems to be addressed to the muse of his youth, or to his youth itself; either way, this muse is hard to separate from its poet:

> Where is the dread prophetic heat,
> With which my bosom wont to beat?
> Where all the bright mysterious dreams
> Of haunted groves and tuneful streams,
> That woo'd my genius to divinest themes?

(stanza 1)

As in the *Pleasures*, it is hard to separate the admired from its admirer, the pleasing from the pleased. The landscape is faintly eroticized, but now it seduces the muse with the hauntings of the young poet, not vice versa. While there appear to be two entities, there are really three: poet, muse, *and* poetic double. In stanza 2 he rejects female beauty as a source of poetic power, along with fame and sensuous music. Since this nearly amounts to rejecting the muse, the acceptance of Milton, his "double," in stanza 3, ostensibly as a means of recovering the muse but arguably as the muse itself, indicates that once again the feminine has subtly been elided, and some of the human with it, and replaced here by two versions of the poet himself. The poet associated with happier unions, equally sexual and political, is addressed in a context of solipsistic elision, divorce, and disillusionment.

Ode IX: To Curio. 1744 is no less "disappointed." It begins like an elegy, with an elegy's ritualistic repetition: "Thrice hath the spring beheld thy faded fame / Since I exulting grasp'd the tuneful shell." Akenside had done for Pulteney what poets ought to do for their patrons and addressees; he had immortalized him, and through association of his name with his, immortalized himself as well. But Pulteney has disappointed both of them:

> How hast thou stain'd the splendour of my choice!
> Those godlike forms which hover'd round thy voice,
> Laws, freedom, glory, whither are they flown?
> What can I now of thee to Time report,
> Save thy fond country made thy impious sport,
> Her fortune and her hope the victims of thy own?
>
> (stanza 1)

The "ode" is in fact an "elegy" for what Pulteney had been, the falseness of which is described in the next stanza, in terms of an Akenside commonplace: "thy arm extended but to dart / The public vengeance on thy private foe." This is the erect, phallic arm of a Brutus, like the arm in *The Pleasures of Imagination*, but "corrupted" to private ends. But Akenside's public parts always resemble the private ones that, through obsessive imagery and excessive energy, they subsequently betray. In the third stanza another voice depicts Pulteney as a demagogue, supported by the "rash many" he misled and betrayed. Pulteney is different from demagogues of the past, for "begging" a worse infamy than he ever earned.

In the fourth stanza Akenside begins to recount Pulteney's career, how he offered some at least apparently better alternative to Walpole's flagrant abuse of power. Among Pulteney's duped admirers Akenside lists one like himself: "The learn'd recluse, with awful zeal who read / Of Grecian heroes, Roman patriots dead, / Now with like awe doth living merit scan." Another is encouraged by Pulteney's example to enter public life and "knows to be a man." After Pulteney further disappoints everyone in stanza 8, he is compared, significantly, to a "wretched suitor for a boon abjur'd."

Unlike the French who "By courtly passions try the public cause," the English "Shall ne'er the loyalty of slaves pretend" and so disown him. But he replaces their lost affection with a spurious "Honour," depicted "Couch'd in thy bosom's deep tempestuous gloom / Like some grim idol in a sorcerer's cell." This spurious honor eventually yields to the judgment of "old Time, imperious judge," who reconciles virtue and honor again by sweeping false honors away and whose hands "crush their trophies huge, and raze their sculptur'd names." As Pulteney's shade is received by dead traitors like Wentworth and Clifford, Akenside commands "ye, whom yet wise Liberty inspires" to "drive ye this hostile omen far away." In the final stanza he reminds liberty's defenders that their state is established not on "Numa's manners, Plato's laws" but on English constitutional law: "a wiser founder, and a nobler plan, / O sons of Alfred." The lateness of Pulteney's disgrace, and the abstract way Akenside achieves it, seem to underline the impotence of poetry, the disharmony of poetry and power, and the serious disjunction of honor and virtue, the very pairs that it is the object of his whole system to reconcile and unite.

Similarly addressed to a Whig politician, *Ode 12: To Sir Francis Henry Drake, Baronet,* is mainly a celebration of Whig achievements, but slightly melancholy or even nostalgic, as it associates regret for a Tory past with heterosexual feelings for one "Olympia" who probably never existed. Winter in the country is contrasted with more genial winter in the city, the former exacerbated somewhat by uncongenial Tory politics (stanza 3). The poem is also an invitation to homosocial conviviality on 5 November, the anniversary of both the Gunpowder Plot and William's arrival, though these men will celebrate only the latter (stanza 4). It ends on a Shakespearean note, as the "smitten" older poet contrasts himself with the "unsmitten" youth. The latter's noncommittal promiscuity or "freedom" seems to parallel the political freedom achieved for him by William, as the older poet's unquestioning loyalty to "fair Olympia" seems almost a vestige of that "Gothic" order which he poet deplores. While the poem ostensibly unites public and private, it typically suggests that the poet's public views are at odds with his private behavior: "I, a true and loyal swain, / My fair Olympia's gentle reign / Through all the varying seasons own" (stanza 8). Less abstractly the poem suggests a youth who probably really loves women, and an older man in love with an ideal.

Several of Akenside's later odes, also addressed to men, continue to explore the relationship of poetry and power in terms of an ideal of union resembling some sort of marriage, but with an increasingly violent and militaristic content. These indicate even more the character of what replaces the softer, more human, less abstract, and usually feminine relationships that he elides above. These include *Ode 18: To the Right Honourable Francis Earl of Huntingdon* and *Ode 2.11: To the Country Gentlemen of England*.

The *Huntingdon Ode* celebrates the marriage of poetry and power through such great exemplars as Homer, Pindar, and—of course—Milton. In the second-to-last trio Akenside recounts how Hastings's ancestors "led the rustic youth to arms." However heroic, their exploits represented "private strife," to which Hastings's prospects are "loftier scenes . . .Where empire's wide establish'd throne / No private master fills" (stanza 5.1). Akenside refers for the first time to the British Empire as a divinely ordained place that for size must be republican, because no one is big enough to "fill" its throne:

> Where, long foretold, the People reigns:
> Where each a vassal's humble heart disdains;
> And judgeth what he sees; and, as he judgeth, wills.
>
> (stanza 5.1)

Akenside's potential for conservative reaction is discernible in the next stanza, where he suggests that Hastings' role is to see that democracy never goes too far, to "guide / The swelling democratic tide" (stanza 5.2). Democracy is allowed provided there is no dissent, which here appears as Jacobite "faction." It is odd to think that he would later identify himself with precisely this faction by supporting the earl of Bute. Akenside concludes this trio by arguing, at his most bloodthirsty and bellicose, that virtue is preferable because "what ensnares the heart should maim the hand"; in other words, virtue is preferable because it is openly violent, while vice is covert and sparing. Virtue is true to "glory," synonymous with violent deeds, all in the name of "Freedom":

> But look on Freedom: —see, thro' every age,
> What labours, perils, griefs, hath she disdain'd!
> What arms, what regal pride, what priestly rage,
> Have her dread offspring conquer'd or sustain'd!
>
> (stanza 5.3)

The second-to-last trio concludes by commemorating aristocrats who, a footnote tells us, "privately concerted the plan of the Revolution" (Akenside 1845, 295). The last trio celebrates this revolution more directly in the current political arrangement, the near loss of which it deplores in lines insulting to Scotland (and to Tobias Smollett):

> Did one of all that vaunting train,
> Who dare affront a peaceful reign,
>   Durst one in arms appear?
> Durst one in counsels pledge his life?
>
> (stanza 6.2)

His enemies' identification with these "cowards" makes Hastings himself look all the more patriotic. In the final lines Akenside matches his praise against that of these alleged "cowards and the lying mouth"; his is genuine, theirs "reproach." Thus, he returns to his initial theme of the proper relationship of poetry and power, while advising Hastings whom to listen to.

The most bellicose of these poems to male politicians is *Ode 2.11: To the Country Gentlemen of England. 1758.* While not explicitly celebrating a "marriage," it obliquely deals with the relationship of poetry to power and celebrates the only sort of human relationship Akenside ever seems to have had much tolerance for. If not art a closely related "luxurious Plenty" has corrupted youth and made imperial power rotten at the core:

> If luxurious Plenty charm
> Thy selfish heart from Glory, if thy arm
> Shrink at the frowns of Danger and of Pain,
> Those gifts, that treasure is no longer thine.
> Oh rather far be poor!
>
> (stanza 4)

His countrymen rely too much on geography to protect themselves and their newly gotten imperial stores. Rather than trust their freedom's safety to anyone or anything, they should "In War's glad school their own protectors rise." Akenside imagines a country militia of young swains led by patrician patriots, power based on land, and the intimate masculine relationships and harmonious patronage that such an organization would encourage:

> Ye chiefly, heirs of Albion's cultur'd plains,
> Ye leaders of her bold and faithful swains,
> Now not unequal to your birth be found:

> The public voice bids arm your rural state,
> Paternal hamlets for your ensigns wait,
> And grange and fold prepare to pour their youth around.
>
> (stanza 7)

> the farmer and the swain
> Met his lov'd patron's summons from the plain;
> The legions gather'd; the bright eagles flew:
> Barbarian monarchs in the triumph mourn'd;
> The conquerors to their household gods return'd,
> And fed Calabrian flocks, and steer'd the Sabine
> plough.
>
> (stanza 9)

He laments the widespread lack of interest in warfare among the young: "No more with scorn of violence and wrong / Doth forming Nature now her sons inspire" (stanza 10). He attributes to "scorn of violence" what to us looks a lot like love of it, possibly the same bloody-mindedness noted by contemporaries. Instead of training, the scions of country families go to London where they are corrupted by all kinds of urban vice:

> The young grove shoots, their bloom the fields
> renew,
> The mansion asks its lord, the swains their friend;
> While he doth riot's orgies haply share,
> Or tempt the gamester's dark, destroying snare,
> Or at some courtly shrine with slavish incense bend.
>
> (stanza 12)

Meanwhile, back in the country the lower classes imitate their social superiors.

Akenside's panacea for the deterioration of the state is "warlike prudence," inculcated by a lot of marching:

> But mark the judgment of experienc'd Time,
> Tutor of nations. . . .
>   . . . There would civil sway
> The rising race to manly concord tame?
> Oft let the marshal'd field their steps unite,
> And in glad splendour bring before their sight
> One common cause and one hereditary fame.
>
> (stanza 14)

Marching together encourages ruling together; clearly Akenside bases national unity on intimate male bonding. The modern form of this is scouting; in the 1930s a more sinister form was the Nazi youth camp.

Akenside's ideal of a national militia is clearly dated, even antiquarian, for his time, . In his scorn for the "new refinements, fiercer weapons tell, / And mock the old simplicity, in vain" (stanza 15) is the potential slaughter of many "country gentlemen" for an amateur's ideal, consistent with which is the "aristocratic" disdain for technical training, the naive assumption that "To the time's warfare, simple or refin'd, / The time itself adapts the warrior's mind; / And equal prowess still shall equal palms obtain" (stanza 15). One suspects, as contemporaries did, that Akenside knows nothing about war, if only because for him war is an ideal like an Olympic Games, a contest of physical skill for gentlemen athletes and their retainers.

Together these odes suggest that, despite his desire to unite and harmonize "the forms or processes of human life and those of true or ultimate reality" (Marsh 1965, 15), Akenside is not, after all, a dialectical poet but truly the poet laureate of elision and displacement. Perhaps his desire for unity merely serves as a disguise for its opposite, which in Akenside's case is clearly *not* a desire for the opposite sex. Whether in an abortive real marriage, in a successful ideal one, or in a public allegiance with a group of men, Akenside seems to "unite" with the same thing every time. As in Harmodius's *Tale*, or as in Smollett's satire in *Peregrine Pickle*, the multifarious "forms" of life are not united to "true reality," the real to the ideal, but sacrificed to it, or even, alas, to something else.

A CODA: THE HARMODIUS OF COLLINS'S *ODE TO LIBERTY*

According to Richard Wendorf in *William Collins and Eighteenth-Century English Poetry*, William Collins would have found Akenside's *Odes* (published in 1745) not only "of great interest" but "a stimulus" (Wendorf 1981, 33), if only to do better. While other inspirations for *Ode to Liberty* would have included James Thompson's *Liberty*, Akenside's *Odes* would also have provided a model, in their preoccupation with relationships like that of poetry and power, and in their exploitation of certain commonplaces, the Harmodius figure in particular.

The *Ode to Liberty* begins by invoking the poet, who in turn shall invoke young men:

> The Youths, whose Locks divinely spreading,
> Like vernal Hyacinths in sullen Hue,

> At once the Breath of Fear and Virtue shedding,
>> Applauding *Freedom* lov'd of old to view?
>>> (Collins 1979, lines 3–6)

While the poem is ostensibly addressed to Liberty, we do not see "her," except through what "she" sees or saw: "love'd of old to view" (line 6). We approximate liberty by attraction to the same thing, by adopting a relationship to the youths comparable to hers, which is potentially erotic. That "we" are men implies a homosexual relationship, as if that were the latter-day form of the more direct heterosexual relationship that the youths themselves enjoyed with the goddess. Whether today we cannot stand such a direct relationship or simply do not want it, the feminine goddess is elided, as Sedgwick and others have argued women generally are, from mechanisms of male homosocial desire. Obviously I believe that some such mechanism is operative here.

Homosexuality is implied in the comparison of the youths to hyacinths, and more strongly in the reference to Alcaeus in line 7 and the Harmodius and Aristogeiton of the poem attributed to him. Lines 8–12 paraphrase that poem's depiction of Harmodius's killing of the tyrant, which according to Thucydides "began in the resentment of a lover":

> Harmodius was in the flower of youth, and Aristogeiton, a citizen of the middle class, became his lover. Hipparchus made an attempt to gain the affections of Harmodius, but he would not listen to him, and told Aristogeiton. The latter was naturally tormented at the idea, and fearing that Hipparchus who was powerful would resort to violence, at once formed such a plot as a man in his station might for the overthrow of the tyranny. (*Peloponnesian Wars* 6.54.217)

It is useful to recall that in Thucydides' version the lovers resolve to assassinate Hipparchus and his brother, the tyrant Hippias, at the festival of Panathenaea, when citizens may wear arms without arousing suspicion. The plot is foiled by a false alarm, but the two lovers manage to slay Hipparchus. Harmodius himself is slain immediately after. In "Alcaeus's" version the festival that provided a cover for the attempt is reduced to a myrtle branch concealing Harmodius's sword, Hipparchus is erroneously designated "tyrant," and the attempt successfully restores democracy.

For these reasons Collins's version of the fragment, or his use of it at all, seems to have been a source of embarrassment to some of his critics. P. L. Carver defends Collins against Garrod's charge of "bad scholarship" for attributing the fragment to Alcaeus, but finds Collins guilty of something far worse "in his selection of Harmodius and Aristogeiton as typical champions of Athenian liberty" (1967, 117). While Carver attributes their actions entirely to "private injury," he seems reticent about what that injury was. One might wonder at a degree of uncharitableness towards the lovers, whose motives even Thucydides seems to allow were rather more *mixed*. It is even possible that Collins would have approved of such a mixture of public and private motivation, or had his own private motivations for endorsing it, however guardedly, in public. Finally one might wonder if critics like Carver do not find Collins "wrong" because they find homosexuality "wrong" too, a "private injury."

In Collins's version, based mainly on "Alcaeus's" fragment, the occasion seems to become a place, "*Wisdom's* Shrine," and the deed, rather than disguised by wisdom, seems prompted by it and therefore wise itself. Doubtless aware of *both* versions, Collins downplays aspects of both; "Alcaeus's" emphasis on brave and forceful deception becomes spiritual consecration (the sword not disguised but anointed), which transforms Thucydides' parable of private and public folly into an allegory of wisdom.

Through such transformations, through Collins's very efforts to redeem it, one can perceive the persistence of a homosexual subtext. In the rest of the *Strophe* he indicates what he will *not* sing of: the loss of Liberty "When Time his Northern Sons of Spoil awoke, / And all the blended Work of Strength and Grace, / . . . to Thousand Fragments broke" (lines 22–25). In the *Epode* he describes how even in these fragments, like the city-states of Italy, "Some Remnants of Her Strength were found" (line 29). The shattered statue, a metaphor for ruined classical culture, is metaphorically connected to the partial renaissance of the arts in Florence at line 34, and eventually to the current difficulties of city states like Genoa. The language and the series of reincarnations of Liberty reach a climax together, as they are meant to, with the invocation of Britain at line 63: "The perfect spell shall then avail, / Hail Nymph, ador'd by *Britain*, Hail!" (line 62–63). The antistrophe describes how Britain was separated from the continent to create a "last Abode" (line 88) for Liberty, and the "Second Epode" precisely situates that abode at once in a Druidic past and in some ahistorical Platonic "reality" where

> The Chiefs who fill our *Albion's* Story,
> In warlike Weeds, retir'd in Glory,
> Hear the consorted *Druids* sing
> Their Triumphs to th'immortal String.

> (lines 109–12)

When in the next stanza he describes in greater detail Liberty's "hoary Pile" (line 89), once again he synthesizes the Gothic and the classical:

> Ev'n now before his favor'd Eyes,
> In *Gothic* Pride it seems to rise!
> Yet *Graecia's* graceful Orders join,
> Majestic thro' the mix'd Design;
>
> (lines 117–20)

After he welcomes "Concord" to Liberty's "blissful Train" (line 131) in the final stanza, it is hard to tell whether he is addressing Liberty or her, or indeed whether one goddess hasn't in fact been subsumed under the other.

The poem's main motif, its structural principle, could be the creation of wholeness out of fragmentation. The fragmentation described in the *Strophe* actually seems to be endorsed in the *Antistrophe,* as a means of preserving the fragments from further disintegration. The naturalness of the geological fragmentation of Britain from the continent in the *Antistrophe,* in contrast to the artificial or "man-made" fragmentation of Rome in the *Strophe,* is probably a further endorsement: the artificial is redeemed by the natural.

A similar contrastiveness characterizes the relationship between the first and second *Epodes.* The former discusses Rome's cultural "fragments" historically, chronologically; the latter discusses one fragment ahistorically (mythologically and philosophically), and introduces "Concord" as if that one fragment had become many and subsequently whole again.

The structure of the poem suggests union and growth where logically there is none. The part cannot become the whole, even by valorizing incompleteness as Collins does in the horrific *Antistrophe*. The poem's retreat from history to fantasy in the *Second Epode* underlines this impossibility. History is the realm of growth and change, but British liberty is fixed in a realm beyond history where it seems as incapable of present regeneration as of past degeneration. The poem's dialectical structure actually disguises the *absence* of dialectic. In its retreat from time, biology, and history, and moreover in its substitution of real union by a disguised "oneness," an elevated insularity, it becomes a political corollary of homosexuality.

Michael Meehan in *Liberty and Poetics in Eighteenth-Century England* suggests that the poem itself becomes another "Sword, in Myrtles drest," liberty reincarnated in words:

> The song itself becomes a sword for liberty; the syntactical structure of the second line ["Shall sing the Sword, in Myrtles drest" (8)] offers an ambiguity that retains the idea both that the poem is celebratory, singing *of* the sword, and that in doing so it will become a sword itself, raised again each time the episode is recounted. (1986, 61)

Obviously I offer another reading of the "sword." Moreover, I suggest that this liberty is homosexual, not just the freedom of the love of Harmodius and Aristogeiton from the tyrannical impositions of Hipparchus, but the freedom of such love generally. The "Sword, in Myrtles drest" is also, obviously, phallic; to sing one is to sing the other.

SOME HYPOTHESES

Collins is simply another example of a politically similar, nearly contemporary poet who also proves to be an "elider"; this is probably more than coincidental, given that several contemporary critics believe that Collins was homosexual. It is arguable that Collins and Akenside could write no other way, at least on certain topics. More generally the recent work of many critics on eighteenth-century aesthetics, in England and elsewhere, indicates that neoclassicism probably facilitated something amounting to a fairly widespread "poetics of elision," that was often homoerotic in nature or even homoerotically driven. For example, Chloë Chard finds a kind of "elision" at work in eighteenth-century commentaries on art that simultaneously exclude the feminine and reintroduce it under a more masculine rubric:

> These commentaries keep the threat of effeminacy at bay through a rhetorical ruse that depends on an elision between two slightly different concepts. . . . Since the concept of sublimity, being closely linked to that of aspiration, attaches itself to divinity even more readily than to manliness, its affiliations with the masculine are dissolved. The god-like sublime is then able to merge, much more easily than the manly could have done, with the smooth-limbed grace and beauty that travellers discern as one of the sculpture's salient characteristics. (1994, 150)

Thus the feminine is erased, at least nominally, under the heading of the divine. I think it is implicit in Chard's remarks that the feminine persists, along with a degree of homoerotic desire masquerading as aspiration for Godhead.

From Thomas Crow's discussion in "A Male Republic," it appears that the late-eighteenth-century French painter, Jacques-Louis David, pursued an agenda not dissimilar from Akenside's of uniting art with republican principles:

> His immediate circle, rather than the hidebound Royal Academy of Painting and Sculpture, would provide their [his and his protegés'] primary

locus of intellectual discussion and moral identity. And together they would act on the belief that modern French artists could play the same role as had the artists among the ancient Greeks, who (so it was argued) were granted creative liberty and thus were inspired to express the ideals of their communities in perfected physical form. (Crow 1994, 204)

Perhaps, because of obvious political differences, David was able to carry the dream a lot farther than Akenside ever did. Perhaps too, for this very reason, his subsequent disillusionment, as many of his own intimate male friends were executed under the Terror, was greater and more obvious. Ewa Lajer-Burcharth discusses, in "The Aesthetics of Male Crisis," how the icons and symbols of the Revolution were grotesquely parodied, sometimes by David himself, in a period of aesthetic "abjection" following the Terror and the political reaction:

Through this aesthetic reversal, a semantic reversal takes place: "Taunay's" image turns inside out that Jacobin space of republican unity and (Rousseauist) transparency that the Davidian festival helped define thus, revealing its dark underside. (Lajer-Burcharth 1994, 222)

Crow describes in some detail how women, largely excluded from works like *The Death of Socrates*, acquire greater prominence (in *The Lictors Returning to Brutus the Bodies of his Sons*, for example) as David's political experience darkens and homosocial tragedies within the studio context prefigure much larger ones in the state. Along with women, the body, not the smooth and contoured classical one but the bloody, mutilated body of the caricaturists of republicanism, is also excluded from the earlier David and also returns, but is in some ways always present (if only in its noteworthy absence):

In the case of David's *Brutus* . . . it was the lining that could be said to have been there from the beginning, but remained repressed. The Stockholm sketch for the painting, in which the bleeding severed heads of Brutus's sons executed on their own father's order appear on the lictors' pikes, suggests just that. (Lajer-Burcharth 1994, 223)

Women and the "real" body are as conspicuously excluded from Akenside's poetry as from David's painting, but they never return, perhaps because Akenside never really had to face the political, indeed the very human, consequences of their banishment. Nevertheless, there is the same sense in Akenside as there is in David (and, for that matter, satirized in Smollett), of a republicanism that is secretly bloody and violent, because of its elision of so much reality.

At the same time one should notice the secretiveness, since that is one of the "beauties" of elision and since Akenside's contemporaries noticed it, or something like it, too. Thus, George Hardinge, a nephew of the Caleb Hardinge to whom Akenside addressed an ode, characterized Akenside's politics as "illegible" (Dyce 1845, lix), or indeed as the *standard* of illegibility. He might have meant simply that Akenside's verse was apolitical, but "illegible" implies something that exists, though it can only be read with difficulty, if at all. Knowing, as he certainly did, of Akenside's "zealous" republicanism and equally zealous conversion to Toryism in the 1760s, Hardinge also seems to have implied a "politics" quite distinct from such public behavior. If his politics had anything to do with the *poetics* described above, it *had* to be illegible. A politics, like a poetics, of *elision* must in some ways remain illegible.

The story from *Memoirs of Thomas Hollis* (quoted in Dyce 1845, li–lii), of how Akenside received the gift of John Milton's bed might help us to characterize Akenside's politics, especially in the last years of his life. Hollis gave the bed to Akenside in June 1761, and with it a note indicating that "if the Doctor's genius . . . having slept in that bed, should prompt him to write an ode to the memory of John Milton, and the assertors of British liberty, that gentleman would think himself abundantly recompensed." The biographer reports, almost indignantly, that while Akenside was delighted with the bed, he never acknowledged the present or wrote the ode, because "an encomium of Milton, as an assertor of British liberty, at that time of the day, was not the thing." The idea of Akenside luxuriating in Milton's bed while pragmatically declining to write him an ode is bathetic.

What both Hollis's biographer alludes to, and what Hardinge elsewhere deplores (see Dyce 1845, lvi), is Akenside's conversion to the ministry of Lord Bute, possibly for the very sort of reasons—sexually suspect opportunistic preferment-seeking—that Bute's detractors most liked to allege against him. Upon the accession of George III, Akenside's patron, Dyson, converted to the Tories and his client followed suit, becoming "Physician to the Queen" in 1761. It is impossible to know for certain whether Akenside's conversion was principled or not, but it is interesting that it could be construed to conform to the sexual and indeed homosexual aspersions that, as we shall see in later sections, Wilkes and Churchill worked to cast upon the Hanoverian court by comparing it (thanks partly to Bute's being a Stuart) to the supposedly "sodomitical" and preferment-ridden court of James I. The potential agreement between the way Akenside and Dyson's conversion might have been construed, if anyone hostile enough had been paying attention, as the natural turning of a homosexual pair toward an innately homosexual court, and the similar slanders that Wilkes and Churchill were making about that court, suggests that such slanders might have had some basis, not exactly as Wilkes and Churchill alleged, and not necessarily in the nature of George III's supposedly Stuart-contaminated and therefore "sodomitical" court, but in the nature of eighteenth-century political culture.

Part III:

Wilkes, Churchill, and George III:
The Politics of Homophobia (2)
(A Late-Century Coda)

8

Essays on Men and Women: Homophobia and Misogyny in Wilkes's Satire of Pope's *Essay on Man*

Aubrey Williams describes in *Wilkes* how George III's ministers may have obtained a copy of John Wilkes's privately printed *Essay on Woman,* and used the same to initiate libel proceedings against him. To my knowledge no one has looked very closely at the contents of Wilkes's alleged libel. While this poem is neither great nor even complete, it expresses attitudes to sexuality, and especially to women, that are probably typical of a class of libertines (Williams 1974, 99). These attitudes themselves are curious for both their criticism of, and their complicity in, an eighteenth-century homocentric system.[1] Not unlike the men who held them, the attitudes of *An Essay on Woman* both are and are not a part of their society.[2]

The "Advertisement by the Editor" to *Essay on Woman* begins with the sort of pun that has led some critics to characterize Wilkes's humor as adolescent: "The truth I take to be this: Mr Pope might indeed, and in all probability he actually and frequently did handle this subject in a cursory way, but I dare say he never *went deep* into it" (Wilkes 1871, 5). The curious thing about such a reference to Pope is the way it suggests that the great, sometimes misogynistic satirist, a professional of his kind, was really an amateur at sex; specifically, it suggests that he had no sexual experience of women. The literary amateur (Wilkes) depicts the sexual nonlover or the heterosexual amateur (Pope). With some dexterity Wilkes makes nonprofessionalism, specifically the nonprofessionalism of the aristocrat, which Pope himself occasionally resorted to as a stance to distinguish him from Grub Street hacks, something to be ashamed of. Amateur *writer* though he may be, Wilkes is at least professional about sex and certainly about *women*, with a heterosexual emphasis that alone would be enough to make Pope's title, *Essay on Man*, look homosexual by analogy; he implies that inexperience is positive when sex is a metaphor, negative when it comes to the "real thing." The area where sexual metaphors do *not* apply is sex itself, at least *heterosexual* sex. Thus he attributes a degree of nonessentialness to Pope, with the difference that such a handicap might be a blessing in disguise, at least for one who is a writer before everything else, even "man."

Nevertheless, Wilkes immediately deploys a whole "body" of his own homosexual metaphors to embarrass Warburton. Warburton could not have written the *Essay,* because at the time of writing he

> was on the other side of the *Pyrenees*, employed in a more *priestly way*. I do not mean to disparage his abilities. They are really *great*, and so indeed they ought to be to keep under the Members of *his* Church and others who have been known to *rise against* him. The case probably was, that he did not choose to exert himself on this subject, but left it to the Laity, and gave them at the same time the truest pattern of humility, in condescending to be mounted in the same manner as his Master was when he entered Jerusalem. (Wilkes 1871, 6)

I quote the passage at length principally because of its blatantly homophobic anticlericalism, expressions of which we have already encountered: the "*priestly way*" is buggery. The Pyrenees, a footnote tells us, is "[t]he space between the Anus and Vulva in women, and Scrotum in men." Obviously, if Warburton could not have written the *Essay* because he was on the "other side," he was buggering someone, literally mounted on an "ass." Warburton's great "ability" obviously signifies his penis, which facilitates a pun on "Members" as both rival penises and rival churchmen. Subsequently church hierarchy becomes a matter of assuming the active role relative to the passive stratum below. That Warburton leaves this "subject"—woman—which he "does not choose to exert himself on" to the laity, merely tends to reinforce the identification of the clergy with homosexuality by contrasting them with a heterosexual laity. The idea that he "gave them at the same time the truest pattern of humility" is both demonic as it parodies Christ and topical as it reproduces earlier complaints about hypocritical clergymen with pretensions of reforming society by example. While the issue goes directly back to Swift in his *Project* and his *Argument Against the Abolition of Christianity,* as we have seen, it involves later (and Whiggish) ecclesiastics like Edmund Gibson, bishop of London, a.k.a. "Dr. Codex," himself attacked for attacking the laity while defending homosexual clergymen.

Finally, Wilkes's disavowal serves as tacit admission of Warburton's membership in a sodomitical "third sex." The authorial requirement for the *Essay on Woman* is to be a man:

> As to my own abilities for such a work, modesty commands my silence. I could produce *two* satis idonei Testes, though I believe one in our law is sufficient. I am ready to *stand the Test*. . . . (Wilkes 1871, 6)

Since homosexuals, like Warburton, fail to meet this requirement, we can assume that, to this author, they are *not* men, regardless of whether or not they have both testicles. Since the "test" for being a man is the same for being an Anglican Protestant and vice versa, satisfying the "Test Act" and having testicles, Wilkes's assertion that he is ready to *"stand the Test"* and his promise to "amiable female readers" that they will not have to bow to him, glance deftly back at a series of "associations": the "Pyreneanism," the quasi-Catholicism and—above all—the *homosexuality* of Warburton. Such associations have also been encountered before.

THE DESIGN

In *The Design* the writer's meaning begins to be complicated by fairly close parody of Pope's *Essay on Man:*

> Having proposed to write some Pieces on human life and manners, such as (to use my Lord Rochester's expression) come home to men's business and breeches, I thought it most satisfactory to begin with considering *Woman* in the abstract, her *Nature*, her Art, her Condition, and Relation to use, and the true *End* and Purpose of her *Being*; since to enforce anything properly we ought first to know all the particulars relating to it. (Wilkes 1871, 9)

The tendency of the parody is indicated by the substitution of Rochester for Bacon, breeches for bosoms. The effect of it is to simultaneously expose and reinforce the deviousness of the universal, "Man." In the context of Pope and Warburton's inexperience of "Woman," and of the latter's alleged homosexuality, the "Man" of Pope's title acquires homosexual connotations. Parody is subsequently almost justified as a "straightening" of the implicitly homosexual original. But while the maleness of Pope's "Man"

is exposed, Wilkes's "Woman" is not an alternative universal but an auxil-
iary, or perhaps even a "particular," whose subordination is painfully more
noticeable for the allusion to universals in Pope's original. "Woman" might
seem better off left out of the poem as she is of the system, but Wilkes's
version is probably closer to the reality underlying Pope's poem and exposes it better. Wilkes seems to express better than Pope that, not a universal herself, the "true *End* and Purpose of her *Being*" is getting fucked by
other universals. The idea that such subordination is really the object of an
oppressive system is reinforced by the substitution of Pope's "moral pre-
cept" by sheer "enforcement":

> since, to prove any moral duty, to enforce any moral precept, or to exam-
> ine the perfection or imperfection of any creature whatsoever, it is neces-
> sary first to know what *condition* and *relation* it is placed in, and what is
> the proper *end* and purpose of its *being*. (Pope 1984, 502)

Wilkes's parody does more than simply mock the moral loftiness of Pope's
Essay. It exposes Pope's *own* "design," by suggesting that the noble principle Pope would inculcate through science is no different from the ig-
noble object of the most carnal knowledge, and perhaps more generally
that the real "design" of any system is not to enforce precepts but to "force"
people.

The Poem

The capacity of Wilkes's imitation to "homosexualize" Pope's original
is felt in the opening lines of the poem proper, the author's invitation to
"Fanny":

> Awake, my Fanny, leave all meaner things;
> This morn shall prove what rapture swiving brings!
> Let us (since life can little more supply
> Than just a few good fucks, and then we die)
>
> (lines 1–4)

The heterosexual tableau emphasizes the homosocial quality of Pope's
poem, suggests (however fleetingly) Pope and Bolingbroke literally awak-
ing—not in some abstract philosophical "dawn"—but in bed together. Pope's
metaphor of rising game for "Manners living as they rise" (line 14) becomes the poet's rising penis: "Observe how Nature works, and if it rise /

Too quick and rapid, check it ere it flies" (lines 13–14). Typically, the god-like ways that Pope attempts to justify to "Man" are condensed here into the godlike ways of "Man" himself: "Spend when we must, but keep it while we can: / Thus godlike will be deem'd the ways of man" (lines 15–16). The parody is not simply clever; it is genuinely satirical of the tendency of self-interested systematizing to exculpate itself by disguising its own agency, by attributing it to some externalized "god." The ways that Pope justifies to "Man" by attributing them to God are here seen as "Man's" from the beginning.

In section 1 the poet replaces Pope's elusive spiritual knowledge with carnal knowledge (with "cunt," actually), his insatiable curiosity with insatiable appetite and sheer promiscuity:

> Say, first of woman's latent charms below
> What can we reason but from what we know?
> A face, a neck, a breast, are all appear
> From which to reason, to which refer.

(lines 17–20)

Similarly, the "Presumptuous Man" of section 2 becomes what makes "Man" male (and presumptuous):

> Presumptuous Prick! the reason would'st thou find
> Why form'd so weak, so little, and so blind?

(lines 35–36)

Pope's remarks about "Man's" relative weakness in the scheme of things are tellingly transformed into mockery by Wilkes's readdressing them to the source of "Man's" power:

> First, if thou canst, the harder reason guess
> Why form'd no weaker, meaner, and no less?

(lines 37–38)

Immediately, the basis of "Man's" power (such as it is) becomes "Man" himself, personified in the earl of Bute. Pope's sometimes offensive moral quietism becomes indignation that such a "prick" should occupy a position of power (as George III's prime minister):

> God-like erect, BUTE stands the foremost man,
> And all the question (wrangle e'er so long)

> Is only this, if Heaven placed him wrong.
> Respecting him, whatever wrong we call,
> May, must be right, as relative to all.
>
> (lines 48–52)

Of course, one position of such a first minister would be up the anus of his king, the ancillary of his power, the source of his "erection" or elevation. Finally, if the right arrangement of the "system" is seen in the adaptation of penis to cunt ("Say rather, man's as perfect as he ought; / His Pego measured to the female Case" [lines 70–71]), the fact that the "system" also produces the earl of Bute implies at least a certain ambivalence about it.

The third and final section of Wilkes's parody continues the theme of the displacement of spiritual by carnal knowledge. More specifically, the original *Essay*'s sparing ignorance of fate is replaced by a rather less sparing ignorance of physiological and biological processes, the stupid lamb at the slaughterhouse by the unwitting virgin on the love bed:

> Thy lust the Virgin dooms to bleed to-day
> Had she thy reason would she skip and play?
> Pleased to the last, she likes the luscious food,
> And grasps the prick just raised to shed her blood.
>
> (lines 81–84)

Wilkes himself seems to make the same implication that it would take critics another two hundred years to make—that Pope's "Reason" is male. Similarly, the indifference expressed in lines 87–90, attributed to a god who "sees with equal eye, as God of all, / A hero perish, or a sparrow fall," is also transparently, self-servingly male:

> Oh! Blindness to the Future, kindly given,
> That each may enjoy what fucks are mark'd by Heaven.
> Who sees with equal Eye, as God of all,
> The Man just mounting, and the Virgin's fall.
>
> (lines 85–88)

While Wilkes is certainly no feminist, the poem is interesting for the way it not only expresses late-century attitudes to homosexuality, but also for the way it indicates some of the period's insights into its own commonplaces. In many ways, of course, the *Essay* is an adolescent piece, but at its best, in its satirical parody of Pope's *Essay on Man*, it articulates the injustice of systematizing and the awareness, within a period famous (even infamous) for its systems, of the tendency of systems to exploit, to exclude, to self-justify, and finally to self-perpetuate. Such articulation of injustice deserves to be seen as an early, necessary preliminary to its correction, even if Wilkes does not seem inclined to do much about it himself.

Several tracts about the *Essay* and the circumstances of its publication illustrate the function of its erotic and pornographic contents, or at least illustrate some disagreement about the ends such contents served. In *A Genuine and Succint Narrative of a scandalous, obscene, and exceedingly profane LIBEL,* Reverend John Kidgell defends himself for exposing the *Essay* in the name of "every social Virtue" that he feels it violates. At the same time, he draws suspicion to his own character when one Faden (at whose house he happens to be visiting) assumes that he would be interested in the proof sheet of such a dirty poem, or when he almost coyly admits that he is chaplain to one of the lords behind the inquiry. Similarly, his reason for not writing almost immediately a "SERIES OF LETTERS" (Kidgell 1763, 7) against the tract, as "it would have been unavoidably requisite for me to repeat the grossest Indelicacies" (7), would seem to apply to the present *Narrative* as well, unless he had some other motive besides the good of society. On this he insists in ways that one cannot avoid suspecting him of a much narrower interest.

In *A Full and Candid Answer to a Pamphlet called A Genuine and Succint Narrative,* by someone calling himself "a Friend to Truth," the whole point of the *Essay* is seen to be social or, indeed, what we today would call homosocial; the writer describes its function entirely as a sort of facilitator of homosocial conviviality, of society (however limited):

> A pamphlet is written, by a society of men, mad with wine, and wanton with desire; designing, no doubt, to create a laugh among themselves. One, more hardy than the rest, ventures to print a dozen copies (for more I am well informed were not printed) and that with the utmost precaution possible; even to the seeing them struck off himself, in order to prevent the evil from spreading. He gives every one of his companions a copy, which, by the by, is only a copy of their own private conversation, and meant as a joke among themselves. (*Full and Candid Answer* 1763, 8)

By publicizing and publishing the pamphlet as he does, Kidgell actually violates both the smaller "homosociety" and the larger one, turning what was only a source of mirth and harmony in the one into a source of anger and discord in the other. The whole point of the composition, which itself, for all its "shockingness" and its insult to women, seems to retreat into the background, is the homosocial, which its very heterosexual lewdness tends to decontaminate of every trace of the homosexual. For attacking it Kidgell's own manliness is implicitly questioned, as he is himself associated with a corrupt priesthood, the sodomizing tendencies of which have already been satirized in the *Essay* itself, and with the "vile *Scotch faction*" around the earl of Bute, consistently identified with the sodomizing Stuarts, James I in particular. The homosocial becomes the key issue in the debate over the *Essay,* and the homosexual is its foil. Through the association of homosexuality with misogyny, and of both with typical eighteenth-century social arrangements, Wilkes exposes and attacks an unjustly homocentric "system." It is intriguing that such associations would have found a degree of corroboration in the works, and indeed in the career, of a prominent writer like Akenside, while remaining in themselves characteristic of a homocentric system.

9

Formal Strain: Homophobia
in Churchill's *The Times*

While his satirical forebears, Swift and Pope in particular, saw modernity doomed aesthetically, in *The Times,* his verse satire of the 1760s,[1] Churchill sees it doomed sexually, biologically. Churchill extends the Swiftian absence of posterity from the political and the aesthetic realm and applies it to the lower—and arguably more important—depths. *The Times* is Churchill's *Epistle to Prince Posterity.* The hack's world cannot survive aesthetically, but Churchill's world is doomed biologically, sexually. The hack's world is one where no one grows old, but Churchill's is one where everyone does—and at the same "time."

The Times begins by invoking a time when, if we were not really better, we seemed better. While this past time is depicted as a boy,

> The time hath been, a boyish, blushing time,
> When modesty was scarcely held a crime[2]
>
> (lines 1–2)

the point is not that this "boy" was without sin,

> —the most wicked had some touch of grace,
> And trembled to meet Virtue face to face.
> ... those, who, in the cause of Sin grown gray,
> Had served her without grudging, day by day,
> Were yet so weak an awkward shame to feel,
> And strove that glorious service to conceal
>
> (lines 3–8)

but that he had a conscience:

> Time was that men had conscience, that they made
> Scruples to owe what never could be paid.
>
> (lines 33–34)

Consequently, while great men sinned, they did not do so with impunity; if rogues could not resist them on principle, they could out of pride:

> Was one then found, however high his name,
> So far above his fellows damn'd to shame,
> Who dared abuse, and falsify his trust,
> Who, being great, yet dared to be unjust—
> Shunn'd like a plague, or but at distance view'd,
> He walk'd the crowded streets in solitude;
> Such rigid maxims (O, might such revive
> To keep expiring honesty alive!)
>
> (lines 35–42

> Made rogues, all other hopes of fame denied
> Not just through principle, but just through pride.
>
> (lines 45–46)

While the first kind of sin Churchill entertains is economic, illustrated by the failure of men like Faber (the earl of Halifax?) to pay their debts, this is soon dismissed for other *worse* kinds:

> But why enlarge I on such petty crimes?
> They might have shock'd the faith of former times,
> But now are held as nothing—we begin
> Where our sires ended, and improve in sin;
> Rack our invention, and leave nothing new
> In vice and folly for our sons to do.
>
> (lines 103–8)

The lines express a homophobic pun, since while they generally suggest a kind of wickedness that is unsurpassably bad, they more specifically suggest homosexuality, biologically unsurpassable simply because it is—according to Churchill and his "times"—sterile.

Curiously, after complaining about other economic sins, like privilege, Churchill complains about a "vice" that has no respect for it either:

> E'en in our temples she hath fix'd her throne,
> And 'bove God's holy altars placed her own.
>
> (lines 117–18)

Ultimately, homosexuality will be shown to be the worst of the "[c]urses which neither art nor time can heal" (line 122). For now, the "meanness" that Churchill inveighs against is depicted in terms of a sexual sterility that makes it synonymous with homosexuality:

> All shame discarded, all remains of pride,
> Meanness sits crown'd, and triumphs by her side;
> Meanness, who gleams out of the human mind
> Those few good seeds which vice had left behind,
> Those seeds which might in time to virtue tend,
> And leaves the soul without a power to mend;
> Meanness, at sight of whom, with brave disdain,
> The breast of manhood swells, but swells in vain;
>
> (lines 123–30)

Meanness leaves the soul without "power to mend" because meanness is the attribute of an implicitly homosexual vice, so is sterile. While the activities of vice and its accomplice are ostensibly spiritual or moral, they are consistently depicted in the more physical terms of sexual procreation or of its failure—impotence. Vice inadvertently leaves behind a few "seeds," chances for future renewal, but "meanness"—homosexuality—eradicates even these. Finally, spirit has no "power" because it has no matter.

As it is with patronage and preferment in the *Codex* pieces, homosexuality is identified with other vices more widespread, and perhaps more explicitly economic. It is the heinousness of homosexuality that is supposed to be operative here, as a vehicle for the nature of these other widespread evils, but as with those earlier pieces, more becomes operative than intended. Something about the social crimes begins to characterize and even normalize that most heinous crime; moreover, once the focus shifts from the world of "normality" to homosexuality, by virtue of the same sort of "polyvalency" we witnessed in *Mr. Bradbury's Case,* it never fully returns. It is as if some accidental shock, the unexpected "contamination" of the tenor by the vehicle, attracts the attention of the reader to something more interesting, from which it cannot be diverted.

Churchill subsequently describes a society in which parents, themselves reduced to virtual (if not literal) prostitution, sell their daughters to old lechers, or to "Ligoniers"—old, decorated war heroes—for whom they advertise in the newspapers:

> Husband and wife, (whom avarice must applaud)
> Agree to save the charge of pimp and bawd;
> These parts they play themselves, a frugal pair

> And share the infamy, the gain to share;
> Well pleased to find, when they the profits tell,
> That they have play'd the whore and rogue so well.
>
> (lines 149–54)

A footnote nervously explains, "It should be noted that neither here, nor in line 558, does Churchill imply that Ligonier was homosexual" (Churchill 1956, 408). These impotent marriages, while not explicitly homosexual, are used as a foil for the greater impotence of homosexuality, which is gradually introduced, almost *insinuated*, through the series of similarly related vices that follows.

In his survey of global wickedness, Churchill harnesses xenophobia to homophobia. He seems to want things both ways, to import vices from their more wicked sources abroad and to depict England herself as their unparalleled home:

> To different lands for different sins we roam,
> And, richly freighted, bring our cargo home,
> Nobly industrious to make vice appear
> In her full state, and perfect only here.
>
> (lines 181–84)

The satire is double-edged, exploiting stereotypes and topical animosities to suggest not just that England has imported other countries' vices but that she has "excelled" them too; subsequently, as England emulates and surpasses the cruelty of the Dutch at Amboyna, Holland becomes positive again—by comparison. Similarly France and Spain give England vanity and pride respectively, although they were never exactly scarce.

What the remaining countries, Italy and the east, give is progressively complicated, sexual, and homosexual. For example, Italy gives opera and castrati, who stand for all Italian and, now, some English men:

> Half-men, who, dry and pithless, are debarr'd
> From man's best joys—no sooner made than marr'd—
> Half-men, whom many a rich and noble dame,
> To serve her lust, and yet secure her fame,
> Keeps on high diet, as we capons feed,
> To glut our appetites at last decreed;
>
> (lines 235–40)

Finally, the east gives the sin so terrible—so Churchill pretends—it has no name, or at least no name men can utter without embarrassment: homosexuality:

Sins of the blackest character, sins worse
Than all her plagues, which truly to unfold,
Would make the best blood in my veins run cold,
And strike all manhood dead; which but to name,
Would call up in my cheeks the marks of shame;
Sins, if such sins can be, which shut out grace;
Which for the guilty leave no hope, no place,
E'en in God's mercy; sins 'gainst Nature's plan
Possess the land at large; and man for man
Burns in those fires which hell alone could raise
To make him more than damn'd. . . .

(lines 265–70)

Men, whom the beasts would spurn, should they appear
Among the honest herd, find refuge here.

(lines 283–84)

What we have here is really a homosexualized version of the *translatio studii*, or a version of a version of it, what Williams calls the *translatio stultii*—the movement not of civilization from the east to the west, but of barbarism from east to west, such as we read of in Pope's *Dunciad*. Here the uncivilizing force is not barbarism, of course, but homosexuality. Again, through the telling revision of an Augustan cliché, the aesthetic has been replaced with the biological, dullness with sterility and extinction.[3]

Churchill tries to get his "middling" audience on side, if they are not already, by identifying homosexuality with their own natural enemy, privilege:

The sin too proud to feel from reason awe
And those who practise it too great for law.

(lines 299–300)

While this might seem to be an effective ploy, the alleged ubiquity of homosexuality wreaks havoc with the presentation of other vices, like prostitution—negatives that now begin to look positive, or at least now have to be presented that way, since it is so difficult in bipolar satire to blame opposites equally:

Go where we will, at every time and place,
Sodom confronts, and stares us in the face;
They ply in public at our very doors,
And take the bread from much more honest whores.

(lines 293–96)

Similarly, a little later, he must express sympathy for a notorious woman of the town, eclipsed by an even more notorious catamite:

> [Aynam] neglected wanders, whilst a crowd
> Pursue and consecrate the steps of Stroud.
>
> (lines 339–40)

While Churchill might have wanted to invoke one evil to suggest a relatively greater one, using conventional negatives as positives—even *relatively*—can backfire by not shocking us over vice but slowly acclimatizing us to it. The problem is only aggravated when, a little later, Churchill tries to indicate the spread of homosexuality through the eradication of prostitution and of pimps:

> Let her [the old-fashioned mother] discharge her cares,
>   throw wide her door,
> Her daughters cannot, if they would, be whores;
> Nor can a man be found, as times now go,
> Who thinks it worth his while to make them so.
>
> (lines 533–36)

When, after comparing the benefits of having daughters to the dangers of having sons (obviously Churchill saw homosexuality as a *male* crime), at the very end of his poem Churchill is forced into something almost unthinkable, though certainly anticipated in works like Gilbert's *A View of the Town,* a direct defense of promiscuity in a formal verse satire:

> —if, hot and wild,
> He [a typical mother's son] chance to get some score of
>   maids with child,
> Chide, but forgive him; whoredom is a crime
> Which, more at this than any other time,
> Calls for indulgence. . . .
>
> (lines 653–57)

Churchill's first direct mention of homosexuality is immediately followed by an encomium of "Woman." Unlike the feminine in preceding xenophobic passages, the feminine is here seen not as the enemy but as the support of masculinity:

> Woman, by fate the quickest spur decreed,
> The fairest, best reward of every deed

> Which bears the stamp of honour; at whose name
> Our ancient heroes caught a quicker flame,
> And dared beyond belief, whilst o'er the plain,
> Spurning the carcases of princes slain,
> Confusion proudly strode. . . .

(lines 311–17)

The problem is, obviously, that "Woman is out of date" (line 319); yet, curiously, in the next lines, with typical inconsistency, Churchill suggests that there is no problem, since "Woman's" replacements, Hylas and Ganymede, are themselves "supports" of masculine gods and heroes:

> Women are kept for nothing but the breed;
> For pleasure we must have a Ganymede,
> A fine, fresh Hylas, a delicious boy,
> To serve our purposes of beastly joy.

(lines 331–34)

This, incidentally, solves the procreative problem too.

Just as the juxtaposition of one sex crime with another, but as negative and positive, creates problems for satire, so does the juxtaposition of different vices. Thus, the Apicius of lines 349–430, a former glutton turned homosexual (if only because, in the argument of the poem, one form of "meanness" leads to another), could easily be interpreted as not having regressed to a worse vice, but as having progressed from thoughtless *eating* to a genuine passion capable of promoting some thought in him, if partly because it is harder to satisfy:

> Whence flows this sorrow, then? Behind his chair,
> Didst thou not see, deck'd with a solitaire
> Which on his bare breast glittering play'd, and graced
> With nicest ornaments, a stripling placed,
> A smooth, smug stripling, in life's fairest prime?
> Didst thou not mind, too, how from time to time,
> The monstrous lecher, tempted to despise
> All other dainties, thither turn'd his eyes?
>
> . . . .
> His cause of grief behold in that fair boy.
> Apicius dotes, and Corydon is coy.

(lines 417–30)

As Churchill shifts his attention from Apicius to Corydon, he offers a list of alternatives, all equally damning, that alludes to a number of contemporary homosexuals and their affairs. Finally, the only way for the young man to preserve himself from bestiality is to become a beast:

> There's not one brute so dangerous as man
> In Afric's wilds—'mongst them that refuge find
> Which lust denies thee here among mankind:
> Renounce thy name, thy nature, and no more
> Pique thy vain pride on manhood: on all four
> Walk, as you see those honest creatures do,
> And quite forget that once you walk'd on two.
>
> (lines 495–504)

This movement seems to be the concomitant of the west to east movement described as a passage of *translatio* above; as unnaturalness moves from east to west, naturalness moves from west to east.

Just as, in the inverted order Churchill describes, the one way to be human (not bestial) is to literally be a beast, so the one sure way to be male (not effeminate) is to be literally feminine. In a world of homosexuals, drag is the "real man's" perfect disguise; it would be sissy to *not* wear it:

> Be not in this than catamites more nice,
> Do that for virtue, which they do for vice;
> Thus shalt thou pass untainted life's gay bloom,
> Thus stand uncourted in the drawing-room;
> At midnight, thus, untempted, walk the street,
> And run no danger but of being beat.
>
> (lines 519–24)

Churchill is uncommonly good at dramatizing the paradox whereby, once conventions have been sufficiently disrupted, the unconventional becomes the refuge of the conservative and the reactionary.

Churchill's *The Times* would be interesting simply as a late-century reapplication of Swift and Pope's fears for a posterityless, barbarous modernity from aesthetics to the realm of the biological and the (homo)sexual. But it is much more. Within the confines of formal verse satire it demonstrates a surprising degree of unity, most of it derived from Churchill's ability to imply homosexuality in other, not obviously homosexual "vices"— like "meanness," or "impudence," or vice itself.

More significantly, the poem's value can be seen in the way it accurately and energetically depicts how homosexuality disrupts the categories of good and evil, not just in eighteenth-century satire but in eighteenth-century culture in general. Critics from Lockwood to Bertelsen have remarked and appreciated the clarity with which—however inadvertently—Churchill depicts moral muddle.[4] His ability to dramatize a culture under stress is, if anything, more obviously demonstrated by his treatment of homosexuality here.[5]

THE ANTI-TIMES

The writer begins by wanting to chastise Churchill a little, to correct him not for being entirely wrong but for having gone astray this time:

> When Churchill writes with barefac'd impudence,
> And deviates from the path of common sense,
> Then is the time, to wield the lashing Pen,
> And scourge him back to reason once again.
>
> *(Anti-Times* 1764, 3)

The repression of libels is associated with manliness:

> The *Time hath been*, a manly good old Time;
> When writing Libels wou'd be deem'd a Crime:
> *When impious Wretches had some Sparks of Grace,*
> *And trembled* to bely all BRITAIN's Race:
>
> (3)

Thus, at this point, toleration as well as the content itself of Churchill's poem is identified with "unmanliness"; it is as if the allegation of homosexuality were as bad as homosexuality itself, in ways that might remind us of the Thistlethwayte affair. Opposition to the homosexual must not be allowed to become so virulent that it jeopardizes the homosocial, here in the form of the whole society or nation, which Churchill is perceived to have slandered.

Moreover, while overtly attacking homosexuality, Churchill is seen to have encouraged it (or at least effeminacy), in many of the same ways discussed above. *The Anti-Times* suggests that Churchill's subversiveness is not merely a function of modern (or indeed postmodern) sensibility. The writer is particularly offended by Churchill's proposal that youth protect themselves by donning dresses: "Lay by thy sex, thy safety to procure; / Put off the Man, from Men to live secure" (lines 509–10); obviously he would not have agreed that it were possible to redeem so flagrantly outward behavior by an inward motive, that one could "Do that for Virtue, which they do for vice" (line 520), especially when the outward manifestations of effeminacy seem to be almost causally related to more inward homosexuality:

> [Churchill] Raves out aloud, (like frantic Bedlamites,)
> And calls all Britain's sons rank Sodomites;
> But yet betrays the letch'ry of his heart,
> In good old earnest takes damnation's part;
> Wou'd shake the manly Bulwark of our State,
> Wou'd have our Youth become effeminate:
> The beastly seeds of Sodomy would sow,
> Subvert Decorum, and oppose all Law;
>
> (4)

The writer's indignation extends as well to the general realignment of vice and virtue that characterizes the morally equivocal atmosphere of Churchill's poem, an ambiguity (if that is the word) that is clearly not a function of postmodern *aporia*: "[Churchill] Wou'd have each Girl, range like a common Whore; / Each son a Rake, debauching each his score."

The writer recounts how Lucifer, at a meeting of the fiends in hell, needed to choose a champion in England: "A FIEND incarnate, who can name to me? / Deem'd fit our great Ambassador to be." Describing what sort of man this champion should be, he describes Churchill:

> External, he a pastor shou'd appear;
> The cloathing of the gentle lamb shou'd wear;
> Yet be within a rav'nous wolf, or bear.
>
> (6)

Churchill's promotion of homosexuality, whether inadvertent or not, is helped in several ways by his being a priest; his divinity functions as a disguise, as an endorsement, and also probably as an advertisement, given the identification of the church with sodomy that we have found elsewhere. The writer's resorting at this point to a triplet suggests that what he is describing is especially significant, a trope.

That the political corollary is described in another triplet suggests that it is also a trope: the false patriot, the counterweight to the equally immoral and sodomitical courtier personified by the earl of Bute:

> Shou'd under Patriotism's noble veil,
> Perturb the British happy commonweal;
> Promiscuous shou'd both friends and foes assail:
>
> (6)

The champion should himself be a kind of Lucifer, a fallen angel of the pen who would "win the giddy thoughtless rabble rout" after he had "pour'd some works of matchless merit forth, / At thirty pence, their gen'ral sterling worth," and then "tack about, and laugh . . . cram his malice on the Town." While Ashmodeus suggests that Sterne would fit the bill ("A parson, scholar, rake, a wit beside; Sterne is the man, in whom we shou'd confide"), and Moloch suggests Wilkes ("Belove'd, caress'd, and almost deify'd; / Who fitter then, his countrymen to guide"), what Lucifer describes is clearly Churchill's own career as it was understood by this writer: the career of a hypocritical if brilliant demagogue who wins an audience only to betray it to the immorality he pretended to defend it from:

> To speak, Hell's mighty monarch now prepar'd,
> And all Hell's conclave with attention heard.
> Th'apostate Churchill, then must be the man,
> Most aptly suited for our dev'lish plan.

(11)

Lucifer prophesies *The Times*, which the fiends will encourage him to write:

> His countrymen, he'll sons of Sodom call;
> Persuade the world, in his opprobrious ire,
> Lords, masters, servants, burn with Sodom's fire;
> Sons, fathers, brothers, shall not be excus'd,
> Nay, ev'ry British mall shall be abused.

(12)

Lucifer then prophesies that realignment of vice and virtue remarked above, as he tempts mothers to "turn their daughters out, as common whores," and teaches "Britain's females how they ought to live"—probably a reference to Churchill's request that women "chide but forgive" young men for seducing their daughters. Churchill is seen not as the enemy but as the friend of homosexuality, or at least its accomplice, as he is seen to advocate measures and to inculcate an attitude that would have a similar effect: "To stop the propagation of mankind" (12). The subversiveness of Churchill's poem is seen to be not an effect of the nature of the vice he is dealing with, but of Churchill's venality and hypocrisy: "[I]n pompous lines, / Whilst artful, he conceals his base designs" (13). Finally, "The Deputation" Lucifer sends Churchill, the ostensible foe of sodomy, becomes its "chiefest advocate" (15), principally because his ironic recommendation to youth to be effeminate, "To go forth a woman to the public view, / And with their garb assume their manners too" (15) is understood as tantamount to an injunction to be homosexual.

In the energetic second part the writer imagines a prostitute, specifically a "mother bawd," picking up a copy of Churchill's poem and remarking that its "cutting strains" would make "brothel girls" blush, and that "They'll turn his serious rant to farce, / With lines splenetic wipe their —
——." Obviously she assumes that Churchill's satire is a conventional attack on conventional immorality.

Accidentally the madame reads the lines remarked above, which the poet condenses to suit the "Hudibrastic Stile":

> Tutorless throw him to a punk;
> Trust not his morals to a monk, &c.
> Nor trust him to the priestly gown,
> 'Tis oft a cov'ring in this town,
> For base designs. . . .
> . . . .
> His servant's female, young and fair;
> If nature's pride shou'd spur thy heir
> To deeds of ven'ry, hot and wil,
> Perchance he gets twice ten with child;
> Chide, but forgive, whoredom's a crime,
> Which more at this, than any time,
> Demands indulgence, 'mongst such race,
> A bastard is some sign of grace.
>
> (18–19)

The lines are only a slight distortion of lines 635–58 in *The Times*, where their tenor is that bad as whoring is, it looks good compared to sodomy. A key word, deleted in the distorted version, is "rather": "Give him no Tutor—throw him to a punk, / Rather than trust his morals to a Monk" (lines 639–40); deleting it transforms Churchill's advice into more positive adjuration. Reading such lines, the madame immediately alters her opinion of Churchill: "To like the man, I now begin, / She simp'ring said, and stroak'd her chin." When she glances at a second passage, this time about daughters, "Unguarded, let 'em range the town, / And run all carnal pleasure down" (19), a distorted version of lines 543–50, her good opinion of Churchill is assured. She buys a copy, remarking "Like goos, and gander, so appear! / We both for half crowns, sell our ware."

Our poet shows *The Times* becoming a hit among all the prostitutes of London. Seducia commissions her friend Flagelinda to assemble them all, to convert as many daughters as possible to prostitution, since anyone who stands in their way can now be accused of being "Th'obstructing cause of Sodomy" (21). They then write Churchill a "Congratulatory Epistle," in which they decree Churchill their "gen'ral pimp" (23). They object, however, to the lines (509–20) starting "Lay by thy sex, thy safety to procure," since,

> With trinkets, each He Molly wears,
> Let him put on our languid airs
>
> .   .   .   .
>
> The mingling males will feel strange fire,
> Swim down the torrent of desire.

(24)

Churchill's proposal, flattering as it is (in a way) to feminine charm, is like trying to defuse a powder house with "brands of fire."

Clearly one of this writer's motives for attacking Churchill in such a qualified way, so carefully distinguished from his great friend Wilkes, is to maintain the support of a middle class that had probably been shocked not just by the wholesale allegations but by the equivocal morality of *The Times*. Attacking Churchill, the (overt) enemy of homosexuality, he must also take care not to appear to defend homosexuality, perhaps by suggesting that Churchill is, if not exactly homosexual himself, at least in complicity with homosexuality. The length the writer goes to to protect the movement from an advocate who has become tainted merely by expressing *opposition* to homosexuality, and by the complicated form such expression probably *had* to take, indicates how problematic the idea and the expression were. At the same time, in exempting a series of known libertines from the depravity required to write *The Times*, the writer reproduces some of the same moral confusion, that "realignment of vice and virtue," that he charges Churchill with. He, too, is tainted.

10

The Homosexual Stage:
The Rosciad

In *Sexual Suspects: Eighteenth-Century Players and Sexual Ideology* Christina Straub argues that eighteenth-century discourse about players provides both a gauge of contemporary attitudes to sexuality and an early development of "the powerful gendered tropes of the male spectator and the female spectacle" (1992, 19). While she begins her study with an appropriate quotation from Churchill's *Apology,* referring to the relationship of actors' public roles to judging spectators that is central to her theme, she does not address in detail the way the theatrical world is depicted in Churchill's most important poem on the subject, *The Rosciad*. This world, I will argue, is consistently a homosexual one. At the same time, Churchill's "unreal" world of the stage is used to stigmatize the "real" one. Churchill's poem is yet another good example of the way homosexuality could be detached from a specific sexual practice and applied to others, social and political.

The poem's initial crisis is establishing criteria with which to determine Roscius's successor. Perhaps because this is the world of actors, where appearances are emphasized over reality, there are simply too many different criteria, as many as there are people, because criteria are now entirely external and nonessential. Moreover, each judges not just by appearances but more specifically by his or her own appearance. In its nonessential narcissism this actors' world resembles the world of the sodomite and the homosexual encountered in earlier polemical literature and pamphlets:

> The town divided, each runs sev'ral ways,
> As passion, humour, int'rest, party, sways.
> Things of no moment, colour of the hair,
> Shape of a leg, complexion brown or fair,

196

> A dress well chosen, or a patch misplac'd,
> Conciliate favour, or create distaste.
>
> (lines 37–42)

It is no coincidence that many of these people are also depicted as homosexual. Regardless of what their sexual orientation might have been, theirs is a homosexual world, a nonessential world. Churchill's poem is one of those early places where many of the iconographic traits of the sodomite and the homosexual come together without explicitly signifying sodomite and homosexual. Many of Churchill's victims probably were literally homosexual, but his target seems more generally to have been a kind of figurative homosexuality that could only have been possible in a world where the literal was already well known.

Look, for example, at the portrait of Alexander Wedderburn,

> A pert, prim Prater of the *northern* race,
> Guilt in his heart, and famine in his face,
> Stood forth, —and thrice he wav'd his lilly hand—
> And thrice he twirl'd his Tye—thrice strok'd his and—
>
> (lines 75–78)

with its symbolic aristocratic and effeminate white hand; or look, again, at the portrait of John Hill,

> For who, like him, his various pow'rs could call
> Into so many shapes, and shine in all?
> Who could so nobly grace the motley list,
> Actor, Inspector, Doctor, Botanist?
> Knows any one so well?—sure no one knows,—
> At once to play, prescribe, compound, compose?
> Who can?—But WOODWARD came,—Hill slipp'd away,
> Melting like ghosts before the rising day.
>
> (lines 109-16)

a man of many roles and bad at all of them, because lacking in substance and so really no man at all, but an amphibian like Hervey or the foppish young sodomites of *Plain Reasons*. Wedderburn's effeminacy also has strong political associations, as (an endnote explains) he "supported the prosecution of Wilkes for the publication of the *North Briton*, No. 45, in 1763" (Churchill 1956, 459). Hill received patronage from Bute.

At their worst these actors are characterized by membership in that "third sex" discussed by Trumbach. Thus Fitzpatrick, heralded by various homosexual emblems like "*smooth* FALSEHOOD" (line 120), aristocratic pallor, fawning, simpering, etc., is denied the dignity of the universal male pronoun and referred to instead as "It":

> A Motley Figure, of the FRIBBLE Tribe,
> Which heart can scarce conceive, or pen describe,
> Came *simp'ring* on; to ascertain whose sex
> Twelve sage impannell'd Matrons would perplex.
> Nor *Male*, nor *Female*; *Neither*, and yet both;
> Of *Neuter* Gender, tho' of *Irish* growth;
> A six-foot suckling, mincing in his gait;
> Affected, peevish, prim, and delicate;
> Fearful *it* seemed, tho' of Athletic make,
> Lest *brutal breezes* should too roughly shake
> *Its* tender form, and *savage* motion spread
> O'er *its* pale cheeks the horrid manly red
>
> (lines 141–52)

Fitzpatrick is depicted as a homosexual because he has no capacity for sound judgment, because he has no criteria, because he has no essence, *not* because he is homosexual in any other way. The other attributes of homosexuality, like the affectedness and "delicacy," are merely used to draw our attention to this nonessential essence which is what he does share with sodomites and homosexuals generally. Nonessential as he is, when he attempts to "perk" on Roscius's throne, Fitzpatrick is vaporized by a single feminine frown from "Plain COMMON SENSE."

Similarly, Arthur Murphy is described not as a man but a "thing,"

> When motionless he stands, we all aprove;
> What pity 'tis the THING was made to move
>
> (lines 565–66)

or a fake man:

> When he attempts, in some one fav'rite part,
> To ape the feelings of a manly heart,
> His honest features the disguise defy,
> And his face loudly gives his tongue the lye.
>
> (lines 573–76)

Churchill is at his most tragic when he describes Murphy's appetite for fame, the irony being that one of no intrinsic worth should *not* desire this very extrinsic thing, and that no one wants it more. Fame is an "outer" that, without something "inner," collapses into its opposite, infamy:

> How few are found with real talents bless'd,
> Fewer with nature's gifts contented rest.
> Man from his sphere eccentric starts astray;
> All hunt for fame, but most mistake the way.
>
> (lines 585–88)

Later, the (understandable) opposition of the actors to *The Rosciad* will be made to appear all the more ridiculous because of their nothingness, at the same time it is identified with aspects of the "real" order, like "privilege" (497), which must have been particularly offensive to Churchill and his middle-class audience:

> What! shall opinion then, of nature free
> And lib'ral as the vagrant air, agree
> To rust in chains like these, impos'd by Things
> Which, less than nothing, ape the pride of kings?
> No, —though half-poets with half-players join
> To curse the freedom of each honest line;
>
> (lines 501–6)

Line 505, "though half-poets with half-players join" suggests a homosexual union with overtones of Platonic myth.

A curse on Fitzpatrick is followed by a passage describing the "Critic Race" in terms strikingly similar to the terms used to describe the much dreaded spawn of the degenerate sodomites, as if this too has been detached from its original "signified":

> Cold-blooded critics, by enervate sires
> Scarce hammer'd out, when nature's feeble fires
> Glimmer'd their last; . . .
>
> . . . .
> . . . A servile race,
> Who, in mere want of fault, all merit place.
>
> (lines 179–84)

Typically, their criterion is negative, a *lack* of character or essence rather than anything positive or substantial. This group resembles the Covent Garden troops, the chief of whom symbolically weds Novelty, with Folly on one side and Lun or John Rich (famous for playing Harlequin):

> Harlequin comes their chief!—see from afar,
> The hero seated in fantastic car!
> Wedded to Novelty, his only arms
> Are wooden swords, wands, talismans, and charms;
>
> (lines 663–66)

Typical of the narcissism of this world, Lun virtually sits opposite himself; just as typically, one of the monsters drawing his chariot is mounted by a hermaphrodite.

This monstrous, quasi-sodomitical race, of which Fitzpatrick is unofficially a member, serves as a foil for Lloyd, whose young manliness and ability to judge by sound criteria are both made all the more striking by contrast. Significantly, while the actors he is contrasted to are entirely external, his essence, his "worth," is discernible even before his appearance, his "person":

> from amidst the throng, a Youth stood forth,
> Unknown his person, not unknown his worth;
> His looks bespoke applause; alone he stood,
> Alone he stemm'd the mighty critic flood.
>
> (lines 191–94)

Since part of his essence is "Englishness," he naturally defends English culture against slavish neoclassicism. His manly essentialism has an aesthetic corollary:

> Where do these words of Greece and Rome excel,
> That England may not please the ear as well?
> What mighty magic's in the place or air,
> That all perfection needs must center there?
>
> (lines 201–4)

He persuades the crowd to appoint native English judges: Johnson and Shakespeare.

The "Order" that marches in the procession on the day of the tribunal (I wonder if this is the "Order" of Akenside's revision) is characterized, as the "homosexual" actors have been, as entirely preoccupied with appearances and without essence. That this is a "homosexual" order seems only the more probable given how Churchill characterized the political order of Bute and George III. This order, like that of the critics above, is associated with a degenerate race, with the sterile "alternate creation" of the sodomites, like what the writer of the *Observations* feared:

> First, Order came,—with solemn step, and slow,
> In measur'd time his feet were taught to go.
> Behind, from time to time, he cast his eye,
> Lest This should quit his place, That step awry.
> Appearances to save his only care;
> So things seem right, no matter what they are.
> In him his parents saw themselves renew'd.
> Begotten by sir Critic on saint Prude.

(lines 295–302)

The "real" order is also obsessed with appearances, which take the form of hard material standards like "cash"—compared to which the actors have only the appearance of appearances, or perhaps not even that. The authority represented by the king has become the king represented on coins, of which the players have only too few:

> What can an actor give? in ev'ry age
> Cash hath been rudely banish'd from the stage;
> Monarchs themselves, to grief of ev'ry play'r
> Appear as often as their image there:

(lines 19–22)

Perhaps such a lack of the real world's currency would naturally claim his indulgence, but it is typical of Churchill's ambivalence, or ambivalence is so typical of him, that he expresses some sympathy for the actors' lack of essence, of reality. At times such a lack even resembles a refinement of what is really gross:

> SHUTER keeps open house at Southwark fair,
> And hopes the friends of humour will be there.
> In Smithfield, YATES prepares the rival treat
> For those who laughter love, instead of meat;
> FOOTE, at Old House, for even FOOTE will be,
> In self-conceit, an actor, bribes with tea;
> Which WILKINSON at second-hand receives,
> And at the New, pours water on the leaves.

(lines 29–36)

However, the judgment that Churchill initially faults is not just superficial but narcissistic, since the superficial criterion is always a characteristic of the bad judge him- or herself: "We praise and censure with an eye to self" (line 54). Thus "smart" ladies admire an actor named Palmer who, from an endnote, must have been a rather effeminate man: "Mr. Palmer has life and sprightliness,—and executes some of his parts very prettily" (Churchill 1956, 458).

More of Churchill's ambivalence is apparent when he describes the "great day" on which the judges are to choose a successor:

> Full in the centre of a spacious plain,
> On plan entirely new, where nothing vain,
> Nothing magnificent appear'd, but Art,
> With decent modesty, perform'd her part,
> Rose a tribunal:
>
> (lines 247–51)

Coming not many lines after Wedderburn's "Nothing," it is hard not to read this "nothing magnificent" as a double entendre, a "Magnificent Nothing" like Wedderburn himself, underlining the ironic process whereby the very intensity of the desire to avoid superficiality actually recreates it worse than ever. His identification of the actors with a kind of effeminate and implicitly homosexual obsession with surfaces and appearances is tempered by his sense that this concern is something of a shared affliction. He is analogous to the homophobe who is sophisticated enough to apprehend that what he fears in others is really his own nonessentialism. Such instability is typically aggravated by history, since the "Mansfield" who concludes this passage historically played such a negative role in his and Wilkes's subsequent career that it is hard not to read the final lines as ironic— as if history was determined that Churchill's poetry would be subtler than he intended.

Besides being ambivalent about the actors' kind of superficiality, Churchill is arguably confused about the superficiality of acting. At times he seems to advocate greater inwardness—

> The actor who would build a solid fame,
> Must imitation's servile arts disclaim;
> Act from himself, on his own bottom stand.
> I hate e'en GARRICK thus at second hand
>
> (lines 33–36)

and to oppose imitative "Fashion":

> Fashion—a word which knaves and fools may use
> Their knavery and folly to excuse.

> To copy beauties, forfeits all pretence
> To fame—to copy faults, is want of sense.
>
> (lines 455–58)

At other times, however, as in his criticism of James Love for always play-ing himself, he seems to reverse himself:

> In a peculiar mould by HUMOUR cast,
> For FALSTAFF fram'd—Himself the First and Last,—
> He stands aloof from all—maintains his state,
> And scorns, like *Scotsmen*, to assimilate.
>
> (lines 483–86)

> Nature, in spite of all his skill, crept in:
> Horatio, Dorax, Falstaff,—still 'twas QUIN.
>
> (lines 985–86)

Finally he seems unclear whether acting should be extrinsic or intrinsic, a matter of pretending or of being what one really or "essentially" is.

Women, who are allowed to contend for Roscius's chair because "Brit-ain owns no Salique Law" (682), are so noticeably exempt from the super-ficiality of the men as to reinforce the identification of this vice with men and the vice, homosexuality, principally (if often only implicitly) associ-ated with them here; for Churchill female homosexuality was not an issue. The superficiality that characterizes the *Rosciad* is specific to the male gender for very good reason.

The change of tone is obvious with the introduction of Catherine Clive, for the very good reason that she resolves the principal tension of the poem, the alternation (or altercation) of inner and outer. Clive's "outer" agrees with her inner originality (despite some physical handicaps) by concealing itself:

> Original in spirit and in ease,
> She pleas'd by hiding all attempts to please.
> No comic actress ever yet could raise,
> On Humour's base, more merit or more praise.
>
> (lines 691–64)

She also reconciles one of the principal inconsistencies indicated by the poem, that between "merit" and "favour": "But though bare Merit might in Rome appear / The strongest plea for favour, 'tis not here" (lines 13–14). It *is* though, where Clive—and women generally—are concerned.

Woman are here the touchstone of the intrinsic, the natural. The un-naturalness of (always homosexually suspect) opera is seen in its capacity to transform even a "naturally" pleasing woman like Charlotte Brent into a source of displeasure:

> Let him reverse kind Nature's first decrees,
> And teach e'en BRENT a method not to please;
> But never shall a TRULY BRITISH Age
> Bear a vile race of EUNUCHS on the stage.
> The boasted work's call'd NATIONAL in vain,
> If one ITALIAN voice pollutes the strain.
> Where tyrants rule, and slaves with joy obey,
> Let slavish minstrels pour th'enervate lay;
> To BRITONS, far more noble pleasures spring,
> In native notes, whilst BEARD and VINCENT sing.
>
> (lines 719–28)

Women are usually associated with balance, as in Susanna Maria Cibber's depiction,

> Form'd for the tragic scene, to grace the stage,
> With rival excellence of Love and Rage,
>
> (lines 777–78)

or as in Hannah Pritchard's:

> PRITCHARD, by Nature for the stage design'd,
> In person graceful, and in sense refin'd;
> Her Art as much as Nature's friend became,
> Her voice as free from blemish as her fame.
>
> (lines 803–6)

Pritchard, in fact, occasions Churchill's fiercest diatribe against our own unbalanced preoccupation with appearances, as he defends her against the charge that she is "too old" for comedy:

> Are foibles then, and Graces of the mind,
> In real life to size or age confin'd?
> Do spirits flow, and is good-breeding plac'd
> In any set circumference of waist?
>
> (lines 825–28)

THE FRIBBLERIAD

Straub argues that this poem was Garrick's attempt to construct himself "in opposition to ambiguous or suspect forms of masculinity" (1992, 61). While this might well have been his intention, the actual effect of the poem must have been somewhat different, an illustration of the uncertainties of what she elsewhere terms "the struggle to control the politics of spectatorship" (15). A "Fribble" might well have been just an effeminate and, indeed, homosexual, male, but Garrick cannot avoid the implication, given his prior identification with Fribble in *Miss in Her Tees* and his invocation of *The Rosciad*, that such homosexual males have a tendency to be actors and vice versa (Staves 1982, 416).

A prose introduction recounts how Fitzpatrick insulted Garrick in the *Craftsman*:

> In this said paper a *certain gentleman* who subscribes himself X, Y, Z, a volunteer too in the service, has thrown about his dirt in a most extraordinary manner, and has attacked our stage here, with unwearied malevolence both in his public and private character. . . . It would be endless and out of place here to point out his want of taste, and even common truth, in his account of the manner of Mr. *Garrick's* speaking and acting in his various characters; of his most ungentlemanlike, as well as unjust abuse of his person, voice, age, &c, &c, &c.; (Garrick 1761, iv–v)

What immediately occasions Garrick's reply is Fitzpatrick's having sent copies of his collected papers in the *Craftsman* to some of Garrick's friends.

The attack on Fitzpatrick is largely directed against his sexuality. His "homosexuality" is foregrounded by an illustration that shows him with hands conspicuously raised, face thrust forward, and protuberant ass: the "round smirking face" and "jut with your bum" of the epigram from the *Ledger* quoted in the brief preface. The face and the ass amount to commonplaces of such literature, the latter for obvious reasons, the former because of the identification of homosexuals with surfaces, appearances—*faces*, as it were. A quotation also foregrounds the issue of his sexuality: "Femina, Vir, Neutrum."

Fitzpatrick's writing against Garrick is marked by "unnaturalness" and sterility for not having been written to obtain the necessities of life, and for being incapable of doing so anyway:

> Say, *Garrick*, does he write for bread,
> This *friend* of yours, this X, Y, Z?

> For pleasure sure, not bread—'twere vain
> To write for that he ne'er could gain:
> No calls of nature to excuse him,
> He deals in rancour to amuse him;
>
> (1)

It is motivated by "pleasure" that in its separation from "bread" here seems analogous to sodomitical pleasure itself, removed from other "necessities of life," like procreation:

> A *Man* it seems—'tis hard to say—
> A *Woman* then?—a moment pray—
> Unknown as yet by sex or feature,
> Suppose we try to guess the creature;
> Whether a *wit*, or a *pretender*?
> Of *masculine* or *female* gender?
>
> (2)

While the last lines connect his sexuality to his politics, the next lines connect it to his writing as well:

> Some things it does may pass for either,
> And some it does belong to neither.
> It is so fibbing, slandering, spiteful,
> In phrase so dainty, so delightful;
> So fond of all it reads and writes,
> So waggish when the maggot bites:
> Such spleen, such wickedness, and whim,
> *It* must be *Woman*, and a *Brim*.
>
> (2)

Narcissistic and delicate as he is, he attempts to appear masculine by borrowing from truly male writers, filling up "gaps with *Pope* and *Swift*," though the manner and the motivation of such borrowing are themselves feminine, "As cunning housewives bait their traps, / And Take their game with bits and scraps." Significantly, the final result is at best a mere *resemblance*:

> By here and there a patch of learning,
> The creature's *Male*—say all we can,
> It must be something *like* a man—
>
> (3)

This seems consistent with the idea, expressed in the earliest tracts, that what defines the homosexual is *nonessentialism*, being *like* a man perhaps, but *not* a man. Appearance that it is, this resemblance is belied by deeper things:

> What, like a man, from day to shrink,
> And seek revenge with pen and ink?
>
> .   .   .   .
>
> *Hate* join'd with *Fear* will shun the light,
> But *Hate* and *Manhood* fairly fight—
> 'Tis manhood's mark to face the foe,
> And not in ambush give the blow;

(3)

Fitzpatrick has a certain amphibiousness, but one that is a parody of the masculine adaptability and competence in many spheres represented by Churchill:

> With colours flying, beat of drum
> Unlike to this, see *Churchill* come!
> And now like *Hercules* he stands,
> Unmask'd his face, but arm'd his hands;
> Alike prepar'd to *write* or *drub*!
> This hold a *Pen*, and that *Club*!
>
> .   .   .   .
>
> If such are manhood's feats and plan
> Poor X, Y, Z, will prove no *man*.
> Nor male? nor female?—then on oath
> We safely may pronounce it *Both*.

(4–5)

The "fribbling race, / The curse of nature, and disgrace" to which Fitzpatrick belongs is a homosexual race.[1] His lack of erotic interest in women leaves him with "every passion" but "no pleasure," as if "no pleasure" were the analogue of sterility. Sterility becomes "want of power," as sexual impotence is identified with political impotence that expresses its frustrated desire in a fondness for forms of arbitrary government: "want of power, all peace destroying." Just as want of power leads to power (or *powerlessness*) of a different sort, his softness—"smiling, smirking, soft in nature"—leads to (or perhaps disguises) the worst kind of hardness:

> But touch its pride, the *Lady fellow*,
> From sickly pale, turns deadly yellow—
> *Male, female*, vanish,—fiends appear—
> And all is malice, rage and fear—
>
> (5)

The writer then wonders why this homosexual race bears such an enmity for Garrick: "Say for what cause these Master-Misses / To *Garrick* such a hatred bore. . . . Are things so delicate, so fell / Can Cherubim be imps of hell?" He then describes what a momentous thing it is for the "Fribbles" merely to "TO DO A DEED" and schedules their conference for a characteristically effeminate time and place:

> 'Twas when the balmy breath of May,
> Makes tender lambkins sport and play;
> When tend'rer Fribbles walk, and dare
> To gather nosegays in the air—
> 'Twas at that time of all the year
> When flowers and butterflies appear,
>
> (7)

When Fitzpatrick is chosen to be their leader, his homosexual characteristics—smoothness, prominent face, protuberant breast and ass, flaunting hands, etc.—are emphasized again:

> At which, ONE larger than the rest
> With visage sleek, and swelling chest,
> With stretch'd out fingers, and a thumb
> Stuck to his hips, and jutting bum,
> Rose up!—All knew his smirking air,—
> They clap'd, and cry'd—the *chair*, the *chair!*
> He smil'd—and to the honour'd seat,
> Padled away with mincing feet.
>
> (11)

One Philip Whiffle relates the reason of the quarrel with Garrick. In 1748 he

> made OUR SEX a shew;
> And gave us up to such rude laughter,
> That few, 'twas said, could hold their water:
> For He, that play'r, so mock'd our motions,

> Our dress, amusements, fancies, notions,
> So lisp'd our words and minc'd our steps,
> He made up pass for *demi-reps*.
>
> (12)

Whiffle is not explicit about which "activity of doubtful legality" makes him a "demimondain[e]," but perhaps he does not need to be. It is significant that he refers to the Fribbles here as a "sex," and that their mannerisms are so closely identified with that "sex" as to constitute mockery of it in particular. For obvious reasons, they are wrought up to a particular excitement by Whiffle's conclusion: "But how attack him? far, or near? / In front, my friends, or in the rear":

> All started up at once to speak
> As if they felt some sudden tweak:
> 'Twas quick resentment caus'd the smart,
> And pierc'd them in the tenderest part.
>
> (13)

One "valiant captain, PATTYPAN" waves his sword, at which "all cry out,— NO NAKED THINGS!" (15); a "reverend Mister MARJORAM" reports the publication of Churchill's *Rosciad,* in which "every *Actor is a thin, / A Merry Andrew, paper king*" and recommends poisoning Garrick; but Fitzpatrick opts for assassination by the pen, in what reads like a parody of Caesar's assassination à la Akenside, as if this sort of republican kitsch was admired in "Fribble" circles:

> My patriot hand, like *Brutus* strikes,
> And stabs and wounds where most it likes:
> *He*, as a *Roman*, gave the blow;
> I, as a FRIBBLE, stab your foe;
> He mourn'd the deed, would not prevent it,—
> I'll do the deed—and then lament it.
>
> (19)

They join hands "like fairies form a magic round," kiss, and go to bed.

11

George III as "Schoolboy King"

Given the prevalence of a sexualized pedagogical relationship in different areas of eighteenth-century culture, several of which (*Mr. Bradbury's Case,* Akenside's *Pleasures,* and Shaftesbury's *Characteristics,* for example) we have already encountered, it should not be so surprising to find it here, in eighteenth-century political satire. It is, however, rather surprising, considering that in this case the "ephebe" and his "satyr" are the young George III and his prime minister, John Stuart, the earl of Bute.

Obviously certain unusual circumstances contributed to the configuration. First, George III's father, Frederick, Prince of Wales, died in 1751, leaving the twelve-year-old prince in the care of an overly protective mother, Augusta, dowager princess of Wales. According to Stanley Ayling, "For the three or four years following his father's death . . . there is no doubt that the young Prince of Wales was protected by his mother from those influences, physical, social, and intellectual, which enable a boy to grow up" (1972, 37). John Stuart, earl of Bute, became Frederick's lord of the bedchamber in 1750, and after his death, Augusta's closest advisor. Historians now do not believe that their relationship was a sexual one, but many of their contemporaries did. More important, in 1755 the princess dowager appointed Bute George's personal tutor. Thus, again in the words of Stanley Ayling, "The future King had become infatuated with the man the world took to be his mother's lover" (41):

> By the spring of 1756, the conquest of the Prince's heart and mind was so complete that among the letters which he now poured out to Bute can be found the sort of language that a lover might use to his mistress. (44)

Ayling assures us that "George's idolisation of his mentor by no means indicated any lack of normal sexual susceptibility" (52), but in the following tracts we are dealing with perception rather than reality, or rather with the manipulation of people's perception by writers, propagandists who must have felt they knew how far they could manipulate it and still be believed. At times this seems far indeed. The distance is largely a function of the basic configurations of George's relationship with his mother and his mentor, and (of course) of associations (homosexual and otherwise) that such a configuration must have possessed.

THE FALL OF MORTIMER

The quotation from Shakespeare on the title page of *The Fall of Mortimer*[1]—"Forbad my Tongue to speak of Mortimer, / But I will find him when he lies asleep, / And in his Ear I'll holla *Mortimer!*"—indicates an intention to embarrass the dedicatee, the earl of Bute, as much as possible, simply by broadcasting the analogy. Wilkes, who wrote the dedication of this revision of William Mountfort's play (sometimes ascribed to William Hatchett), pretends to object to its "odious" application, while applying it more contrastively: "I have felt an honest indignation at all the invidious and odious applications of the story of ROGER MORTIMER" (Wilkes 1763, ii):

> The former Prince [Edward the Third] was held in the most absolute slavery by his Mother and her Minister, the first Nobles of England were excluded from the King's Councils, and the Minion disposed of all places of profit and trust. (ii)

A second quotation following the dedication hints again at the weakness and possible effeminacy of the king, alluding as it does to Richard II.

In reality, the differences that Wilkes presents between Mortimer and Bute only suggest that the English under George III and the earl of Bute are much worse off than they ever were under Edward III and Mortimer: "The young King had been victorious over the *Scots*, who were in *that* reign our cruel enemies, but are happily in *this* our dearest friends" (ii). The positive differences are all sarcasms:

> With the highest rapture I now look back to that disgraceful era, and I exult when I compare it with the halcyon days of *George the Third*. This excellent Prince is held in no kind of captivity. All his Nobles have free access to him. The throne is not now besieged. Court favour, not confined to one partial stream, flows in a variety of different channels, enriching *this* whole country. (iii)

A mere change of the demonstrative pronoun from "this" to "that" reveals Wilkes's real meaning; substituting an article for the negative of the next sentence has the same effect: "[A] Court Minion now finds it necessary, for the preservation of his own omnipotence, by the vilest insinuations to divide either the royal, or any noble families" (iii). Finally, "To compleat the Contrast, we have now an *advantageous*, a *glorious* Peace, fully adequate to all the *successes*, to all the *glories* of the WAR" (iv).

Employing a configuration that reminds me of Straub's "trope of the schoolboy," Wilkes implies that as Bute's former pupil George remains in a subordinate position, even as king: "This happy state of things we owe to your Lordship's unexampled care of His Majesty's youth. The great promise you made us, that we should frequently see our Sovereign, like his great Predecessor William the third, presiding in person at the British Treasury, has been fulfilled to the advantage and glory of these times" (v). With even worse implications of royal passivity and ministerial wickedness, Wilkes contrasts Arthur Murphy's acting ability with Bute's and concludes that "in the famous scene of *Hamlet*, where you *pour fatal poison into the ear* of a good, unsuspecting King," Bute was not acting.

This comparison enables Wilkes to insinuate that the tragedy of Mortimer is really Bute's tragedy, for which his life has been a kind of rehearsal: "While Mr. *Pitt*, Lord *Temple*, and others, your contemporaries, were preparing themselves for the national business of Parliament, and already taking a distinguished part there, you were treading a private stage in the high buskings of pompous, sonorous Tragedy" (ix). Wilkes balefully indicates that he hopes Bute's career will end as ignominiously as Mortimer's: "It is the warmest wish of my heart that the Earl of BUTE may speedily compleat the story of ROGER MORTIMER. I hope that your Lordship will *graciously* condescend to undertake this arduous task, to which *parts* like yours, are so peculiarly adapted" (xii).

It is hard to believe that anyone in this propagandistic play really has the "national interest" in mind, any more than the scheming war profiteers in Brecht's *Threepenny Opera*. The comparison to Bute is blatant, Mortimer having made as compromising a peace with King Robert of Scotland as Bute was thought to have made with France. Lord Mountacute imprudently fumes over Mortimer's insults to the peerage, citizens complain about the bad effects of the peace on business, and everywhere the pretense of loyalty to the king, but not the king's minister, wears thin: "Our faithful annals thus transmit to Fame / A *Villain-Statesman*, not the *King* to blame," says the speaker in the prologue. The citizens agree, Bumper especially: "Here, Masters, here's *God bless the king, and send him better Counsellors.* —No

Mortimer for me. . . . 'Tis a Shame the Nation should any longer be impos'd upon" (Mountfort 1763, 19).

The king himself is introduced in a supine state, dreaming of his father's ghost and his murderer, Mortimer. The king continues to rave about the contents after his dream, even after the messenger enters the room, probably indicating a tendency for inwardness and an inability to swiftly respond and adapt to circumstances. "Headless *Kent*, my beloved Uncle" (20) no doubt stands for the duke of Cumberland.

The homosexuality of Edward II implicitly becomes Edward III's, as the two are identified at a caesura in the king's speech. The rhetorical figure, the reversal of "Edward," underlines the king's "reversed" sexuality, at the same time it implies that Edward III might be able to reverse it again to redeem the monarchy:

> If Dreams presage, or Visions can forbode
> The Fate of *Edward*, *Edward* must succeed,
> If so you've fix'd it; yet I'll face this Storm,
> Stand like a King 'gainst my rebellious Doom,
> And perish worthy of my Dignity.
>
> (21)

When the nobles inform the king of Mortimer's wrongdoing, he is roused to even greater manliness:

> I find myself enlarg'd: Each Artery
> Beats double Time, as if my Spirits strove
> To be in Action: My Father's Soul
> Shoots in my Blood, and prompts to Resolution.
>
> (24)

Immediately following this burst of energy, we are given (at second hand) the queen's version of Edward, which looks all the weaker by contrast:

> "Insolence! and Treason to the State, cry'd she!—
> "Howe'er, the Boy shall bend to all my wishes:
> "'Tis a half Soul, bred in the Lag of Love,
> "And spiritless as the Desire that got him—
> "Bid Mortimer not fear what's crush'd so soon.
>
> (25)

By implication, George III is not a man but a "boy," a "half Soul," and as "spiritless" as his father. Edward II's "spiritless" desire for his queen seems to allude to his homosexuality, his greater desire for Gaveston. I think at this stage Edward III really is his father, politically and sexually, although he is clearly about to differ from and surpass him; consequently, his modern equivalent, George III, is also, however obliquely, tainted with homosexuality. Edward III is different from his father in that he is younger, unsettled, and in relationship to Mortimer something like a Greek ephebe; his homosexuality, such as it is, really is a "phase" that he will soon break out of. George III, on the other hand, can go either way; he can be Edward III and throw off the feminizing yoke of his tutor, or he can remain Edward II and end up like him too. The Mortimer analogy offers a kind of "double typology," a negative and a positive Edward, of either of which George III could be the antitype, depending upon his behavior. The negative type remains largely hidden, for obvious reasons; indeed, the positive is negative enough.

Mortimer's seduction of Serjeant Eitherside's niece, Maria, later in act 2, seems intended to present his manliness in stark contrast to the king's "boyishness," at least for now. When Mortimer hears in act 3 that the king is with three lords—Leicester, Berkeley, and Exeter—he curses: "How's this? so cunning, Boy? Damnation!" (37). As Mortimer rouses Isabella by describing what she will be if Edward takes control, it becomes apparent that to her the king's advisers, if not the king as well, have assumed the part of her homosexual husband's lovers, Gaveston in particular:

> Be thou as once, when *Spencer, Gaveston,*
> The Minions of my Husband, did attempt
> To curb my Will, and I defy'd them all. . . .
>
> (39)

It also becomes apparent what a subordinate role the king has played for her and continues to play, at least in imagination:

> Can the froward Chit believe, because my Son,
> I'd still him with a Play-thing call'd a Crown,
> And live myself on Curtesy of State,
> The Fragments of the Grandeur I had left?
> Perish ten Sons e'er such a Fit possess me!
>
> (39)

Toward the end of the scene she reaffirms the identification between father and son, which had been implicit from the beginning: "If in the Father's Time I rul'd alone, / I'll never yield that Honour to the Son" (40).

After Serjeant Eitherside, using his daughter Maria to get preferment from Mortimer, loses the scroll with the order to dispatch Mountacute and Maria gives it to the same in act 4, the identification of Edward III with his father becomes all the stronger, with the very important difference that he can break with it at any moment. By implication George III, at a similar crossroads, but with the difference that he has not one but *two* Edwards, either of which he could emulate, can choose to fulfill the positive type, Edward III, or, by doing nothing, inevitably fulfill the negative and lose both throne and life to Bute. If with only a negative example Edward III still managed to choose a positive role, George III has all the more reason to do the same. Thus, Sir Thomas Delamore urges Edward III, as both together (indirectly) urge George III:

> Your murder'd Father, whom we oft admonish'd,
> Nay, told him plainly what hath since ensu'd,
> Laugh'd at our Caution: sir, you must be careful,
> Or all is lost beyond Recovery.
>
> (56)

The queen interrupts their meeting, rather like an angry den mother. The irony of her insult, that these lords stand in the relationship of tutors to the king, is obvious and highlights the fact that this is precisely the relationship in which she and Mortimer themselves have stood to the king. Her bitchy exchange with the lords indicates how much George III had become a kind of "schoolboy king" to Bute's tutor, with many of the same negative sexual or rather *homosexual* connotations described by Straub, here aggravated by the double typology of the two Edwards:

> Queen: There is a better Man to answer me
> Than *Delamore*, thou Usher to these Schoolmen,
> Who in their Absence sets my Son such Lessons.
> Mountacute: Then, since your Majesty—
> Queen: Boys I could never listen to—
> Go, prattle with my Page.
>
> (57)

Here the king proves himself no Edward II, by asserting homosocial solidarity over the more or less dead body of his mother. Isabella has some great lines, however, perhaps because there is something to her position that today sounds strikingly like that of all women in a patriarchy: "Have I no Place? Am I a Cypher grown? / Will none afford a Place for Dignity?"

(58). When no one will sit with her at the head of the table, she soliloquizes:

> What, am I left alone?
> Am I infectious? Dare none sit near the Plague?
> Ungracious Boy! Is this thy filial Love?
> This the Return for all the Pangs and Throws
> I suffer'd at thy Birth? This the Reward
> For all my sorrows, Cares, Anxieties,
> Which through thy sickly Infancy possess'd me,
> When, many a weary Night, bereft of Rest,
> I've slumber'd o'er thy Cradle, and bemoan'd
> My own hard fate?
>
> (59)

The lords drag the king away before he can weaken, the queen begging Nemesis to make her revenge "masculine."

LE MONTAGNARD PARVENU: OR, THE NEW HIGHLAND ADVENTURER IN ENGLAND

The author of *Le Montagnard Parvenu: Or, the New Highland Adventurer in England* uses a similar analogy to describe the relationship of George III to his first minister. Again, with the pretense that the analogy is negative or contrastive, he compares Bute to the duke of Bourbon:

> It is but fair to believe that his conduct arose from the purest motives, and not from any views similar to those which had actuated the late duke of *Bourbon* in procuring a queen (the now living) for the present *French* monarch. (1763, 18)

The principal point of the analogy, besides Bute himself, is the king. This writer is a little more directly incriminating about what the relationship means for *him*:

> [T]he duke of *Bourbon*, father of the present prince *Condé*, and one of the royal blood, insinuated himself so adroitly with the young, implicit, and unexperienced king, as to establish himself prime minister, to the general surprise as well as dislike of the nobles and people of *France*. (18)

The writer does not say exactly *how* the duke insinuates himself into the affection of his king, but the king himself (by implication George III) is obviously young and impressionable and not beyond being imposed upon sexually as well. Whatever his feelings for his minister, he is sexually imposed upon simply by virtue of having his marriage arranged for him, a marriage to someone who is ugly and poor, not the best choice for him but for Bute because she will owe her status entirely to the latter. In such an arrangement, he is virtually married to the duke. Thus, in the Mortimer analogy the king is "unmanned" by his mother, in the duke of Bourbon analogy by his wife. In a similar way the king's relationships are seen to merely cement a more important relationship with his minister.

When the French queen is informed by her "court-ladies" how and why the duke arranged her marriage, she confronts him in a way that is clearly intended as an example to Queen Charlotte. The analogy concludes with a prayer that what happened in France may never happen in England to "screen" English majesty from the public eye, but that if it should, "then may every Whiggish heart direct a constitutional arm to tear off the encroaching and presumptuous weed" (24).

LETTER TO HER ROYAL HIGHNESS THE PRINCESS DOWAGER OF WALES

The *Letter to Her Royal Highness the Princess Dowager of Wales,* with its epigraphs from Rowe and others about this "Busy talking World," suggests that the insinuations of the above works had become widespread; moreover, it draws attention to such insinuations as its own rather sordid background material. However reasonable most of the *Letter* might appear, it has this rather lurid context which the writer wishes the reader to be aware of.

From the beginning, when the writer remarks that "a good Prince must advance the security of [the British constitution], and promote the happiness of [the country]" (1762, 1), the real subject of the *Letter,* as well as in some ways its addressee, is not the princess dowager but her son, George III. The fact that a pamphlet about royal government is at least ostensibly addressed not to George but to his mother itself indicates something the matter with the king. Either he is not the real power, or the princess dowager has created a circle around him isolating him from his people, as the writer of the last tract suggests.

After some scarcely controversial points, such as "that a perfect una-
nimity between prince and subject, is the best foundation for the happiness
of both" (4), or that "a Prince should be particularly careful in the choice of
his ministers" (5), the writer deals with just this issue of addressing the
princess dowager so publicly. His ostensible reason, not surprising considering the above portrayals of George III as a schoolboy, is her contribution
to the royal education, which he praises in a little poem:

> [You have taught] The opening genius of our Royal
>   Youth,
> And form'd their footsteps to the paths of truth;
> Gave each expanding bosom how to beat,
> With all the princes and the patriots heat;
> And nobly raised an emulative fire. . . .
>
> (10)

His real reason must be that this contribution has been rather more negative, otherwise there would no need "to offer a few plain and rational hints
upon the prospect of an approaching Peace" (11). Such "plain and rational
hints" would *not* be necessary if she had educated George properly. That
the writer addresses her and not the king implies that this negative tutorial
relationship is still in effect.

The writer seems to offer Charles II's Restoration as an example of a
bad reign that failed "to consider our situation as a maritime power" and
was characterized by things that, by implication, could threaten the present
government: "Our citizens were effeminate, our nobility riotous, and our
monarch dissolute" (13). Something like the masculinity of all Englishmen is at stake, still contaminated as it is by the Stuarts:

> The effects of CHARLES'S administration, notwithstanding a succes-
> sion that does honour to the name of royalty, are not yet totally removed,
> and it required all the virtues of a BRUNSWICK Family to wake in us
> that regard which we now entertain for our liberty as BRITONS, and our
> characters as MEN. (15)

Obviously "our characters as MEN" are in reality threatened by a feminizing princess dowager who is, moreover, in league with one of these very
Stuarts, the earl of Bute. If the writer is not explicit about such things, it is
because it would be imprudent to be so; moreover, he does not need to be,
having already drawn the attention of the reader to things like the Mortimer
analogy in the epigraphs.

Of course, the real addressee of the tract would not be the princess dowager at all but the Whiggish merchants and citizens who supported Wilkes already. To them none of the reasonable "points" would have been new, but for them they were not the main points anyway. For them the real content of the tract would have been its insinuations that the princess dowager was a usurper, that she had miseducated and weakened the king, that she was in league with Bute against her own son, that together she and Bute represented a threat to English manhood and were as potentially dangerous a feminizing force as anything at the court of Charles II, etc. No doubt they found it inspiring.

THE *NORTH BRITON*

One of the principal weapons of the *North Briton*'s propaganda campaign against Bute and "ministerial" papers like the *Briton* is analogy, the proper use of which is the theme of the very first number. The writer reprimands the *Briton* for failing to observe the difference between illustration and application, which the reader is invited to ignore but which the writer must observe, especially when the application is unflattering to his cause. The *Briton* has erred by applying an analogy from Roman politics too directly to British affairs, and by completing it in a way that directly incriminates the king:

> The MONITOR has indeed charged the cannon, but the BRITON has pointed it against his sovereign. He pretends to have discovered the source of his calumny in the MONITOR of Saturday May the 22d. . . . A minister may in all points resemble SEJANUS, or Count BRUHL, and yet his royal master need not be a TIBERIUS, or AUGUSTUS III. (Wilkes and Churchill 1763, 2)

The *North Briton* simultaneously protects itself and invites its readers to do some of its work for it, at least in imagination; moreover, such imaginative freedom of application (provided it be read, not written) is identified with freedom of the press itself, which is immediately invoked to defend the *North Briton's* use of such damaging but always only *implicit* analogies. The right to illustrate ought not to be restricted by anyone's application, especially that of the minister himself most concerned (or of his hirelings):

> The *liberty of the press* is the birth-right of a BRITON, and is justly esteemed the firmest bulwark of the liberties of this country. It has been the

terror of all bad ministers; for their dark and dangerous designs, or their
weakness, inability, and duplicity, have thus been detected and shewn to
the public, generally in too strong and just colours for them long to bear
up against the odium of mankind. (1)

Of all these analogies which the *North Briton* exploits, the Mortimer
analogy is perhaps its most "imaginatively" telling, its most insinuating,
with its homosexual implications reinforced by other analogies, to James I
in particular and to the Stuart court in general. The latter constitute a kind
of "matrix," a background or foil for the more specific points Wilkes and
Churchill wish to score. Having warned the *Briton* against asserting (if not
reading) implicit applications, the *North Briton* argues for freedom of the
press—indeed, the right to make implicit applications—with yet another
implicit application, this time of the corrupt Stuart court to the court of
George III:

> Under the government of a STUART, which has been so fatal to EN-
> GLAND, the most daring encroachments have been made on the favourite
> liberties of the people, and the freedom of the press has been openly vio-
> lated. Even a *Licenser* of the press has been appointed. Nothing but the
> vilest ministerial trash, and falsehoods fabricated by a wicked party, had
> then the sanction of this tool of power; nor of consequence could any
> production, breathing the spirit of liberty, have a chance of being ushered
> to light. The *imprimatur* of the minister was scarcely ever given, but to
> compositions equally disgraceful to letters and humanity. I do not how-
> ever recollect that any of these hirelings have ventured, as the *Briton* of
> last Saturday has done, magnificently to display the *royal arms* at the
> head of their papers. (1)

The Mortimer analogy is the main topic of "Number 5." The problem
of political favorites had already been illustrated in the *Monitor*, by "the
kings of France and Poland, who have lately fallen victims to a confidence
misplaced in an enterprising minister by the latter, and in an intriguing
mistress by the former" (11). Such negative examples can backfire, especially when they are read and *misapplied* by wicked people (the earl of
Bute himself, no less):

> Instances of this kind may produce very proper effects in the minds of
> those who are not so self-sufficient as to believe, that in similar situations
> their abilities would enable them to convert those very incidents, which
> have been the ruine of others, into solid foundations. (11)

The *Monitor* having tried to encourage "glorious actions" by negative example, the *North Briton* proceeds to do so with examples of positive virtue:

> It may therefore perhaps be more expedient, instead of painting the mis-
> eries which a country must be involved in, if governed by an insolent
> *favourite*, to shew the peculiar felicity of a prince and people rescued
> from the tyrannous slavery of a *court minion*, exemplified in the deliver-
> ance of this country by the noble and manly conduct of EDWARD the
> THIRD. (11)

Of course, such examples are positive *and* negative—this one especially
so, for reasons discussed above; any allusion to Edward III was also, however indirectly, to his more infamous father Edward II, who for a while the
son almost seems to have been:

> The reign of his Father and predecessor, EDWARD the SECOND, is dis-
> tinguished in history as the reign of *favourites*; to his unbounded affec-
> tion for them, may be ascribed the various misfortunes that afflicted this
> country at that time; and by those attachments, the affections of the old
> nobility were so alienated for him, that he became involved in disputes
> which terminated with the loss of his crown and life. (11)

The allusion to *positive* examples is only a pretense, and a double one at
that, since Edward III himself is only *partly* positive:

> The deposing of this prince [Edward II] was not productive of all that
> happiness which the nation was taught to expect from it. . . . [The people]
> knewe what the government of a weak and imprudent King could do, but
> they were unexperienced as to the effects of a minority under the direc-
> tion of a *Mother*, actuated by strong passions, and influenced by an inso-
> lent minister. (11–12)

By implication, Bute feminized George III through the influence of the
princess dowager, as Mortimer feminized Edward III through the influence
of his mother, Queen Isabella:

> *Mortimer*, afterwards Earl of March, was, through the ascendancy he had
> obtained over the *Queen Mother*, in fact the sole Regent. . . . Thus edu-
> cated under the guidance of his *Mother*, thus secured by the custody of
> *Mortimer*, he was easily persuaded to believe that *Mortimer* was a faith-
> ful *friend*, and a consummate minister. (12)

Again, by implication, through such means Bute achieved a peace, as
Mortimer did with Robert Bruce:

> [A] shameful *peace* was concluded for him by the influence of *Mortimer*;
> such a *peace* as, historians say, was profitable to the *Queen Mother* and
> *Mortimer*. (12)

The rest of the number describes how Edward ultimately regains control,
and has Mortimer executed. The depiction of the way he regains power
stresses again his manliness, his forcefulness:

> [H]e, with a resolution and judgment unequaled in history, in person seized
> *Mortimer* in the presence of the *Queen Mother*, and sent him to the Tower;
> then called a Parliament, told them, "That though not yet arrived at the
> age prescribed by law, yet, with the consent of his subjects, he designed
> for the future holding the reins of government in his own hands." (13)

The writer emphasizes the contrast between his prior disgrace and shame
and his newly won dignity:

> Thus did EDWARD wipe off the blemishes which had sullied his minor-
> ity; thus, taking the reins of government into his own hands, did he give a
> happy presage of the glory and prosperity of his future reign, the bright-
> est perhaps in the annals of England. (13)

However, in his conclusion, the writer could be alluding either to Edward
II or to Edward III, since both suffered for the "pretensions of a *court minion*," though with different degrees of responsibility.

> O may Britain never see such a day again! when power acquired by profli-
> gacy may lord it over this realm; when the feeble pretensions of a *court
> minion* may require the prostitution of royalty for their support; or if,
> which heaven avert! such a day should come, may a Prince truly jealous
> of the honour of his House, and armed with the intrepidity of EDWARD
> THE THIRD, crush the aspiring wretch who mounts to power by such
> ignoble means. (13)

George could be Edward III, or he could be Edward II; Bute could almost
be Gaveston, as well as Mortimer, as various other pieces suggest (though
carefully). The author of *A Letter to the Author of the North Briton* does so
indirectly, by attributing the comparison to the hyperbole of others, while
obviously making it himself:

But what has lord Bute done to deserve such uncommon persecution? to be branded with the most odious names; to be compared to the earl of Mortimer, between whom and him there is this material diffrence, the accusers themselves being judges, that the one was an Englishman, and the other a Scot. Why not compare him to Gaveston, to the Spencers; to bishop Gardner, to cardinal Wolsey, or to bishop Bonner . . . ? (1763, 31)

The author of letter 12 of *A Select Collection of the Most Interesting Letters on the Government, Liberty and Constitution of England* makes the same insinuation, contrasting Bute's with Elizabeth's administration, and thereby identifying him with James I's Buckingham as well:

When I read the actions of Gaveston, or the Spensers, my indignation rises against them, yet sure no man will call it personal prejudice; I knew them not, nor does my hatred arise from their refusing me an employment for which I was not qualified. —On the other hand, when I approve and commend the administration of Queen Elizabeth's counsellors, it is not because they were of the same principles as to party with myself. . . . (1763, 36)

In "Number 8" of the *North Briton* a different analogy, that of William de la Pole and Henry VI, is used to make similar points about the effeminacy of the king and the dangerous ascendancy of his minister. Again, the analogy works through both positives and negatives. The writer argues that there currently are no favorites, by "instancing particularly the three great men on whom prejudice, envy, or interest have fixed this name, and proving that, as a term of reproach, it cannot be applicable to either of them" (Wilkes and Churchill 1763, 20). He then lists the duke of Newcastle, Pitt, and a third about whom he suddenly becomes coy. Instead of naming this party as a clear instance of "non-favouritism," he describes him by means of analogy, this time to William de la Pole, earl of Suffolk, *"favourite* of Queen MARGARET and HENRY *the Sixth"* (25). For all the *North Briton's* warning about application, every analogy is clearly an invitation to make one:

[Henry VI] had a very mean genius, and but little like his father's. He easily suffered himself to be governed by those about him. . . . he was distrustful of himself, and chose rather to follow the counsels of others than his own. . . . honour, virtue, and religion, which indeed made him wish he could always act justly, but often served for a foundation and pretence to his counsellors to draw him into many acts of injustice. As he wanted penetration, he was deceived with appearances. (25)

As the earl of Bute was alleged to have done, the earl of Suffolk "hit upon a scheme which for a time answered his purpose, *though in the end it proved his ruin*" (25):

> [H]e fancied that the best way to support himself was to give the king a *wife*, and a wife of such a kind, who having no ground naturally to aspire to such a marriage, and being intirely indebted for it to the managers, might be always ready to support her benefactors. Such a person he found in *Margaret*, daughter of a beggarly duke and titular king. (25)

As the writer of the *North Briton* no doubt hopes will happen to the earl of Bute, the earl of Suffolk was eventually given up to "the resentments of an exasperated people" (26).

The nature and degree of Bute's influence over the young king, not as minister but as teacher or tutor, is the issue of "Number 34":

> One very remarkable reason, for such it is called, assigned to justify the exorbitant greatness of the present minister, is the great care which he exerted to form the mind of his most excellent majesty in his early years. . . . I am not yet sufficiently deep in the history of LEICESTER-HOUSE, to be quite certain that the Favourite hath any just claim to our acknowledgements in this respect. (112)

Some of Bute's perceived arbitrariness is seen to be connected to his having been a tutor, which role in turn is used to caricature his role in government. The writer exploits previously existing associations of the tutor with arbitrary punitiveness and of his "pupil" with the passive and even degrading submission of a "subject," who in this case happens to be the king:

> A very good schoolmaster may make a very indifferent statesman: pedantry is of little service in politics, and I should have a very contemptible opinion of an English administration, who should submit in their several departments to the imperious dictates of an overbearing tutor. (112)

The quotation from David Mallet is no doubt intended to highlight the danger that the submissiveness involved in this tutorial relationship has continued into government, and to suggest that Bute's being second in this way is just a preliminary to his being first, or a formality disguising his being first already: "In the *political poem* of ELVIRA, now *acting* at *Drury-Lane* Theatre, are the following lines: *He holds a man, who train'd a king to honour, / A second only to the prince he forme'd*" (112). The relationship is not explicitly sexual or homosexual, but always *implicitly* so, especially given the association of schoolboys and tutors with sodomy and effeminacy, which critics like Straub argue was prevalent, especially in the theatrical world so familiar to the writers of the *North Briton*. At the very least George is politically "unmanned" by Bute. In "Number 126" this relationship is illustrated by analogy to another tutor to the king, with an even more disastrously influenced pupil:

> They [the rights of the Stuart line] will always be asserted with dignity by our august family, and we are the more assured of it, because another noble *Scot*, our cousin, lord *Dunbar*, of the loyal stock of *Murray*, when he was *groom of the stole* to his royal highness, formed the mind of our most dear son, CHARLES, prince of Wales, to all virtues, and above all, to the two princely virtues of our race, strict *oeconomy* and exemplary *piety*. (126)

SOME HYPOTHESES

Considering the above texts and the continuous presence of homosexuality in them, politics as metaphor for a homosexual stage and vice versa, I think it is reasonable to suppose that most of Churchill and Wilkes's homophobia was politically motivated. It should be understood as part of a (largely obsolete) political mythology that merely served to differentiate them from the court. I think too that like any mythologizing activity, it was never meant to be taken literally. The very effectiveness of the stories they used—the earl of Bute as a homosexual Stuart bogey like James I; George III as Edward (II or III or both) to his Roger Mortimer—depended on their obviously being just stories, which related to the reality they described *only* metaphorically. On one level at least—the level of public morality—it seems certain that neither really feared homosexuality any more than he really feared a restoration of the Stuarts. And according to George Nobbe (1939) neither Wilkes nor Churchill feared any such thing.

Perhaps, therefore, the very virulence of Churchill's attack on homosexuality in *The Times* indicates that on another, more personal level, as a writer increasingly conscious of and disturbed by his own kind of "nonessentialness," Churchill genuinely feared homosexuality. One should not *need* to rail so at a mere fiction, especially of one's own creation. Here, as in earlier tracts, the idea of homosexuality lends itself to political applications and even to propaganda, while retaining much of its original meaning and, consequently, its power to disturb. Thirty years after the *Codex* business, homosexuality retains the capacity to switch from illustration to "thing itself," or like Harmodius's sword, from private to public and back again. It remains a dangerous weapon to wield at all.

12

Toward a Rhetoric
of Sodom

I assume that by now it is clear that I have organized my material as I have because such organization—Akenside (representing "high culture") sandwiched between two sets of polemical literature (relatively "low culture," I think most readers would agree)—besides appealing to my own sense of symmetry, maintains the chronology of the period, symbolizes what I see as the "centrality" of homosexuality in pivotal midcentury works, and generally reflects the arguments that I see emerging.

The material displays a rather surprising consistency of tropes and commonplaces, amounting to what will one day almost certainly comprise a "rhetoric of homosexuality." Perhaps this will be among its first handbooks.

Above all, the material reveals the pervasiveness of such a rhetoric in the period. Among these pervasive tropes are various kinds of artistic expression (opera, for example), the clergy, preferment and patronage, and education—to list only a few.

Many of these and other tropes are polarized according to the point of view of the writer. Sometimes they enjoy (or suffer from) a kind of alternating polarity within the same inconsistent and obviously "disturbed" work. Women, for example, can at once be negative as feminizing influences and positive insofar as their presence indicates a positive heterosexuality. Similarly, an emphasis on appearances, a certain "exteriority," is at once a bad thing in the homosexual and a good thing in his polemical opponent, who himself dwells on externals in order to expose the homosexual (allegedly) obsessed with appearances.

One of the most recurrent of these tropes, and the most implicitly political, is pedagogical. This resembles Straub's trope of the schoolboy, but is encountered in other areas besides the stage. Thus, we have Akenside's "high culture" allegorical version of it in the Harmodius/Spirit of Mankind relationship, Costard's (and others') "low culture" version in their accounts of the Thistlethwayte affair, and Wilkes and Churchill's "middling" version of it in the Bute/George III relationship. Such "pervasive troping" on the large scale, like what we find on a smaller scale in tracts like those of the *Codex* business, is characteristic of ideas of homosexuality in the period.

Other continuities will occur to other readers; my own readings are intended to facilitate such connections, which I leave to others to make.

For now, in as few as possible words, I observe that eighteenth-century homophobic and homoerotic texts tend to be one or all of these three things: oppositional, transpositional, and self-reflective. These general traits affect their commonplaces, which themselves tend to be paired as opposites; but they are *unstable* opposites, liable to reverse themselves, and often are presented as or already in themselves significatory.

Thus we encounter many pairs: many abstract "marriages" like misogyny and (for want of a better word) uxoriousness, fertility and sterility, procreativeness and (again, for want of a better word) retrocreativeness, truth and beauty, and philosophy and poetry, etc.; and many relatively concrete, like patrons and clients, teachers and students, preachers and members of their congregation, etc. However, these are mainly *unstable* couplings, whose oppositions blur, merge, and even reverse themselves.

We encounter another set of commonplaces concerned with appearances, with surfaces: clothing, hair, and makeup, on one level; but on a more exalted plane, more symbolic (and what I mean by "self-reflective") appearances, writing for example, and language itself. Some of this preoccupation with appearances is intensified or aggravated (depending on how one receives it) by the tendency of writers to use sodomy almost simultaneously as thing illustrated and as vehicle, thereby foregrounding signification by problematizing it.

For sodomy destabilizes most texts in which it appears, drawing attention to their own being as texts, their textuality, their own form of "nonessentialness." While this is obviously characteristic of the more homophobic texts, it also marks, though (of course) in different ways, positively homoerotic texts like Akenside's *Pleasures*, in which the beautiful youths, the pleased subjects of the poem, themselves become pleasing objects. It is hard to know precisely why such reversals occur, but one can hazard a few guesses.

Perhaps in both kinds of work, homophobic and homoerotic, the thing itself is simply extremely "charged." Whether in physics, aesthetics, or ethics, extreme charges tend to reverse themselves. And perhaps it is human nature to want things *both* ways, to illustrate moral extremes with very good or very bad things, and very good or very bad things with moral extremes.

Of course, the particular evil or good one illustrates sodomy with, or that sodomy illustrates, can be many different things, depending on the attitude of the writer: insubordination of the church, patronage, pedagogy, wisdom, folly, etc. The subsequent effect of this metaphorical range and variety is actually the proliferation of sodomy along the lines of whatever it illustrates or that illustrates it, in effect the sodomization of important areas of culture. When something is offered as evil or good it is at least significant; and the same must be said of sodomy, when it illustrates such things, or they it.

Notes

Chapter 2. Formal Strain: Problems of Homosexual Expression in William Arnall's *Letter to Dr. Codex*, Philalethes' *The Parson and His Clerk*, and Thomas Gilbert's *A View of the Town*

1. The insert, on the first page of the *Daily Journal* for Wednesday, 27 February 1734, is brief enough to quote in full: "In the second Volume of Bishop Burnet's History, p. 119. publish'd a few Days since, there is this remarkable Passage, viz. 'The State of Ireland leads me to insert here a very particular Instance of the Queen's pious Care, in the disposing of Bishopricks: Lord Sidney was so far engaged in the Interest of a great Family of Ireland, that he was too easily wrought on to recommend a Branch of it to a vacant See. The Representation was made with an undue Character of the Person: So the Queen granted it. But when she understood, that he lay under a very bad Character, she wrote a Letter, in her own Hand, to Lord Sidney, letting him know what she had heard, and order'd him to call for six Irish Bishops, whom she named to him, and to require them to certify to her their Opinion of that Person: They all agreed, that he labour'd under an ill Fame. And, 'till that was examined into, they did not think it proper to promote him; so that Matter was let fall. I do not name the Person; for I intend not to leave a Blemish on him; But set this down as an Example, fit to be imitated by Christian Princes.'"

2. The *Dictionary of National Biography* reports that Arnall "(1715?–1741?) political writer, was bred as an attorney, but took to political writing before he was twenty. He was one of the authors in Walpole's pay who replied to the 'Craftsman' and the various attacks of Bolingbroke and Pulteney. He wrote the 'Free Briton' under the signature of Francis Walsingham, and succeeded Concanen in the 'British Journal'. . . . Pope attacked him in the 'Dunciad' (Bk. ii. 315), where his name was substituted for Welsted's in 1735, and in the epilogue to the 'Satires' (Dialogue ii.129: 'Spirit of Arnall, aid me whilst I lie!'"

3. Arnall refers to a *Letter to the Clergy,* which he says "was *generally reported* to have been written by the R. R. *Dr.* G[ree]n then L[ord] B[ishop] *of* L[inco]ln" (1734, 19). He suggests that Gibson may have been misled by a passage "in the *first* Division of his Discourse, Par. IV. that *it had been* his Majesty's *continual and prudent Rule to* Consult or be DIRECTED *by his Bishops, in the Disposal of Preferments of every Rank in the Church*"

(19), which if taken at face value is inconsistent with the subordination of church to state that Green argues for elsewhere.

Chapter 3. The Wadhamites: Homosocial versus Homosexual in *College-Wit Sharpen'd* and *A Faithful Narrative*

1. An article in the appendix of the *Universal History*, "The Opinions of the most celebrated Philosophers with respect to the Creation of the World," probably by Swinton (P. J. Marshall in a chapter, "Oriental Studies" in Sutherland and Mitchell 1986 writes that "John Swinton was responsible for some of the essays on the history of Asian peoples in what came to be known as the 'ancient' sections" [556]), expresses greater gratitude than Costard ever does to Egyptian learning. For example: "This cosmogony . . . agrees in substance with the former [the Phoenician], but is more large [as later commentators used to be] in particulars, and nice attempts to a mechanic explication of the generation of the world, without any help from God" (131); "From this imputation of acknowledging no deity besides stupid matter, the Egyptians have been strenuously defended by a very able man [Dr Cudworth in his Intell. System, P. 317]" (132). The attitude is equally generous in other volumes, such as the first: "whoever considers how difficult it is to lay the first foundations of any science, be it ever so small, will allow them great commendation" (244). In *A Letter to Martin Folkes, Esq; President of the Royal Society, Concerning the Rise and Progress of Astronomy among the Ancients*, George Costard takes a very different, remarkably less generous tack: "That the *Greeks* borrow'd the Foundation of their Astronomical Skill from the *Egyptians* and *Babylonians*, is a Point in which all their Writers are universally agreed, and need not be prov'd to one so well acquainted with them as Yourself. This Concession of theirs, and the Want of understanding it with its proper and necessary Restrictions, has contributed amongst almost all Sorts of Writers to rob them of that Reputation they undoubtedly deserved" (1). Whether Swinton wrote passages laudatory of Egyptian astronomy I do not know for certain, so I cannot know for certain whether Costard aimed his remarks especially at him, but I notice that passages in Costard's *Letter to Martin Folkes* seem to echo the *Universal History* almost tauntingly. In the first volume of the latter we read "the Egyptians . . . by reason of the constant serenity of the air, and the flatness of their country, might observe the motion of the heavenly bodies earlier, and with more ease, than other people" (245). In Costard's *Letter* we find this: "That Mankind began very early to lift up their Eyes to the Heavens, and observe that beautiful Canopy so richly adorn'd, is not at all surprizing; but that these Observations, before the Flood at least, contain'd any Thing more than meer Curiosity, may very easily be doubted" (2). It is likely that these two "proto-Orientalists" disliked one another for more than sexual reasons. If for *them* the homosexual was not subordinated to the homosocial, it was probably because for *them* the homosocial had never been very strong.

2. I realize that this is a "Foucauldian" idea, although I am not interested in explicating Foucault. In his chapter, "The Perverse Implantation," in Foucault 1978, he adumbrates the complicity of power with what it is not really interested in controlling, or if in controlling not in eliminating.

3. For example, William Arnall's *Letter to Dr. Codex* (Edmund Gibson), in which there is a tension between sodomy as an abuse in itself and sodomy as an illustration of a much more pervasive abuse of patronage in the church. The effect of such illustrating is, I think, to backfire a little, to make *sodomy* seem pervasive. Comparisons work "both ways."

Chapter 4. Sporus before Us: Some Versions of Hervey

1. For some additional background on Hervey's "pamphleteering," see Halsband 1973, 107–20.

Chapter 5. *Mr. Bradbury's Case Truly Stated*

1. In 1739 George Baker accused both Robert Thistlethwayte, warden of Wadham, and John Swinton, a fellow, of sodomy. Thistlethwayte was convicted and fled, but Swinton, while quite probably "guilty," managed to outwit Baker by confusing the principal witness and by tricking Baker into writing a recantation that was subsequently published in the London newspapers. Baker wound up looking like a vicious slanderer. Thus, Swinton successfully turned the enormity of the accusation back upon the accuser. Sodomy is not something that one could be wrong about with impunity.

2. In the original, Nokes is sometimes spelled "Noakes," and Whitaker sometimes spelled "Whittaker."

Chapter 6. Narcissism and Homoeroticism in Akenside

1. Readers might want to take a look at Rousseau 1989. While Rousseau offers some circumstantial evidence that Akenside belonged to a homosocial and possibly partly homosexual university club, and that he and Dyson might have been lovers, he unfortunately says nothing about Akenside's poetry. This part of *Swords* tends to corroborate Rousseau's hunches about Akenside (i.e., his homosexuality) but without being *premised* on them, or on the kind of "evidence" that *they* were premised on.

2. For a discussion of Akenside's "republican" significance, see Jump 1989, 207–24.

3. This view of the "tyrant slayers" is not uncontroversial. See, for example, Taylor 1991. Taylor explains that both Herodotus and Thucydides emphasized the compromising, "crime of passion" aspect of the tyrannicides. Thucydides did so in order to make a point about the disastrous role that passion and impulsiveness had played in Athens's recent defeat by Sparta in the Peloponnesian War.

4. See Hart 1959, 69. He remarks Akenside's inversions, but sees them as a compensation for simpler poetic diction.

5. Curiously, this is one of those passages that Hart faults (1959, 69).

6. Hart is one of the few critics to note the political implications of this: "By calling his sage Harmodius, Akenside associated him with the young Athenian rebel who was killed in an attack on the tyrant Hippias. The name Harmodius thus suggested libertarian political sentiments" (1959, 73). The same name must also have suggested the homosexual passion of Harmodius and Aristogeiton, violated by the homosexual passion of the tyrant's brother Hipparchus for Aristogeiton.

Chapter 8. Essays on Men and Women: Wilkes's Satire

1. For women's exclusion from enlightenment systems, see (for example) Salvaggio 1988.

2. See Bleackley 1917. The position of the poem's attackers seems to have been no less equivocal. Bleackley describes how, at the beginning of the proceedings against Wilkes,

"Assuming the pose of virtuous indignation, in a voice that thrilled with pious horror, the new Secretary of State informed the House that John Wilkes had published an obscene and blasphemous poem, some passages of which he proceeded to read aloud. In spite of their amazement at this new specimen of ministerial craft, the humour of the situation was not lost upon the audience, for the orator himself was a notorious rake, whose repertoire of ribald songs was the delight and pride of the Sublime Society of Beef Steaks" (133–34). Apparently, any attempts to interrupt the reading were opposed with gleeful cries to "Go on! Go on!"

CHAPTER 9. FORMAL STRAIN: HOMOPHOBIA IN CHURCHILL'S *THE TIMES*

1. Brown 1953. Brown places *The Times* with the poems that Churchill wrote to express "ideas and interests apart from the incentives of politics and his friendship for Wilkes" (1953, 144). While the poem is not explicitly political, homosexuality elsewhere in Churchill's poetry is closely identified, through the Stuarts, with political absolutism and the perceived abuses of George III and his Scottish minister, the earl of Bute. It is probable that by 1764 homosexuality had a political value not just for Churchill but for most of his readers as well. Within the text there are connections between homosexuality and political abuses like privilege.

2. Quotations from *The Times* are taken from Churchill 1956.

3. Williams 1955, 44–48. Naturally, given contemporary notions of the sterility of homosexuality, its appearance in a "progress-piece" is highly problematic. The "progress of homosexuality" is, for the period, an even worse contradiction in terms than *translatio stultii*. Homosexuality is the ultimate "modern" denial of "a place in a continuous tradition going back to Greece and Rome" (45)—despite the significant presence of homosexuality in Greek and Roman culture.

4. See Lockwood 1979. Lockwood argues that what he calls Churchill's "nominalism" can "partly be explained by his theory of moral decay. The old virtues are gone, things are not what they used to be. As a matter of fact, Churchill devotes an entire poem (*The Times*) to the *O tempora* theme. His readiness to personify abstractions serves him well in developing this idea, because very often a 'true' or 'original' virtue will be contrasted with its latter-day descendant" (84). This also helps to explain how Dutch "charity," for example, can be both ironic and nonironic—ironic in terms of genuine, old-fashioned charity, nonironic in terms of a spurious modern kind, which exists entirely as a contrast to English meanness. Generally there is a tension in Churchill between a virtue that is transcendent and one that is merely relative and, consequently, at least slightly corrupt. Churchill's epistemology is already shaky before homosexuality disturbs it some more.

5. This "stress" may be reflected in the qualities Smith 1977 finds in occasional hysterical passages, like the one at lines 659–61: "His moral outrage occasionally seems to border on hysteria . . . Churchill may have unconsciously recognized in these aberrant men his own shadow-self" (108–9). Smith quotes George Sherburn to similar effect: "[*The Times*] was an unsavoury depiction of the vices of the day with emphasis at times on vices to which Churchill himself was perhaps not a stranger." One need not resort to biography to argue that formal difficulties imperil the "I" of the speaker. Along these lines, Brown notes that *The Times* is "Churchill's severest exposure of the public evils of his day" and suggests that "he was genuinely outraged by these sexual abnormalities" (148).

CHAPTER 10. THE HOMOSEXUAL STAGE: *THE ROSCIAD*

1. Among the various "tropes" used to characterize actors as a group, Straub identifies social class and ethnicity or race. I cannot agree with Straub that the "deviant" masculinity described in the *Fribbleriad* is really "external to the acting profession." One of the Fribbles, Lord Marjoram, actually quotes Churchill against it: "[E]very *Actor* is a *thing*, etc." (Garrick 1761, 16).

Select Bibliography

PRIMARY SOURCES

Addison, Joseph. 1898. *The Spectator*. Vol. 6, No. 395 – No. 473. London: J. M. Dent.

Akenside, Mark. 1845. *The Poetical Works of Mark Akenside*. Edited by Rev. Alexander Dyce. London: William Pickering.

The Anti-Times: Addressed to Mr. C—— Ch—ch—ll; in Two Parts. 1764. London.

Arnall, William. 1734. *A Letter to the Reverend Dr. Codex, on the Subject of his Modest Instruction to the Crown, Inserted in the Daily Journal of February 27, 1733*. London: T. Cooper.

Bradbury, Charles. 1755. *Mr. Bradbury's Case Truly Stated*. London: M. Lewis.

Churchill, Charles. 1956. *The Poetical Works of Charles Churchill*. Edited by Douglas Grant. Oxford: Clarendon Press.

College-Wit Sharpen'd: Or, the Head of a House, with, A Sting in the Tail: Being a New English Amour, of the Epicene Gender, Done into Burlesque Metre, from the Italian. Address'd to the Two Famous Universities of S—d—m and G—m—rr—h. 1739. London.

Collins, William. 1979. *The Works of William Collins*. Edited by Richard Wendorf and Charles Ryskamp. Oxford: Clarendon Press.

Cooper, Anthony, third earl of Shaftesbury. 1963. *Characteristics of Men, Manner, Opinions, Times, etc.* Edited by John M. Robertson. 2 vols. 1900. Reprint, Gloucester, Mass.: Peter Smith.

Costard, George A. 1746. *A Letter to Martin Folkes, Esq., President of the Royal Society, Concerning the Rise and Progress of Astronomy among the Antients*. London: Jacob Ilive, for T. Osborne and J. Hildyard, at York.

The Countess's Speech to her Son Roderigo. 1731. London: R. Walker.

Dyce, Rev. Alexander. 1845. Introduction to *The Poetical Works of Mark Akenside*. Edited by Rev. Alexander Dyce. London: William Pickering.

An Epistle from a Nobleman. 1734. In *Tit for Tat: To which is annex'd an Epistle from a Nobleman to a Doctor of Divinity*. London: T. Reynolds.

A Faithful Narrative of the Proceedings in a late Affair between the Rev. Mr John Swinton, and Mr. George Baker, both of Wadham College, Oxford. 1739. London.

Foote, Samuel. 1976. *A Treatise on the Passions.* 1747. Reprint, New York: AMS Press.

A Full and Candid Answer to a Pamphlet called A Genuine and Succint Narrative. 1763. London.

Garrick, David. 1761. *The Fribbleriad.* London: J. Coote.

———. 1980. *Miss in Her Teens; or, The Medley of Lovers. A Farce, 1747. Garrick's Own Plays, 1740–1766.* Edited by Harry William Pedicord and Fredrick Louis Bergman. Vol. 1 of *The Plays of David Garrick.* Carbondale and Edwardsville: Southern Illinois University Press.

Garrick, David, and John Vanbrugh. 1980. *The Provok'd Wife. A Comedy, 1744. Garrick's Alterations of Others, 1742–1750.* Edited by Harry William Pedicord and Fredrick Louis Bergman. Vol. 5 of *The Plays of David Garrick.* Carbondale and Edwardsville: Southern Illinois University Press.

Gilbert, Thomas. 1735. *A View of the Town: In an Epistle to a Friend in the Country: A Satire.* London: R. Penny.

Hell upon Earth: Or, the Town in an Uproar. 1729. London, J. Roberts.

Hervey, John, Baron Hervey. 1731. Dedication to *Sedition and Defamation Display'd: In a Letter to the Author of the "Craftsman."* 1731. London: J. Roberts.

———. 1732. *The Publick Virtue of Former Times, and the Present Age Compared.* London: J. Roberts.

———. 1739. *A Satire in the Manner of Persius: In a Dialogue Between Atticus and Eugenio: By a Person of Quality.* London: J. Clarke.

Kidgell, Rev. John. 1763. *A Genuine and Succint Narrative of a Scandalous, Obscene and Exceedingly Profane Libel, Entitled, An Essay on Woman.* London.

Le Montagnard Parvenu: Or, the New Highland Adventurer in England. 1763. London: W. Morgan.

Letters to Two Great Men. 1762. London: A. Henderson.

A Letter to Her Royal Highness the Princess Dowager of Wales on the Approaching Peace. 1762. London: Printed for S. Williams.

A Letter to the Author of the North Briton, in which the Low Scurrilities and Glaring Falshoods of that Paper are Detected. 1763. London: A. Henderson.

A Most Proper Reply to the Nobleman's Epistle to a Doctor of Divinity. 1734. London: J. Huggonson.

Mountfort, William. 1763. *The Fall of Mortimer: An Historical Play.* London: G. Kearlsy. An adaptation ascribed to William Hatchett; dedication by Wilkes.

"Peerless Poetess." 1733. *Flavia to Fanny, An Epistle.* London: T. Reynolds.

"Philalethes." 1734. *The Parson and his Clerk.* London.

Plain Reasons for the Growth of Sodomy, in England. 1730. London: A. Dodd.

Pope, Alexander. 1984. *The Poems of Alexander Pope.* Edited by John Butt. Bungay, Suffolk, U.K.: Methuen.

Pulteney, William. 1731. *A Proper Reply to a Late Scurrilous Libel Intitled, "Sedition and Defamation Display'd."* London: R. Francklin.

A Review of Lord Bute's Administration. 1763. London: I. Pridden.

A Select Collection of the Most Interesting Letters on the Government, Liberty, and Constitution of England; which have appeared in the Different Newspapers from the Elevation of Lord Bute. 1763. Vol. 1. London: J. Almon.

Smollett, Tobias George. 1964. *The Adventures of Peregrine Pickle, in which are included Memoirs of a Lady of Quality.* Edited by James L. Clifford. London: Oxford University Press.

Thomson, James. 1986. *James Thomson: Liberty, The Castle of Indolence, and Other Poems.* Edited by James Sambrook. Oxford: Clarendon Press.

Tit for Tat: To which is annex'd an Epistle from a Nobleman to a Doctor of Divinity. 1734. London: T. Reynolds.

A Treatise, Wherein are Strict Observations upon that Detestable and Most Shocking Sin of Sodomy, Blasphemy, and Atheism. 1728. London: A Moore.

A Tryall of Skill Between a Court Lord, and a Twickenham Squire. 1734. London: J. Dormer.

The Tryall of Skill between Squire Walsingham and Mother Osborne: An Eclogue in Imitation of Virgil's Palaemon. 1734. London: J. Huggonson.

An Universal History, From the Earliest Accounts to the Present Time: Compiled from the Original Authors. 1779–81. 18 vols. London: C. Bathurst.

Weatherly, Edward H., ed. 1954. *The Correspondence of John Wilkes and Charles Churchill.* New York: Columbia University Press.

Wilkes, John. 1763. Dedication to *The Fall of Mortimer: An Historical Play,* by William Mountfort. London: G. Kearsly.

Wilkes, John (and others?). 1871. *"An Essay on Women," and Other Pieces.* Edited by J. C. Hotten. London: privately printed.

Wilkes, John, and Charles Churchill. 1763. *The North Briton: Corrected and Revised by a Friend to Civil and Religious Liberty.* London: n.p.

SECONDARY SOURCES

Ashe, Geoffrey. 1974. *Do What You Will: A History of Anti-Morality.* London and New York: W. H. Allen.

Ayling, Stanley. 1972. *George the Third.* London: Collins.

Bleackley, Horace. 1917. *Life of John Wilkes.* London: John Lane.

Bray, Alan. 1982. *Homosexuality in Renaissance England.* London: Gay Men's Press.

Bradley, James E. 1990. *Religion, Revolution, and English Radicalism: Nonconformity in Eighteenth-Century Politics and Society.* Cambridge: Cambridge University Press.

Brown, Wallace Cable. 1953. *Charles Churchill: Poet, Rake, and Rebel.* Lawrence: University of Kansas Press.

Brunt, P. A., ed. 1963. *Thucydides: The Peloponnesian Wars.* Translated by Benjamin Jowett. New York: Twayne.

Buck, Howard. 1932. "Smollett and Dr. Akenside." *Journal of English and Germanic Philology* 31:10–26.

Butler, Judith. 1993. "Sexual Inversions." In *Foucault and the Critique of Institutions,* edited by John Caputo and Mark Yount, 81–98. University Park: Pennsylvania State University Press.

Caputo, John, and Mark Yount. 1993. "Institutions, Normalization and Power." In *Foucault and the Critique of Institutions*, edited by John Caputo and Mark Yount, 3–23. University Park: Pennsylvania State University Press.

Carver, P. L. 1967. *The Life of a Poet: A Biography of William Collins*. New York: Horizon Press.

Chard, Chloë. 1994. "Effeminacy, Pleasure and the Classical Body." In *Femininity and Masculinity in Eighteenth-Century Art and Culture*, edited by Gill Perry and Michael Rossington, 142–61. Manchester and New York: Manchester University Press.

Crow, Thomas. 1994. "A Male Republic: Bonds Between Men in the Art and Life of Jacques-Louis David." In *Femininity and Masculinity in Eighteenth-Century Art and Culture*, edited by Gill Perry and Michael Rossington, 204–18. Manchester and New York: Manchester University Press.

Dickinson, H. T. 1977. *Liberty and Property: Political Ideology in Eighteenth-Century Britain*. London: Weidenfeld & Nicolson.

———. 1995. *The Politics of the People in Eighteenth-Century Britain*. New York: St. Martin's Press.

Doolittle, I. G. 1986. "College Administration." In *The History of the University of Oxford*, vol. 5: *The Eighteenth Century*, edited by L. S. Sutherland and L. G. Mitchell. Oxford: Clarendon Press.

Duberman, Martin Bauml, Martha Vicinus, and George Chauncey Jr., eds. 1989. *Hidden from History: Reclaiming the Gay and Lesbian Past*. New York: NAL Books.

Dubro, James R. 1976. "The Third Sex: Lord Hervey and his Coterie." *Eighteenth-Century Life* 2:89–95.

Foucault, Michel. 1978. *The History of Sexuality*. Vol. 1, *An Introduction*. Translated by Robert Hurley. New York: Vintage.

Fuller, Ronald. 1939. *Hell-Fire Francis*. London: Chatto & Windus.

Green, V. H. H. 1986. "The University and Social Life." In *The History of the University of Oxford*, vol. 5: *The Eighteenth Century*, edited by L. S. Sutherland and L. G. Mitchell. Oxford: Clarendon Press.

Haggerty, George E. 1992. " 'The Voice of Nature' in Gray's *Elegy*." In *Homosexuality in Renaissance and Enlightenment England: Literary Representations in Historical Context*, edited by Claude J. Summers, 199–214. New York: Harrington Park.

Halperin, David. 1995. *Saint Foucault: Towards a Gay Hagiography*. Oxford: Oxford University Press.

Halsband, Robert. 1973. *Lord Hervey: Eighteenth-Century Courtier*. Oxford: Clarendon Press.

Hart, Jeffrey. 1959. "Akenside's Revision of *The Pleasures of Imagination*." *PMLA* 74:67–74.

Houpt, Charles Theodore. 1944. *Mark Akenside: A Biographical and Critical Study*. New York: Russell and Russell.

Jump, Harriet Devine. 1989. "High Sentiments of Liberty: Coleridge's Unacknowledged Debt to Akenside." *Studies in Romanticism* 28:207–24.

Lajer-Burcharth, Ewa. 1994. "The Aesthetics of Male Crisis: The Terror in the Republican Imaginary and in Jacques-Louis David's Work from Prison." In *Femininity and Masculinity in Eighteenth-Century Art and Culture*, edited by Gill Perry and Michael Rossington, 219–43. Manchester and New York: Manchester University Press.

Lonsdale, Roger. 1984. *The New Oxford Book of Eighteenth-Century Verse.* Oxford: Oxford University Press.

Lockwood, Thomas. 1979. *Post-Augustan Satire: Charles Churchill and Satirical Poetry, 1750–1800.* Seattle: University of Washington Press.

Mack, Maynard. 1985. *Alexander Pope: A Life.* New Haven: Yale University Press.

Marsh, Robert. 1965. *Four Dialectical Theories of Poetry: An Aspect of English Neoclassical Criticism.* Chicago: University of Chicago Press.

Marshall, P. J. 1986. "Oriental Studies." In *The History of the University of Oxford,* vol. 5: *The Eighteenth Century,* edited by L. S. Sutherland and L. G. Mitchell. Oxford: Clarendon Press.

McIntosh, Mary. 1969. "The Homosexual Role." *Social Problems* 16:182–92.

McKeon, Michael. 1995. "Historicizing Patriarchy: The Emergence of Gender Difference in England, 1660–1760." *Eighteenth-Century Studies* 28:295–322.

Meehan, Michael. 1986. *Liberty and Poetics in Eighteenth-Century England.* London: Croom Helm.

Miller, John. 1973. *Popery and Politics in England, 1660–1688.* Cambridge: Cambridge University Press.

Miller, Peter N. 1994. *Defining the Common Good: Empire, Religion and Philosophy in Eighteenth-Century Britain.* Cambridge: Cambridge University Press.

Nobbe, George. 1939. *The North Briton: A Study in Political Propaganda.* New York: Columbia University Press.

Perry, Gill, and Michael Rossington, eds. 1994. *Femininity and Masculinity in Eighteenth-Century Art and Culture.* Manchester and New York: Manchester University Press.

Rousseau, G. S. 1987. "The Pursuit of Homosexuality in the Eighteenth Century: 'Utterly Confused Category' and/or Rich Repository?" In *'Tis Nature's Fault: Unauthorized Sexuality During the Enlightenment,* edited by Robert Purks Maccubbin, 132–68. Cambridge: Cambridge University Press.

———. 1989. "'In the House of Madam Vander Tasse, on the Long Bridge': A Homosocial University Club in Early Modern Europe." In *The Pursuit of Sodomy: Male Homosexuality in Renaissance and Enlightenment Europe,* edited by Kent Girard and Gert Hekma, 311–47. New York: The Haworth Press.

Salvaggio, Ruth. 1988. *Enlightened Absence: Neoclassical Configurations of the Feminine.* Chicago: University of Chicago Press.

Sedgwick, Eve Kosovsky. 1985. *Between Men: English Literature and Homosocial Desire.* New York: Columbia University Press.

Smith, Raymond J. 1977. *Charles Churchill.* Boston: Twayne Publishers.

Straub, Kristina. 1992. *Sexual Suspects: Eighteenth-Century Players and Sexual Ideology.* Princeton: Princeton University Press.

Staves, Susan. 1982. "A Few Kind Words for the Fop." *Studies in English Literature* 22:413–28.

Sutherland, L. S., and L. G. Mitchell, eds. *The History of the University of Oxford,* vol. 5: *The Eighteenth Century*. Oxford: Clarendon Press.

Sykes, Norman. 1926. *Edmund Gibson, Bishop of London, 1669–1748: A Study in Politics and Religion in the Eighteenth Century*. London: Oxford University Press.

Taylor, Michael W. 1991. *The Tyrant Slayers: The Heroic Image in Fifth-Century B.C. Athenian Art and Politics*. Salem, N.H.: Ayer.

Trumbach, Randolph. 1977. "London's Sodomites: Homosexual Behavior and Western Culture in the Eighteenth Century." *Journal of Social History* 11:1–33.

———. 1989. "The Birth of the Queen: Sodomy and the Emergence of Gender Equality in Modern Culture, 1660–1750." In *Hidden from History: Reclaiming the Gay and Lesbian Past*, edited by Martin Duberman, Martha Vicinus, and George Chauncey Jr. New York: New American Library.

———. 1987. "Sodomitical Subcultures, Sodomitical Roles, and the Gender Revolution of the Eighteenth Century: The Recent Historiography." In *'Tis Nature's Fault: Unauthorized Sexuality During the Enlightenment*, edited by Robert Purks Maccubbin, 109–21. Cambridge: Cambridge University Press.

———. 1990. "Sodomy Transformed: Aristocratic Libertinage, Public Reputation and the Gender Revolution of the 18th Century." *Journal of Homosexuality* 19:105–24.

———. 1991. "London's Sapphists: From Three Sexes to Four Genders in the Making of Modern Culture." In *Bodyguards: The Cultural Politics of Gender Ambiguity*, edited by Julia Epstein and Kristina Straub, 112–41. New York: Routledge.

Watney, Simon. 1987. *Policing Desire: Pornography, AIDS and the Media*. Minneapolis: University of Minnesota Press.

Wendorf, Richard. 1981. *William Collins and Eighteenth-Century Poetry*. Minneapolis: University of Minneapolis Press.

West, Shearer. 1991. *The Image of the Actor: Verbal and Visual Representation in the Image of Garrick and Kemble*. London: Frances Pinter.

Williams, Aubrey. 1974. *Wilkes: "A Friend to Liberty."* London: George Allen & Unwin.

———. 1955. *Pope's "Dunciad": A Study of Its Meaning*. London: Methuen.

Index

55–56, 58; politics, 37; and privilege, 58; and public awareness, 50–51; spread of, as *translatio studii*, 187

James I, 225
Jonson, Ben, 81

Kidgell, John, reverend: author of *A Genuine and Succint Narrative of a scandalous, obscene, and exceedingly profane LIBEL*, 181

Lajer-Burcharth, Ewa, 169
Letter to Her Royal Highness the Princess Dowager of Wales, 217–19

Mack, Maynard: idealization of a homophobic stereotype, 85–86; on Pope's reaction to Lord Hervey's attack, 72–73
Marriage: Akenside's version (elision), 152–57; in Harmodius's story, 122–23; heterosexual joys of, 29–31; in Shaftesbury, 123–24; of a young sodomite, 20–21
Marsh, Ronald, 164
Marvell, Andrew, 46, 80–81
Masculinity: attributes of, 18; defined by spirit and essence, 19, 20–21, 23, 25, 86, 200; essentialness of, betrayed, 23; and heterosexual love, 29–31; nostalgia for, 18; nostalgia for, in Churchill's *Times*, 183–84; oppositional emergence of, 19, 20, 21, 205; threatened by earl of Bute, 219; threatened by the Stuarts, 218, 220
Meehan, Michael, 167
Milton, John, 158, 161, 170
Montagnard Parvenu: Or, the New Highland Adventurer in England, Le, 216–17
Mortimer, Roger, earl: double typology involving Edward II and Edward III, 214, 222; in Mortimer analogy, 211, 216–17; in *The North Briton*, 219–23; represented the earl of Bute in *The Fall of Mortimer*, 211–16;
Most Proper Reply, A, 80–81

Nobbe, George, 225
North Briton, The, 219–24

Phaedrus, 118, 120, 128
Pindar, 150
Plato, 125, 132, 199
Pope, Alexander: attacked by Lord Hervey, 71–72; his *Essay* parodied, 177–81; and *The Dunciad*, 187; the homosexual implications of *Essay on "Man"* (vs. *Essay on "Woman"*), 177; invoked by Gilbert, 49; lack of virility of, 175; nonprofessional stance of, as heterosexual inexperience, 175; nonessentialness of, as a writer, 176; and posterity, 190; sexuality of, impugned, 177; version of, of Lord Hervey, 65–66
Pulteney, William, earl of Bath, 129; in Akenside's *To Curio*, 159; attacks Lord Hervey in *A Proper Reply to a Late Scurrilous Libel*, 66–68; depicted as Roderigo in *The Countess's Speech*, 68–69; "homosexualizing" effects of his tract, 87; in *Tit for Tat*, 76

Reading: and anticipating commonplaces, 17; and arbitrariness, 22–23; and context, 8; and implication of reader, 22–23; as looking, 24; of other texts, 11; and sexuality, 7–8; of sodomites' clothing, 22
Rousseau, George, 7, 8
Rundle, Thomas, 37

Smollett, Tobias: satire of Akenside, 116, 129–35, 153
Sedgwick, Eve Kosofsky, 53
Socratic figure, 117, 118, 119, 123
Sodomite: and atheism, 26, 28; attire of, 21–23; Bradbury accused of being, 98; and marriage, 21; misogyny of 25–26, 29; nonessential nature of, 25, 34, 36, 65, 67, 84–85, 87, 115, 196, 199, 202; nonessential nature of, and connection with the theater, 196–97; as outsider, 77, 79, 84–87; and Pope's version, 85; preoccupation with appearances of,